Three Winds of Death

The Saga of the 503d Parachute Regimental Combat Team in the South Pacific

Bennett M. Guthrie

ADAMS PRESS
CHICAGO

FIRST EDITION

Copyright ©1985 by Bennett M. Guthrie

Library of Congress
Catalog Card Number 85-71010
ISBN 0-682-40169-2

Published by
503d Parachute RCT Association
Bennett M. Guthrie
Rt. 5, Box 186
Tahlequah, OK 74464

Dedication

Slipping into history with the 503d Parachute Infantry Regimental Combat Team in World War II

This history of the 503d Parachute Infantry Regimental Combat Team is dedicated to that gallant breed of man, the paratrooper, both past and present, but most humbly, respectfully, and reverently, to our buddies who fell in mortal combat with the common enemy.

Contents

Illustrations

Maps

Photographs

Preface

The history of airborne warfare in the United States Army began with certain men and units of the 503d Parachute Infantry Regiment, the 462d Parachute Field Artillery Battalion, and Company C of the 161st Parachute Engineer Battalion. The 503d Parachute Infantry Regiment was the first regiment of paratroopers to be formed in the United States Army; within the 503d was the 501st Parachute Battalion, the very first paratrooper unit to be organized in the United States Army.

Four decades have passed since airborne warfare became a part of United States Army battle plans. Sadly, the "grim reaper" has harvested his toll of old troopers over the years, including some key personnel without whose reminiscences this report is not complete. This history is written for the purpose of documenting the life of the 503d Regimental Combat Team (RCT) in World War II. Perhaps in that telling it will rekindle the old American spirit of derring-do, challenge, exploration, pioneering, patriotism, and gallant camaraderie. Failure of old memories has necessitated omission of some dates, names, and events. Information that has been recalled or written down as record however, is treated with reverential dignity. The 503d Parachute Infantry Regiment (PIR) initially contained nearly two thousand men; more than three thousand others eventually joined the ranks as replacements for casualties or other unit components that made us a parachute regimental combat team, unattached, in the Southwest Pacific area theater of war. Some old troopers of the 503d Parachute Infantry Regimental Combat Team spent more than three years overseas during World War II. It is impossible to relate all the individual daily patrol actions or the exploits of platoons, companies, and battalions. For writing this history, I acknowlege that each old trooper harbors and treasures individual memories, many more than are included here.

During the Viet Nam War, troopers of the 503d Parachute Infantry spent more than six years in combat operations. It is my hope that in reading this account of the glorious accomplishments of the 503d Parachute Infantry since its inception, each old trooper in his own way, may relive that portion of our history in which he participated. This history of the units of the 503d Parachute Infantry Regimental Combat Team attempts to relate our origin, our dreams, our prayers, and our victories. It relates our fears and frustrations. Perhaps another trooper of the 503d will write an addendum that will bring the glorious achievements of the 503d up to date with its valorous feats during the Vietnam War.

The 503d Paratroopers have witnessed their Armageddon . . . they have walked through the Valley of the Shadow of Death.

Here is their story.

Bennett M. Guthrie
Co. H, 503d Parachute Infantry
Route 5, Box 186
Tahlequah, Oklahoma, 74464
23 December, 1982

Acknowledgements

I wish to express my gratitude to the former enlisted men and officers of the 503d Parachute Infantry Regimental Combat Team of World War II, who have been extremely helpful and encouraging during the seven and one-half years that I have been preparing this unique history. I particularly wish to thank my former comrades-in-arms Andrew J. Amaty, Mike Matievich, and Jesse B. Gandee of the 462d Parachute Field Artillery Battalion, Charles Wasmund and Gene Stautberg of Company C, 161st Parachute Engineer Battalion, my former commanding officer of Company H, 503d Parachute Infantry Regiment, James M. Mullaney, who maintained a diary throughout the war despite U.S. Army regulations prohibiting doing so in wartime battle arenas; and Brig. Gen. George M. Jones, who shared his memoirs and after-battle reports and offered sage advice and encouragement through the years.

All contributors to this saga are enumerated in the bibliography. Nevertheless, special recognition must be given the invaluable assistance obtained from Mrs. Jewell C. Dold and Mr. Gilbert G. Fites, Professors of Library Science at the Northeastern State University Library, Tahlequah, Okla.

Finally, I wish to express my deep love and appreciation to my wife and family for their preseverance, patience, and understanding of my quest over the many years when I selfishly ignored their desires so I could pursue the compilation of this story. They never forsook me.

Three Winds of Death

1
Into The Frying Pan

Airborne warfare became a part of twentieth-century battle plans and training manuals when in November 1939 the Russians introduced parachute troops into the one-sided Russo-Finnish War. The Cossacks had been developing attack units of Parachute troops since early in the decade and took the opportunity to put this new battle organization to the test.

By the late 1930s, France, Germany, Italy, and Japan had developed airborne attack units. American intelligence observers made frequent references to the parachute troops-training programs of these nations, in their reports to the United States War Department.

Finally, on 1 May 1939, American War Department officials began to stir out of their complacency. The U.S. War Department G-3 section ordered the chief of infantry to formulate a feasibility study of the use of air infantry in our armed forces. Ironically, our nation at the time was following a road of isolationism, and this order was shelved to collect dust for several months.

Suddenly, several events occurred in Europe and Asia that shook this nation's startled military leaders into action. In the autumn of 1939, the German army marched into the Rhineland in defiance of the Treaty of Versailles. Shortly afterward, more Germans marched into Poland while the Russian army, doublecrossing the Poles, attacked them from the rear. In November of the same year, Russia committed its unforgivable and dastardly attack on tiny Finland. In the Far East, after conquering Manchuria, the land of Nippon was increasing the tempo of its war against China, and began making alarming gestures toward other Asiatic nations.

Finally, in January 1940, U.S. Army Chief of Infantry Maj. Gen. George A. Lynch assigned Maj. William C. Lee to accomplish the feasibility study of the use of air infantry that had been ordered more than six months earlier. Major Bill Lee was destined to be emblazoned in the annals of history as the "daddy" of airborne troops in the U.S. armed forces, and in less than two years he had become a major general.

Major Lee's assignment was threefold: (1) to develop a parachute training program; (2) to work with the United States Army Air Force

1

Maj. William C. Lee, commanding officer of the Provisional Parachute Group Fort Benning, Georgia, 1941-42.

(USAAF) to develop a parachute that infantrymen could use (earlier parachutes were of the free-fall variety that required jump altitudes exceeding fifteen hundred feet); and (3) to recruit a platoon of infantry volunteers as a test unit.

In May 1940, the German army troops' rapid blitzkrieg through Belgium and Holland, spearheaded by airborne troops, accelerated the efforts of our own infant airborne program, which immediately began a comprehensive study of the German paratrooper, particularly his equipment, training, and methods of exiting aircraft.

Within six months after Major Lee began his task, events began falling into place. A General Headquarters directive of 25 June 1940 authorized formation of a screened cadre of volunteers from the 29th Infantry Regiment, billeted at Fort Benning, Georgia. A platoon of infantry volunteers was quickly obtained (see appendix). Lt. William T. Ryder (West Point class of 1936) was selected as the senior officer to lead these volunteers in this daring new army venture. They were directed by the Infantry Board of Fort Benning.

The test platoon obtained assistance from Harry Wilson of Chanute Field, Illinois, a warrant officer from the USAAF Parachute Riggers School Directory. Beginning in July 1940, Wilson led the test platoon members and their backup men through a tough and demanding eight-week training program that culminated with six required parachute jumps. To condition the training paratrooper physically and mentally, there were daily runs of three or four miles, calisthenics, judo, tumbling, parachute orientation, and parachute packing. The eighth week began with individual "slap-out" jumps.

The drop zone for the test platoon was on Lawson Field in front of the checkered airport terminal buildings. The Civilian Conservation Corps cleared the area to the south of the airfield to create a jump field for the test platoon and thousands of paratroopers who followed. All the prickly plants in Georgia seemed to be amassed there to welcome the descending paratrooper. The jump site received the endearing name of "Cactus Field."

Lieutenant Ryder, the test platoon commander, made the first jump. Ironically, the enlisted man who drew first place in the jump profile "froze" at the door of the airplane on two separate passes of the jump field. William "Red" King, second-place enlisted man, became the first actually to jump, following Lieutenant Ryder. The enlisted man who had refused to jump was packed up and transferred as soon as the aircraft landed at Lawson Field. The final and qualifying jump was a mass exit, in which the entire planeload exits on signal in one mass

3

exodus or "stick." The qualifying jump was accomplished by all the remaining men and the two officers. This momentous event was attended by just about all the "brass" in Washington, including the secretary of war. Having achieved its goals, the test platoon divided into two segments. One group, under Lt. James A. Bassett, travelled to Chanute Field for parachute rigger school; the other, under Lieutenant Ryder, remained behind to formulate a training program for future units.

Strict rules of unquestioned discipline, proffered by this early training unit, were to characterize all future paratrooper training. Passing the arduous training program and having to meet the physical demands of the trainers enabled the conditioned paratrooper cadet to dictate his will over his normal conscience and be able to jump from an airplane in flight.

While these first paratroopers were training, the wars in Europe and Asia had reached alarming magnitudes. On 16 September 1940, the U.S. War Department ordered the activation of several National Guard divisions and Army Reserve units to bolster our national defense system. The same day, an alert was issued to activate the First Parachute Battalion. Volunteers were to be obtained from existing infantry divisions of the U.S. Army. Because of favorable publicity about the test platoon and the adventuresome American nature, it was assumed that it would be easy to obtain volunteers for this battalion. A few days after the alert, the First Parachute Battalion was ordered to become the 501st Parachute Battalion. Thereafter all paratroop units in the U.S. Army were listed in the "500s." The person selected to lead this pioneer parachute battalion was the Fort Benning post athletic officer, Maj. William M. Miley (West Point Class of 1918), holder of numerous athletic awards. William Miley later commanded the Seventeenth Airborne Division during World War II.

The 501st Parachute Infantry Battalion was activated on 1 October, 1940. Ranks were filled by the first week of November with members of the test platoon interspersed throughout the various companies. Lieutenant Bassett and his trained riggers had now returned from Chanute Field. Lieutenant Ryder, however, had but twenty-five instructors, an insufficient number to serve a battalion. More problems arose. Five hundred parachutes had been ordered from the manufacturer, but only ninety had arrived for use. The U.S. Army Air Force would provide only two airplanes. There was only one packing shed. These early snafus were eventually overcome, but until they were, it was impossible to plan an eight-week course of jump training for the entire battalion. The first 330 men and officers of the 501st Battalion

4

Lt. Col. William M. Miley, 1941-1942

The packing shed where paratroopers packed their own parachutes. Picture ca. 1941 or early 1942. This structure was beside Lawson Field, Fort Benning, Georgia.

had to qualify as "expert parachutists" by making individual jumps from 1,500 and 1,000 feet, two jumps from 750 feet, and two mass jumps from 750 feet. The last member of the battalion finally completed jump training in mid-March 1941. The training program had by then been reduced to four weeks and the number of qualifying jumps to five. The anchor line cable in the aircraft had been changed. Once running from side to side, it now ran the length of the plane, from cockpit to tail. The static line had been lengthened to 12 feet in order to lessen the opening shock. Deletions, innovations, and modifications of equipment and training procedures occurred constantly during this early paratrooper training period. The basic procedure of airborne training remains the same today as it was then.

The first death caused by parachute failure occurred on 6 March 1941, when Sgt. Floyd S. Beard of Company C, 501st Parachute Battalion, fell to his death during a mass jump at 750 feet altitude. By the time he pulled his reserve parachute, he was at such a low altitude that there was no time for it to open properly.

Requirements for the first candidates to jump school included being single (officers excepted), age 21-32 years (officers could be no older than 35), between 5 feet 6 inches and 6 feet 2 inches in height, under 185 pounds in weight, previous infantry experience, sufficient intelligence to be recommended by one's commanding officer, and above average in military bearing and ability.

The 501st Battalion was quartered atop the hill just north of Lawson Field in the old Twenty-Ninth Infantry regimental garden area until November and then moved across the street to newly constructed wooden barracks. The hot Georgia climate, coupled with the hot tempo of paratrooper training, resulted in a permanent name for this area — The Frying Pan. Training and the required number of jumps completed, the proud troopers of the 501st Parachute Infantry Battalion were presented with their "wings." This distinguished United States Army paratrooper badge was authorized by a War Department directive of 10 March 1941. The design accepted by the Office of Quartermaster General was submitted by Capt. William P. Yarborough (West Point Class of 1936). He later designed an oval background for the "wings" with appropriate colors and border for each branch of the service: blue for infantry, red for artillery, and so on. He also designed several other items of uniform equipment. Captain Yarborough was later elevated to the rank of major general. He commanded the famous 509th Parachute Battalion during World War II.

Capt. William P. Yarborough designer of the "wings" and the oval background for them, which he is wearing here.

In the months following activation of the 501st Parachute Infantry Battalion, various officers received special group jump training and then command units of the battalion.

The first review of U.S. Army parachute troops was held at Fort Benning, Georgia, on 22 March 1941. Major Miley issued orders that troopers could wear their jump boots off base, but they had to shine like a mirror for one to obtain a pass. Also, a round patch with an embroidered parachute on a blue background could be worn on the left front of the newly adopted, foldable Overseas cap that replaced the old rounded and billed garrison cap.

On 10 March, the First Provisional Parachute Group Headquarters was activated. This unit superseded the earlier unit and was to assume the supervision of training all additional battalions of paratroopers for the U.S. Army. The commander of this newly formed unit was recently promoted Col. Bill Lee.

Jump towers were built for practicing simulated jumps, and a maze of interconnecting pipes was erected that was later referred to as the "plumber's nightmare." The men were supposed to be toughened by crawling, twisting, and lifting their way through this jungle. Other needed facilities were built such as packing sheds, parachute shake-out bins, and other necessities.

In the war in Europe about this time the capture of the island of Crete by an all-airborne German armed force inspired Washington officials to issue orders to increase the tempo of U.S. airborne buildup. Also at this time the number and influence of German civil and diplomatic officials in various Latin American countries was growing alarmingly. To buffer this threat to American security in the Southern Hemisphere, Company C of the 501st Parachute Infantry Battalion commanded by Capt. John B. Shinberger (West Point Class of 1933) was ordered to Panama, Canal Zone, on 28 June 1941. This forerunner unit established a base at Fort Kobbe, located on the Pacific side of the isthmus. Three more companies would arrive by autumn. These men were the first paratroopers to see foreign service during World War II.

A streamlined new parachute training program was now begun in serial units; parachute packing and physical fitness were stressed throughout the entirety of the course. Trainees were not permitted to walk. Wherever one needed to go — the Lister bag for water, the shower, or the next event — he ran. Any action not meeting the approval of the mentors could result in disciplinary measures such as doing one hundred push-ups or digging a foxhole with a GI mess kit. The general progression through the four-week period was as follows:

9

A stage (first week): physical education, hand-to-hand combat, judo, and three-to four-mile runs daily;

B stage (second week): nomenclature of the parachute, training in its use, and an introduction to the mock-up 34-foot towers, which introduced the trainee to jumping into space, exiting from a simulated plane door, and proper landing profile;

C stage (third week): negotiation of the 250-foot towers with training in both captive and free descent attitudes and introduction of the wind tunnel to teach the trainee to exercise control in collapsing his chute in a strong ground wind; and

D stage (fourth week): individual slap-out jumps from airplanes, after which, the parachutes were shaken out and repacked for the next day. The fifth jump was a mass exit of all paratroopers aboard the plane.

In off-duty hours, gallant troopers, old and new, would gather at the old Frying Pan PX (post exchange) for nightly beer busts and to exchange exaggerated accounts of their day's activities. Various older and "wiser" men sometimes traveled to nearby Columbus, Georgia or its sister "sin city," Phenix City, Alabama, where one could obtain liquor, gamble, or dance and play with the "ladies of the night." Any soldier found playing against the rules of the corrupt city government officials, the police, or the controlled liquor and gambling syndicates and houses of prostitution was usually found floating face down in the old muddy Chattahoochee River without a life preserver.

In early jump training, the instructors had the troopers strap on their parachute harnesses too tight. The shock of the opening parachute blossoming out and filling with air caused leg, chest, and shoulder straps to tighten even more and would pinch flesh and cause blood-filled epidermal abrasions called "strawberries." After receiving his wings and being on his own, the seasoned trooper adjusted his parachute harness to fit more comfortably. Early morning of jump days found the troopers in harness, lined up beside their assigned airplanes parked alongside the runway of Lawson Field. This thrilling event was one to remember forever inasmuch as the majority of men probably had never been so close to an airplane before, let alone expecting to leap from one in flight.

Circling the military reservation in our assigned plane was soul-satisfying—that is, until the jumpmaster signaled *you* to the door. Here an equipment check was done to be sure the anchor line snap fastener was secured and locked to the anchor cable, which ran fore to aft in the transport plane. Seconds later, we stood in the door. The plane leveled and passed over the Chattahoochee River, and the red light over the door changed to green when we passed the leading edge of Cactus Field. This was the signal for the jumpmaster to slap our rumps and yell "go"! One would feel the opening shock, glance at the canopy to be sure the panels of the chute were OK and then float enjoyably and breathtakingly to earth. Moments after exiting the plane, the troopers landed in Cactus Field with hearts in their throats, strawberries on their shoulders, and sandbriars in their derrieres.

By midsummer of 1941, several new parachute battalions were activated. On the first of July 1941, the 502d Parachute Infantry Battalion was activated with cadres coming from Companies A and B of the 501st, who were still at Fort Benning. This unit was given to Maj. George P. Howell, Jr. (West Point Class of 1919), the 501st Parachute Battalion executive officer.

On 22 August 1941, the 503d Parachute Infantry Battalion was activated, with Maj. Robert F. Sink commanding. Major Sink was a 501st Battalion member and a West Point graduate in 1927.

At this time, the Parachute Jump School replaced the First Provisional Parachute Group and was placed under command of the Infantry School for jump-training all succeeding thousands of paratroopers. Most of the officers of the newly activated 503d Parachute Battalion were trained jumpers. Screening of the regular army units produced thousands of volunteers, but only 341 enlisted men and 37 officers were selected; they were chosen on merit alone. In September these men and the unqualified officers completed the required courses and began their qualifying jumps. On 3 October 1941, these men took their qualifying jump. The proud battalion then engaged in demolition, sabotage, and other advanced infantry training tactics. Soon the authorized strength of the battalion of 456 men and 36 officers had been attained by tapping the first group of selective service personnel at Camp Roberts, California, for paratrooper training. These draftee volunteers entered paratrooper training on 4 October 1941 and were ultimately assigned to Company A of the 503d Battalion.

On 30 November, Company B was detailed to Orlando, Florida, to test the coordination of parachute troops with the airborne infantry. On 14 January 1942, this same company was dispatched to Salt Lake City, Utah, for infantry paratroop ski training. On 5 October 1941, the 504th Parachute Infantry Battalion was activated. Command of this newest battalion was given to Maj. Richard Chase, a 1927 graduate of Syracuse University, who had entered the U.S. Army in October of

Maj. Robert F. Sink (note infantry decor patch behind wings).

that year as a newly commissioned second lieutenant. He was a member of the 501st Battalion. After promotion to the rank of major he was assigned for two months as executive officer of the 503d Battalion.

Only four officers among the 39 officers and 518 assigned enlisted men had had jump training. The entire 504th Battalion entered and left jump school as a unit. This battalion furnished company-sized classes to the demolition and sabotage school and later to the communication school of the Provisional Parachute Group before its transformation to the Parachute Jump School. Qualifying jumps for this battalion had been scheduled for 15 December 1941, but with the outbreak of war on 7 December, there were no planes available for jump qualifying until 26 January 1942. The battalion made all its qualifying jumps on that date. Its members were also the first to receive their "wings" en masse. This 504th Parachute Battalion would later combine with the 503d to form the 503d Parachute Infantry Regiment — the very first regiment of parachute troops to be formed in the United States armed services.

At this point, a bit of professional jealousy arose. Newly activated tank battalions under command of Brig. Gen. George S. Patton arrived at Fort Benning. These armored infantry soldiers stole the paratroopers' proud jump boots to augment the insignia and dress of their uniforms. The paratroopers were infuriated by this gross infringement of their rights. The sight of unqualified soldiers wearing the cherished jump boots resulted in innumerable skull-busting knock-downs and drag-outs between airborne and armored personnel.

The attack on Pearl Harbor on 7 December 1941 accelerated the tempo of war. Christmas found the 501st Parachute Battalion in Panama and the 502d, 503d, and 504th parachute battalions in Fort Benning, Georgia. These troopers celebrated the holiday with roast turkey, oyster dressing, and accompanying goodies. They all had wings on their chests, stars in their eyes, and a vision of the army's glorious past. Eating lunch with the 503d Battalion that day were the executive officer, Maj. James M. Gavin, and Capt. Joe Lawrie, the plans and training officer.

Because of crowded conditions at Fort Benning, the 503d and 504th parachute battalions were moved to Fort Bragg, North Carolina. Peacetime allocations for army troop strength were lifted at this time, resulting in new War Department orders for the formation of four parachute regiments, with cadres drawn from the existing parachute battalions. On 2 March 1942, the 502d Parachute Infantry Regiment was activated, with a cadre coming from the 502d Battalion, which had been formed nine months earlier. Major Howell, the battalion commander, was elevated to regimental commander and to the rank of

Parachute Group Headquarters

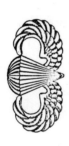

Certificate of Proficiency

This is to Certify That Pvt.1cl ROLLAND P. McGINN, 6923532, Company B, 501st Parachute Battalion has satisfactorily completed the prescribed course in parachute packing, ground training, and jumping from a plane in flight. He is, therefore, entitled to wear the special insignia of the Parachutist and be rated from this date, March 21 1941, as a qualified Parachutist in the Army of the United States.

W. M. MILEY,
Major, 501st Parachute Battalion,
Commanding.

18350—Benning, Ga., 5-7-41—2,500

14

Parachute Group Headquarters
Fort Benning, Georgia

Certificate of Proficiency

This is to Certify That Private RICHARD F. O'BRIEN Jr. (39302339), Co A, 503d Prcht Bn
has effective this 20th day of _____ December _____ 194_1_, A. D.
satisfactorily completed the prescribed course in demolition and
sabotage and is qualified in all phases of demolitions and sabotage
for parachute troops in the army of the United States.

Robert H. Shords

ROBERT H. WOODS
1st Lt, 504th Prcht Bn
Instructor

G.P. HOWELL
Major, 503d Prcht Bn
Comdg Prov Prcht Gp

20619—Benning, Ga., 11-28-41—1,500

15

Lieutenant Colonel. Activation should not be confused with the *formation* of a unit. Troops are needed to form an outfit. Also on 2 March 1942, the 503d Parachute Infantry Regiment was formed by uniting the 503d and 504th battalions. The former became the First Battalion and the latter became the Second Battalion of this very first operable parachute infantry regiment. Lt. Col. William M. Miley was given command.

Months earlier, the remainder of the 501st Parachute Infantry Battalion had departed from Fort Benning by train to join Company C in the Panama Canal Zone. The troopers sailed from Charleston, South Carolina, on 8 September 1941, on the SS *Siboney*. They landed at Cristobal, Canal Zone, on the Atlantic side of the isthmus. Capt. John Shinberger had a train ready to transport the battalion across the isthmus to its new home on the Pacific side, Fort Kobbe, an old artillery post situated so as to guard the Pacific entrance to the canal. The 501st Battalion troopers were elated to enter new barracks provided for them by the Canal Zone commander. At Howard Field, the nearby United States Army Air Force base, they would continue their parachute jump training.

In Panama, the company's number of effectives for training diminished because of illness, transfers, and accidents. Rather than rely on Fort Benning for replacements, the 501st Battalion commander prevailed upon the Canal Zone commander to process transfers from nearby army units to fill vacancies. The 501st Parachute Battalion then organized its own jump-training school in Panama. In the ensuing months of experimental parachute training exercises, one drowning and one death caused by parachute malfunctioning occurred. When Lieutenant Colonel Miley was ordered to return to the United States for reassignment, Maj. Kenneth Kinsler, the battalion service officer, was elevated to become commander of the 501st Parachute Infantry Battalion.

A fruitful search resulted in the battalion acquiring, enlisting, and jumping its mess sergeant, Eddie Bright. In Panama, kitchen police (K-P) duties were performed by San Blas Indians, specifically employed for the job, to free the paratroopers for more essential duties.

The troopers of the 501st Parachute Battalion accomplished several airborne maneuvers, some of which were held near Rio Hato, about 50 miles from Fort Kobbe. Supply and equipment parachutes bore huge emblazoned numbers on the canopies to facilitate their recovery and identification following jumps. The long marches back to base camp caused the troopers of the 501st Parachute Battalion to recognize the

The DC-3 or C-47 trooper transport plane. Picture taken at Lawson Field, Fort Benning, Georgia, early 1942.

Photo Courtesy Joe Walukas

17

importance of discipline in use of water to prevent dehydration in the jungle heat. In August 1941, the 550th Infantry Airborne Battalion, with Company C, 501st Parachute Battalion, conducted the first airborne training exercise in United States Army history. This maneuver, in the Republic of Panama, used the C-39 troop transport planes with B-18 bombers of the USAAF. Critiques following the exercise underlined the need for coordination between Air Corps and airborne paratroopers.

After February 1942, each succeeding graduating class of paratroopers from the jump school was processed to fill the ranks of the authorized units. On 1 May 1942, the 504th Parachute Infantry Regiment was activated, with command going to Lt. Col. Reubin H. Tucker (West Point Class of 1935). Some of the men of this regiment became integral to the future structure of the 503d Parachute Infantry Regiment. On 20 May 1942, less than three months after formation of the 503d, Colonel Miley was ordered by the War Department to provide a parachute battalion for overseas duty in Europe. He released the Second Battalion (originally the 504th Battalion) because it was near the authorized troop strength, and its men well trained in communications, sabotage, and demolition. This group departed from Fort Bragg on 29 May 1942 and arrived at Fort Dix, New Jersey, on 1 June.

These paratroopers left New York Harbor on 3 June 1942 aboard the HMS *Queen Elizabeth*. They landed in Glasgow, Scotland, in late afternoon on 10 June, then boarded a train for an overnight trip to England. This unique and distinguished battalion would later become the famed 509th Parachute Battalion after its initial blood bath in North Africa. Lt. Col. Edson D. Raff (West Point Class of 1933) was commanding.

In March 1942 the famous Eighty-second Infantry Division was reactivated. In June 1942, Brig. Gen. Matthew B. Ridgway (West Point Class of 1917) was elevated to Division commander. Colonel Miley, commander of the 503d Parachute Infantry Regiment, departed to join the Eighty-second Division as the new assistant division commander with a promotion to brigadier general. Lt. Col. Robert F. Sink, the 503d executive officer, assumed command of the 503d on 20 May 1942. The Eighty-second Division was assigned airborne status on 15 August. The 506th PIR was activated on 20 July 1942. Colonel Sink was reassigned to command this new regiment. Colonel Sink, along with numerous other original officers of the 501st, would ultimately gather his "stars." He later led the Strategic Army Command and became commander in chief-South (Panama). When Colonel Sink relinquished command of the 503d, his executive officer, who had recently returned to Fort Bragg from his command of the 501st Parachute Battalion in Panama, became the new commander of the 503d Parachute Infantry Regiment.

Lt. Col. Kenneth Holmes Kinsler, new commander of the 503d, was born 22 June 1901. His early childhood and adolescent years are obscure; he enrolled at the University of Nebraska in September 1923 in a pre-medical program. Kinsler was active in the Reserve Officers Training Corps at the university, serving as a first lieutenant in Company D. Kinsler did not graduate from the University of Nebraska; he dropped out on 29 July 1924. In those uncertain pre-depression years, when employment was difficult to obtain, Kinsler entered the United States military service on 8 September 1926. He was commissioned a second lieutenant and assigned to the Twenty-eighth Infantry.

When the Twenty-eighth and Twenty-ninth Infantry Regiments were screened for volunteers to form the 501st Parachute Battalion, Capt. Kenneth H. Kinsler stepped forward to enter airborne history.

The departure of the Second Battalion of the 503d for Europe left the First Battalion all alone at Fort Bragg. By authorization of the War Department, dated 4 June 1942, the Third Battalion of the 503d was activated. Command went to Major John J. Tolson III (West Point Class of 1937), who later commanded the U.S. Army Eighteenth Airborne Corps and attained a rank of Lieutenant general. Major Tolson had earlier formed Company A of the 504th Battalion. He was battalion executive officer of the Second Battalion when it was ordered to Europe. The night before its departure, Colonel Miley assigned Major Tolson to form the newly authorized Third Battalion of the 503d.

The troopers who formed the new newly activated Third Battalion came from the cadre of the 502d PIR at Fort Benning (actually still the 502d Battalion). On 7 June 1942 all of the 502d troopers, less essential officers and a few key noncoms, were laterally transferred to Fort Bragg to form the Third Battalion of the 503d Parachute Infantry Regiment. This accomplishment was facilitated as follows:

Headquarters and HQ Company of the 502d became HQ and HQ Company Third Battalion; Company A of the 502d became Company G, Third Battalion, 503d; Company B of the 502d became Company H, Third Battalion, 503d; and Company C of the 502d was assigned as Company I, Third Battalion, 503d Parachute Infantry Regiment. A later chapter will describe the differences in structure and organization between a parachute regiment and a regular infantry regiment.

When Lieutenant Colonel Kinsler departed from Panama, he relinquished command of the 501st to the battalion executive officer, Maj.

Maj. John J. Tolson III, commander of the newly activated Third
Battalion.

George M. Jones. Parachuting was now done from C-47 aircraft, the workhorse of the United States Army Air Force, to which paratroopers had given the endearing nickname of "Flying Coffin." A later plane, the C-46, which had both right and left jump doors, was soon stricken from the troop transport list because troopers had to relearn jump exit pivots if they were to jump from the right rear door. Early training exercises with the C-46 saw poor plane exits, poor body positions because of speed and prop-blast, and too frequent parachute malfunctions, also resulting from the prop blast. Its greater payload and lift capacity later made the C-46 of greater use in resupplying ground troops by air drops. Test jumps, supervised by Lt. John B. Pratt, using the Marine, T-5, and T-6 parachutes, were conducted at Fort Bragg. The recommendations by this group of men and officers as to which were the better aspects of the various parachutes tested were later incorporated into the T-7, the parachute the 503d troopers used in their later combat jumps.

One early innovation by the 501st Battalion in Panama and the 503d Battalions in Fort Bragg was the night parachute jump. Numerous such jumps were conducted on the squad, platoon, company, and battalion levels. On a great many occasions at Fort Bragg, however, men and officers would claim to be leaving for night jump training exercises but would don dress uniforms under their coveralls. After arriving in Fayetteville, where the airport was located, the troopers secured their parachutes and outer garments and had a night on the town. Yankee ingenuity "pulled the wool" over the eyes of the commanding brass. The 503d made several exhibition jumps to impress such notables as Franklin D. Roosevelt, Gen. George C. Marshall, U.S. Army Chief of Staff, Gen. Dwight D. Eisenhower, British Prime Minister Sir Winston Churchill, and Lord Louis Mountbatten of the British Expeditionary Forces. After observing the 503d jump at Fort Jackson, South Carolina, in early May 1942, President Roosevelt requested that this unit of paratroopers parade in the Washington, D.C., Memorial Day celebrations. The First Battalion of the 503d made this much heralded march in the nation's capitol. The troopers had a gala weekend on the town, and reports were that the city was never the same again.

A large area of training ground used for maneuvers by various army groups as well as jump sites for paratroopers was located in and around the city of Hoffman, North Carolina, an area at first called Camp Hoffman. On 1 May 1943, this training ground was named Camp Mackall in honor of the Second Battalion trooper Tommy Mackall, who was mortally wounded in that unit's combat jump into North Africa on 8 November 1942. One brisk and memorable day in early October

1942 the First and Third Battalions at Fort Bragg were alerted to prepare for a foreign expedition. Great numbers of men were needed to fill the ranks to authorized strength.

Newly qualified paratroopers from jump school and other airborne units undergoing activation were drained to beef up the First Battalion. The men of the 503d worked long hours to load the baggage cars of the Pullman train backed onto a spur line of the Fort Bragg quartermaster railroad complex. By the eve of 10 October 1942, men and equipment had been entrained. In late afternoon on that day Major General Ridgway, commander of the Eighty-second Airborne Division, personally delivered Company A of the newly activated 504th Parachute Infantry Regiment. As the sun set in the West on this notable Saturday evening, the wheels of our troop train began turning. Major Tolson, Third Battalion commander, was temporarily transferred to the rank of regimental executive officer. He commanded the troop train during the entire journey. The regimental commander, Colonel Kinsler, had left by air for California and thence to Australia to prepare an encampment for us there. These were the early events that began the 503d Parachute Infantry Regiment moving toward its destiny and the annals of the history of airborne warfare.

The erratic week-long train ride was largely uneventful. The seemingly endless days provided the men of the 503d PIR time for a sobering and long gaze at the vastness and greatness of our country. Years would pass before most would again see the magnificent countryside. For untold scores of others, this panorama was their final view of their beloved homeland. A stop in Elko, Nevada, one afternoon to take on fuel and water provided a temporary respite. Troopers tossed sums of money to civilian onlookers, with the request they make a mad dash to a visible liquor store. As our westward-bound train once again began to move, large numbers of civilians were still running both ways with troopers' money and "hootch." By late evening, our Pullman coaches were full of great joy and much noise. Officers ordered a shakedown that netted only a few bottles — the troopers were sly. The few enlisted men who got caught with bottles provided free drinks for the officers.

At last our regiment arrived at Camp Stoneman, near Pittsburg, California, where serious preparations for embarkation overseas were begun. Vaccinations for tropical diseases, ordnance checks, equipment checks, clothing checks, the issuance of a unit of fire for each weapon, security checks, and other checks. A trooper had talked with a guy who had overheard another dogface tell another fellow our future destination — . His name? KILROY! He had been there!

22

On 19 October 1942 at dark, companies of the 503d Parachute Infantry Regiment were assembled and began marching out. Each man carried his weapon, a unit of fire, his helmet, and two heavy barracks bags. The column of men was long and silent. Neither loud talking nor lights were permitted. Soon the troopers began perspiring. Sharp ears would have caught numerous blasphemies. It seemed like eternity before we arrived at our port of embarkation.

This physically demanding night ended as each trooper approached the ship's officers bearing our manifest; each saluted and stated his name, rank, and serial number. He then stumbled up the steep gangplank, descended into his designated hold on the ship, and sought a bed among tiers of bunks four and five high. The crammed holds were extremely odoriferous that hot night. Dawn of Tuesday, 20 October 1942, found the 503d PIR with its First and Third Battalions plus the company of troopers of the 504th PIR steaming under the Golden Gate Bridge and out of San Francisco Bay. We floated low in the ocean because we were heavily laden with troops, food, supplies, and ammunition. Our transportation was one of twenty-nine of the Netherlands East Indies ships that had escaped the Japanese onslaught and were being used to transport troops and supplies between the United States and Australia or between Australia and the islands to the north. Our ship was a converted Dutch freighter, the SS *Poelau Laut*, registered in Batavia, Java. She had been built in Amsterdam in 1929. She had a 61.2 foot-beam, 36-foot 10-inch draft, and was 494 feet long, with an eight-cylinder oil engine. (The old girl survived the war, again ran the trade route between Amsterdam and Indonesia, and finally was sold as scrap to Hong Kong in 1959.) The crew was Indonesian. Our heading was due south along the coast of California, Mexico, and Central America. We docked twelve days later at Balboa, Panama Canal Zone, where the 501st Parachute Battalion less Company C came aboard. Essential noncoms and officers of Company C remained behind to form a cadre of the 551st Parachute Battalion, activated in November 1942. Enlisted men of Company C were laterally transferred to Battalion Headquarters Company, and Companies A and B; and others joined ranks with the men of the 504th company we had attached.

By late afternoon, all men and equipment had been loaded. Canal authorities had the ship escorted out of the channel and into the open sea. The voyage resumed, but this time in a west-southwesterly direction into the vastness of the mighty Pacific Ocean. After leaving Panama, another month would pass before we sighted land. In the interim, the troopers listened to navigational directions given in a strange, guttural language over the intercom. The ship's captain, a man of Dutch extraction, issued commands such as "daumphh de garrrbiddggee," "pipe down de mess," "de smoking lamp is lit," "de smoking lamp is oudt." The old Dutch freighter turned troop transport had no destroyer escort. It sailed south by west at a steady twelve knots per hour, heading downhill and with a tailwind. Approximately halfway to the destination, a fierce tropical typhoon hit with ocean waves higher than the ship's mast. The seiches of the ocean plus the yaws and pitches of the old ship, induced a great amount of seasickness among the paratroopers of the 503d Parachute Infantry Regiment. Tension was heightened by an erroneous submarine sighting late one stormy evening. Smoke pots were fired, and the troop transport circled within the periphery of the smoke. The landlubbers of the 503d were getting anxious to see terra firma. Traveling the vast expanse of the mighty Pacific Ocean on the old troop transport, one could see the skipper, Captain J. van der Meer, at the helm, peering intensely into the seemingly endless western horizon. Gazing sternly over his shoulder was the new commander of the 501st Parachute Battalion, Lt. Col. George M. Jones.

Lieutenant Colonel Jones, the senior officer of the heterogenous group of paratroopers aboard, was the regimental executive officer and commander of all troops aboard ship. This young West Point graduate rapidly began to inculcate disciplinary standards that would well serve the 503d Parachute Infantry Regiment in the months and years to come. Aboard ship at this time were a total of 1,939 men and officers, slightly under the 1,958 men and officers authorized by the War Department for a parachute infantry regiment.

2
Call To Action

Activities on board the troopship were varied and numerous. They included KP duty, calisthenics, reading, writing, swabbing down the decks, cleaning the equipment, and gambling. On that crowded old freighter there was a good chance that each trooper would eventually meet all the others. Bull sessions between men of different companies gave rise to a closeness and brotherhood among the men of the regiment not paralleled in recent military history. A regimental fighting or marching song was written by Cpl. Ken Brown of Regimental Headquarters and Headquarters Company Special Services Section. (See appendix.) The troopers learned the words and joined in singing the march several times during the voyage across the Pacific. The regimental S-2 officer attempted to teach the troopers that the Japanese fighting men were subhuman in size and intelligence. The troopers later discovered that a great many of the Japanese warriors were much larger in stature than most of us. Common Japanese words and phrases were taught, but most of them were derogatory. The troopers soon learned that many enemy soldiers spoke fluent English, which they used to try to throw the Americans off guard during their frequent predawn banzai charges.

At specified intervals, the troopers were given booster shots or vaccinations for tropical diseases to supplement the series begun at Camp Stoneman before they had embarked on the expedition. Inoculations against smallpox, yellow fever, diphtheria, and tetanus were administered by the 503d medics, under the supervision of the regimental surgeon, Maj. Monroe B. Gall. Simultaneous shots into each arm and under the shoulder blade caused a few paratroopers to become faint.

On 21 November 1942, our troopship crossed the International Date Line, and we gained one day in time. We were instructed to set our clocks ahead twenty-four hours. The time change was a topic of conversation for awhile among the dogfaces and created a classroom atmosphere that encouraged the science-trained GI's to display their knowledge of latitude, longitude, sidereal and solar time, and the revolution and rotation of the earth. Another important day, the one when we crossed the equator, gave rise to a carnival atmosphere aboard ship

THE 503ᵈ SONG

Reproduced by Permission 503ʳᵈ RCT Association [WW II]

(See Appendix A)

If you see a Soldier with a parachute on his hat walking proudly down the street I'll

Bet you money that if you say "HEY" Soldier Boy what outfit are you in? He'll turn about and

he will shout with all the pride in him: I'm Proud I'm allowed to be one of the crowd of the Parachute

Infantry! Fighting men are we fighting for our Liberty. We'll lick the Japs, the dirty rats and

S.S. POELAU LAUT

Domain of Neptunus Rex

To ALL SAILORS wherever ye may be
And to all Mermaids, Sea Serpents, Whales, Sharks and other Living
Things of the Sea, GREETINGS: Know Ye that on this Certain day
of *XXX* 1942, in Lat. 00-00, Long. 361' W., there appeared within
our Royal Domain the U. S. A. T. 01 bound Southward for the Equator
and beyond. Be it REMEMBERED said Vessel, Officers and Crew
have been inspected and passed upon by Ourself and Royal Staff; and
Be It KNOWN by all Ye Sailors, Marines and Landlubbers who may
be honored by his presence that—

Private Bennett M. Guthrie

having been found worthy to be numbered as One of our Trusty
Shellbacks, has been gathered to our Fold and initiated into the Solemn
Mysteries of the Ancient Order of the Deep. By virtue of the Power
invested in Me, I hereby Command All of My Subjects to show him
due honor and respect whenever he may enter our Realm.

Disobey this Order under penalty of Our Royal Displeasure.
Given under our hand and Seal this Certain day of *XXX* 1942.

NEPTUNUS REX
Davy Jones   Ruler of the Raging Main.
Royal Scribe.

All the 503d paratroopers received this certificate that they had crossed the Equator.

28

and much horseplay. A canvas hold cover was filled with sea water to form a large pool or tank. A gangplank was installed over the tank, and blindfolded troopers were walked across it and off into the pool, simulating a fall into the briny deep. This ritual was generally accomplished by men who had their heads shaved, were nude, and had their bodies smeared with grease. Neptunus Rex was the ruling monarch that day, and each man aboard ship received a certificate that he had crossed the equator.

Toward the end of our voyage some forty officers purchased several cases of beer from the ship's Steward. Lieutenant Colonel Jones, the executive officer for the regiment and commander of troops aboard ship, had forbidden any drinking en route because our ship was without escort and subject to Japanese submarine attack. When Colonel Jones learned that the officers were drinking in their crowded quarters, he disciplined them by confining them to their hot interior stateroom for about a week, allowing them only to march to and from meals.

Because Colonel Jones had spent time as a Military Police officer in Panama and now had confined officers, he was given the nick-name "Warden." Colonel Jones used his authority several times in the difficult years ahead to bolster morale and to demand and receive unquestioned discipline, but his foremost purpose was to mold us into a fighting force.

The long-awaited day at last arrived when land was sighted from the crows nest atop the masthead. We were originally scheduled to go to Townsville, but our orders were changed to proceed north between the continent of Australia and the Great Barrier Reef. Finally, on 2 December 1942, our troopship steamed into port and docked at Cairns, North Queensland, Australia. Our long voyage ended 42 days after we had left Pittsburg, California, and a month after we had left Panama, Canal Zone.

The troopers were elated and very alert as they disembarked from the smelly old ship. They filed ashore in relays, were loaded aboard lorries (two-and-a-half-ton trucks), and transported in a southerly direction. The long but exciting day ended late at night with the men of the 503d Parachute Infantry Regiment eating crumpets (sweets) and a thick hamburger (a new dish to our hosts), drinking hot tea or tepid cordial (comparable to soda pop in the United States), and sizing up the terrain. This gracious hospitality was attributable to the thoughtfulness of the Australian North Queensland Country Women's Association, the Catholic Daughters of Australia, the Australian Comfort Fund, the

[Not drawn to Scale]

Australian Red Cross, the Salvation Army, and other women's organizations from Mulgrave Shire (county or parish) of North Queensland Province and the nearby village of Gordonvale. They spent much money, time, and effort to welcome us, and we were eternally grateful. While enjoying the refreshments, the exhausted, weary, silent, politely disciplined, but vigilant paratroopers listened in awe to the strange-sounding English accent of their hosts. The troopers attempted to express their gratitude to the Aussie ladies. The bond of friendship, given and accepted that night, has grown stronger even after four decades. Late that humid tropical night, in thickly forested areas assigned to the companies, the men of the regiment bedded down in two-man pup tents or under the canopies of the endless eucalyptus trees, whose branches encompassed all.

The 503d regimental encampment site was one and one-half to three miles southwest of Gordonvale and spread out on both sides of the Gillies Highway. Gordonvale was approximately fourteen miles south of Cairns. The region was in the Lower Riverstone watershed area. The climate was subtropical to tropical, and the foliage of the trees and undergrowth from the ocean to the inland mountains was that of the jungle. Reptiles, koala bears, and peculiar birds called "cuckoo-burrows" or laughing jackasses (because of their weird calls) abounded, and various brilliantly plumed cockatoos and a "wild turkey" that resembled the American crow were also seen.

December 1942 was a busy month. Training was generally suspended while the troopers unloaded the transport ship and erected a suitable camp. The men were placed in pyramidal squad tents for shelter. Early morning calisthenics always preceded breakfast and the day's strenuous activities. The accustomed three-mile daily runs were soon discontinued because of the taxing effect on the training paratroopers of the great heat and high humidity. The Australian Civil Construction Corps built wooden floors in the squad tents. The enlisted men of the companies constructed "corduroy" walkways from saplings, throughout the companies, battalions, and regimental areas.

Our tents were widely dispersed for safety in case of air raids. The Japs at this time were atop the Owen Stanley Mountains of New Guinea to the north of Australia. The people where we were stationed feared the Japs and were happy to see Yankee troops in the vicinity. Several people had already fled south in fear of a possible invasion by the Nips. Heavy monsoon rains soon began falling, flooding our campsite so the troops had to dig drainage ditches throughout the regimental area. These ditches were about six feet wide by five feet deep. One of the most welcome tents to be erected in our camp was that of the PX. Here, the troops could obtain needed toilet articles, boot-shining kits, candy, and beer from the Great Northern Brewery of Cairns. These items were sold after the usual work day ended, about five in the evening.

We discovered that in this land "down under" December was a summer month, and a wide variety of fruits, berries, and vegetables were in great abundance. The canned food, parachutes, rigging equipment, ammunition, and other supplies that had come on our transport ship, were stacked in piles on the downtown square of Gordonvale, covered with tarpaulins. This equipment was soon surrounded by mounds of watermelon rinds, the watermelon purchased locally and eaten voraciously by the energetic troopers. The greater part of the monetary transactions of Yankee dollars for Australian pounds were honest. A few Aussies, however, took advantage of the Yanks, mostly after posted closing hours of the pubs during the day or on weekends, when "sly grog" (bootleg hootch) was in great demand but in short supply.

Each evening about sundown, a local Aussie of Italian heritage traversed the regimental encampment with a horse-drawn cart. Although one of his arms had been amputated, he worked effectively and efficiently with the other, selling papayas, mangoes, pineapples, and bananas to the troopers. It was not long before demand and enterprise resulted in a more coveted item being hidden under the fruit in the cart: a varied assortment of liquid refreshments — gins, rums, brandies, and whiskeys. The brandies were labeled with two stars, three stars, or four stars according to their age and alcohol content. Those who had imbibed each swore that the stars indicated the number of days a hangover would last if one "killed the bottle." This bootleg hootch was a bit higher in price than that available in local pubs. Inasmuch as alcoholic beverages were rationed, demand great, and money available to pay a premium price for a desired bottle, the Italian fruit salesman began to put exorbitant price tags on his wares. He came to be known as the "one-armed bandit." His downfall came abruptly when he was forbidden to enter the regimental area by order of Colonel Kinsler. The troopers then had to rely on their strong legs to carry them to Gordonvale or other nearby places with pubs. Sale of beer at the PX was not allowed on the Sabbath.

A very hot and humid Christmas Day found the men of the 503d Parachute Infantry Regiment eating roast turkey with all the trimmings, prepared by well-intentioned but sadly misplaced chefs. The battalion cooks would have been better certified as truck mechanics, judging from the way they handled our food. Sadly, on the afternoon of this solemn feast day, Pfc. Henry J. Blalock drowned in the Little Mulgrave River while swimming. This accident occurred in a deep pool of the river near the base of Welches Pyramid, a dominating mountain peak of the area. Men of the 503d frequented this spot to wash their clothes and to cool off after a hard day's activities.

After establishing our base camp in Australia, our regiment needed to be reorganized. The original Second Battalion had been dispatched to England, where it became the famed 509th Parachute Battalion after its initial combat operation in North Africa. When the 501st Parachute Battalion came aboard our troopship in Panama, its Company C was left behind. All unessential men of Company C were transferred into other 501st Battalion companies to bring them up to strength. Those C Company men left in Panama, mostly officers and noncoms, formed the cadre for the 551st Parachute Infantry Battalion activated in November 1942. It will be well to remember that when the 503d left Fort Bragg, North Carolina, on the eve of 10 October 1942, Company A of the 504th Parachute Infantry Regiment was among the entourage.

In Australia a new Second Battalion was restructured as follows:

501st Battalion Headquarters Company became Second Battalion Headquarters Company of the 503d.
504th Company A became the Second Battalion D Company of the 503d.
501st Battalion Company A became the Second Battalion E Company of the 503d.
501st Battalion Company B became the Second Battalion F Company of the 503d.

As a newly organized and firmly unified regimental fighting force, we entered a series of concentrated training exercises designed to prepare us for jungle warfare.

The union of the 503d Parachute Infantry Battalion with the 504th Parachute Battalion on 2 March 1942 had resulted in the formation of the 503d Parachute Infantry Regiment, the first parachute infantry regiment to be formed in the United States Army. This was a two-battalion regiment, as authorized by the War Department in 1942. When the Second Battalion (originally the 504th Battalion) departed for Europe on 29 May 1942, the First Battalion (originally the 503d Battalion), remaining in Fort Bragg, was but half a regiment. A War Department directive of 4 June 1942 authorized the activation of a Third Battalion for the 503d, to be filled by men from the 502d Parachute Infantry Battalion, now in cadre among the many companies of the newly activated 502d Parachute Infantry Regiment in Fort Benning, Georgia. The addition of the Third Battalion to the 503d Parachute Infantry Regiment still left the regiment with only two battalions stateside. In October 1942, as the 503d Parachute Infantry Regiment expedited to the Southwest Pacific Area, the 501st Parachute Infantry Battalion in Panama, Canal Zone, joined the regiment enroute to become the essential ingredient for the authorized three-battalion regiment. The restructure of the battalions to form the 503d Parachute Infantry Regiment in Australia was outlined above.

The 503d Parachute Infantry Regiment, with an authorized strength of 1,958 men and officers, was structurally different from its counterparts in regular army infantry regiments. First, it had a Regimental Headquarters and Headquarters Company. Regimental Headquarters was controlled by the regimental commander and his sectional chiefs, whose duties were as follows. The S-1 Section (Executive Section) was responsible for execution of administrative orders, movement of troops, and liaison with all battalions and companies within the regimental structure. The S-2 Section (Intelligence Section) executed assignments for reconnaissance, was responsible for total regimental security, and contained the essential interpreters of the enemy language. The S-3 Section (Plans and Training Section) directed total regimental communications relative to regimental assignments in combat with all battalions and companies. The S-4 Section (Supply and Service Section) was responsible for all supplies and resupplies, including rations, ammunition, clothing, and other essential items. The three battalions' headquarters companies and the rifle companies had sections corresponding to those listed here.

Regimental Headquarters was a complex organization. Within the structure of this unit were communication sections, a postal section, and a demolition section, and attached to but separate from it, was a Service Company. The regimental Service Company consisted of the company commander and his staff plus first-aid men (medics), the regimental chaplains, and the Quartermaster Section. The Quartermaster Section provided a supply sergeant for each of the other regimental companies. The Service Company also contained the Parachute Riggers' Section and the few vehicles for transporting supplies, equipment, troops, and communications directives. All supplies and resupplies of food, ammunition, and equipment were the responsibility of the Service Company.

Each battalion headquarters resembled the primary structure of the regimental headquarters. A Battalion Headquarters Company consisted of the battalion cooks, the battalion surgeon, and his staff with accompanying medics, a communications section, a supply section, and others. Originally, each battalion Headquarters Company had a single eight-gun platoon of light machine guns. This platoon had four squads with two light machine guns per squad. This structure changed after the first combat operation, replaced by three four-gun light machine gun platoons. The battalion Headquarters Company contained a four-squad platoon of 81mm mortars, one gun per squad. Machine guns and mortars were assigned as needed to the rifle companies.

There were three rifle companies per battalion:

First Battalion Headquarters and Headquarters Company:
Rifle companies assigned were A, B, and C
Second Battalion Headquarters and Headquarters Company:
Rifle companies assigned were D, E, and F
Third Battalion Headquarters and Headquarters Company:
Rifle companies assigned were G, H, and I

Each rifle company had three platoons of riflemen and one platoon of 60mm mortars. Each platoon consisted of three squads. The third squad of each platoon of riflemen also was provided with a light machine gun. Troopers of the rifle companies were armed with Garand rifles (M-1s), 1903 model Springfield rifles, .45 caliber pistols, .45 caliber Thompson submachine guns, trench knives, bayonets, and Browning automatic rifles. The mortar platoon had three 60mm mortars, one gun per rifle company platoon. Each rifle company squad had one rifleman equipped to fire rifle grenades. These grenades were of two types: fragmentation and antitank. The later were replaced in late 1944 by the bazooka, a portable rocket launcher.

Minor structural differences existed within each company or battalion to suit the needs of a particular time and place, the manpower available, and the demands of a situation. Medics were normally assigned permanently to the rifle companies, but these gallant troopers suffered casualties, received promotional transfers, or requested transfers from one company to another. The machine gun platoons and 81mm mortar platoons of Battalion Headquarters Company usually followed an assigned rifle company pattern. But in response to pressing demands in a particular combat situation, tough bearers of "strong medicine" could rapidly shift their heavy weapon support from one company to another or combine their total assembly on any given sector in an amazingly brief period of time. Paratroopers of the various commands were versed and rehearsed about the weapons and fire support of all other commands of the regiment, thereby instilling confidence in the individual trooper.

Each paratrooper, upon securing his own safety, would expect to see to that of his fellow trooper. Were it not for this unity, comaraderie, and devoted fellowship among the troopers of the 503d Parachute Infantry, the loss of lives would have been much greater both in practice and in combat jumps. Paratroopers quickly discovered during the war that in a combat operation, when behind enemy lines and amid the foe, there is no one more close than one's buddy. Absolute and unquestionable trust in the fellow trooper was necessary. He became closer than one's own brother. This is the applied but unwritten creed of the United States Army paratrooper. At this time, Col. Kenneth Kinsler was the regimental commander, Lt. Col. George M. Jones was the regimental executive officer, Maj. Joe Lawrie commanded the First Battalion, Maj. John Haltom the Second Battalion, and Maj. John J. Tolson III, the Third Battalion.

In the nearby village of Gordonvale, the United States Army had requisitioned the Gordonvale and Commercial hotels to be used as hospitals and the Central hotel for use by the American Red Cross as a canteen. This canteen, operated by Miss Catherine Irving (who died several months later in southern Australia), provided a place for men to lounge when they were off duty and held dances for chaperoned young Aussie lassies with the Yanks. All drinks, foods, and services were paid for by the troopers. The paratroopers resented this charge very much because they knew their parents, relatives, and friends back in the United States were contributing generously to the Red Cross so their armed forces personnel overseas could have a taste of home while away from home free of costs.

Several parachute training jumps were made into the interior of the North Queensland province, locally referred to as the "never-never" land or the "tableland." This flat land with a savannah climate and vegetation provided good jump sites. On the long marches back to base camp, carrying full field equipment loads of sixty pounds or more, we met numerous field tactical problems. The U.S. Army C rations were of three kinds: hash, vegetable beef, or pork and beans. Many men would purchase canned beef, vegetables, and fruit from local grocers to take along on the training exercises because our limited menu was boring. There were abundant wild and hot pepper plants in the mountains of the "never-never" land. The high mountain ranges cooled rain clouds, causing rain to fall on the seaward or ocean side and leaving the winds that passed over the top to the inland areas quite dry. The mountain effect accounted for the savannah climate of the tableland and also for the vegetation and the rapid runoff of rainfall to the sea during the wet or monsoon season. The Little Mulgrave River had no fish because of the short distance from its headwaters to its mouth. The wild edible plants in the mountains and the peppers provided spice and dietary supplements to the dreary C rations.

The 503d's military field problems usually ended by sunset on Saturdays. Then a celebration by the troopers that consisted of "beer busts" and barbecues would begin. Each payday, voluntary contributions were paid into a company slush fund or "kitty" that was used to buy needed items that were not issued by the U.S. Army. Steers or hogs for our barbecues and the kegs of beer from the Great Northern Brewery in Cairns were some of these items. Cooking details were sent to base camp to prepare the feast at least half a day before the troops were expected. The large wooden barrels of beer with their wooden spigots were centrally located in the company area. Long after eating their fill and into the wee hours of the night, troopers would be found tapping the keg, filling their canteen cups, and shooting the bull. Singing of airborne songs would eventually die down in tempo and enthusiasm; sometimes fights erupted between troopers.

To avoid the confusion and transportation problems of leap-frogging a regiment of men to the packing shed and to allow more time for the men to obtain jungle warfare training, Australian women were employed and trained as parachute riggers. About two dozen of these lassies were given a two-week riggers' training course beginning 17 February 1943. The packing shed was in Norman Park, across the street from the American Red Cross building. It was reportedly the first air-conditioned building on the continent of Australia. One of these riggers, Miss Dulcie Pitts, whose vocal talents were encouraged in the friendly atmosphere of the camp, later became known in international musical shows as Georgia Lee.

On 24 February 1943, during the monsoon season, a three-day maneuver by the regiment resulted in the drowning deaths of two more men in the flooded Little Mulgrave River. "Enemy forces," consisting of Company A plus a mixed platoon, were left stranded on the tableland side of the river. As this group of men attempted to swim across, Pvts. John Kobiska and Bernard Petrie paid with their lives. This unnecessary double drowning aroused ire among both the troops and the civilians. One requirement for paratroopers that was not listed in airborne qualification standards was that of being an able swimmer.

Mrs. Ivy Stokes and Miss Mary Barrett inspecting parachutes at the 503d Parachute Infantry Regiment packing shed, Gordonvale, Queensland, Australia, 31 December 1943.

Parachute jumps were made to satisfy jump pay status, in training exercises, or as exhibitions for visiting VIP's. In noncombat arenas, one jump per month was mandatory to stay on jump pay status. Jump pay or "hazardous" duty pay was now $50 above base pay for enlisted men but $100 above base pay for officers. One must surmise that the extra money was needed to induce the officers to jump out of the airplane door.

Various events punctuated the time in spring 1943. Lt. Gen. Walter Krueger, the U.S. Sixth Army commander of the Southwest Pacific Area, inspected the 503d on 24 March. On 9 April, Sir Leslie Wilson, governor of Queensland province, made a visit. Another sad loss occurred on 2 April 1943, when S/Sgt. Bernard drowned while on maneuvers. On 1 May, General Downing, the British liaison officer who was attached to the Australian army, inspected the 503d regiment. On 5 May, General Lavarack of the First Australian Army visited us. On 6 May, a jump near Cairns resulted in the electrocution death of Pvt. Robert H. White, when he became entangled in electrical transmission lines. A jump field was created by men of the regiment working with machetes and pick-mattocks, to clear the brushy lantana a couple miles east of Gordonvale. Occasionally as they worked, a subterranean marsupial rodent called a bandicoot made its appearance. This jump field was named White Field in honor of our lost comrade.

In any group of soldiers, there are always a few who want to "goldbrick" or relegate their duties to others through faked injuries or illness. The 503d had its share of these men. There were, however, legitimate aches and pains that were not properly cared for by the regimental surgeon, Major Gall. Complaints to the regimental commander and the inspector general resulted in his transfer from the 503d. Highly trained first-aid men took care of most of the strains, sprains, cuts, and bruises and were greatly admired by the troopers. Capt. Robert F. Lamar replaced Major Gall as regimental surgeon.

In the numerous training jumps in the Gordonvale area, the 503d paratroopers "qualified" several company mascots: dogs, cats, ducks, chickens, and even a donkey. The latter nearly tore up a C-47 before it was forced out the door. The smaller animals were usually placed inside our chute equipment bags that were snapped either to our chest or leg harness snap fasteners. These animals were as glad to get to terra firma as were their jumpmasters.

On 25 June 1943, a regimental jump was made for benefit of the Australian general, Sir Thomas Blamey, and Gen. Douglas MacArthur, commander of the Southwest Pacific Area. The C-47 transport planes took off in early afternoon from the airfield at Cairns and flew around for hours waiting for the VIP's to arrive at the jump site. It was dusk before Blamey and MacArthur arrived with all their entourage. Because the darkness caused poor visibility, the jump altitude was lowered from a thousand to six hundred feet. The jump took place en masse, as planned but Pvt. Donald "Shanghai" Wilson fell to his death as a result of not hooking up his anchor line snap fastener. The man who had checked out his equipment stated that Wilson *had* had his static line hooked up. It was surmised that Wilson thought we were jumping at the higher altitude and wanted to "free fall" before pulling his reserve parachute so as to give MacArthur a thrill. He had mentioned this idea to a buddy earlier in the flight. Because the jump altitude was lower, he did not have time to clear his reserve parachute after his delayed count. General Mac Arthur, witnessing this death leap, ordered that Private Wilson be awarded the Order of the Purple Heart. This was the regiment's first Purple Heart, and we had not yet seen combat. Other visitors to view the paratroopers of the 503d Parachute Infantry Regiment were Lt. Gen. Robert L. Eichelberger, U.S. Army First Corps commander, and from the British Army, Lord Louis Mountbatten. The latter gentleman was heard to say that the 503d troopers were too fat to be jungle fighters. Our combat record proves he was wrong. Col. Kenneth Kinsler, our regimental commander, ordered that a prison compound be constructed to accommodate paratroopers who were unruly, AWOL, or would not conform to proper behavior. This fenced-in area was referred to as the Barbed Wire Hotel. The isolated guardhouse was guarded by rotating companies of men under command of the officer of the day. Food, clothing, toilet articles, and other essentials were passed through the gate under close scrutiny of the provost Marshal. Some officers looked the other way when extra goodies were smuggled into the compound. If the officers did not cooperate, the guards had a way to get whiskey inside to their buddies — it was placed inside the cans of milk and carried past the inspecting officers by the prisoners themselves. If the prisoners became too inebriated and rowdy, they were placed inside a "sweat box" located inside the compound. This small house, without windows and with a crawlway door, was in the open sunlight. The menu was bread and water for a designated number of days. The men of the 503d were as one and could always find a way to help a buddy and ease his pain if he landed in the guardhouse. What little pain existed was short-lived.

The paratroopers in Australia had much to learn. The daily three- to four-mile runs were soon eliminated as too taxing. Rigorous calisthenics and long marches, however, were maintained. There were verbal communication problems at first between the Yanks and Aussies. *Sly grog* was illegally sold or consumed liquor. Alcohol for consumption was called *spirits*. A motion picture or movie was a *flick* or a *cinema*. The milk bar in Australia sold only milk products and perhaps sandwiches. Drug stores sold only prescribed medicines or drugs. If an Aussie told you to "keep your pecker up," he meant to keep your chin up. In a restaurant, the Yank should ask for *serviettes* and not napkins. If one were *knocked up*, he was tired.

Holidays, off-duty hours, and weekends found numerous paratroopers migrating to Cairns. In this large coastal city, were to be found women, wine, song, and other recreational attractions. The infamous Trocadero Theatre showed months-or year-old movies. The ultimate in patience and fortitude was to sit through a long cinema on a Sunday evening, sobering up from the previous night on the town, then board the "Toonerville Trolley" for the uncertain trip to Gordonvale. The "Toonerville Trolley" was a Yank nickname for the tram or railway carriage that ran from Cairns to Gordonvale and points beyond. This vehicle made stops at each crossroads to admit or discharge passengers. About half way to Gordonvale, the tram stopped, the steam lines were bled of hot water by the crew for their "spot" of tea, and a lengthy period of time elapsed before the tram moved forward again, much to the chagrin of the unappreciative paratroopers. The coffee-drinking Yanks did not appreciate the traditional Australian ritual.

Some troopers found new friends in other nearby villages such as Babinda, Kuranda, and Innisfail. To get a cold beer on Sunday, the trooper had best obtain an invitation from a civilian friend to the local bowling green. The bowling greens, to Australia, were like country clubs in America. The game of bowling was played outside on short, green grass, hence the name. The sport was very similar to that played in American bowling alleys. These private clubs served alcoholic beverages on Sundays. Once in a great while, after much persuading and bribing, a local pub owner could be enticed to let Yank and Aussie soldiers in the rear door and serve beverages in the darkened bar.

Weekends in Gordonvale sometimes saw fights between the paratroopers and the Australian Militia. The Australian Militia wore olive-drab bands on their campaign hats and were the Home Guards. The soldiers in the Australian Imperial Forces had volunteered to fight outside the continent and wore white hat bands. The latter were highly respected by both civilians and the troopers. The fist fights that occasionally erupted usually were the result of mixing grog with lassies claimed by local swains. The Aussie soldiers who lost lovers while away in New Guinea sometimes bitterly referred to the Yanks as "overpaid, overfed, oversexed, and over here." The same words have probably been heard by the soldiers of Hannibal and Alexander the Great to the present time.

On 7 August 1943, general orders were received for the 503d Parachute Infantry Regiment to proceed to New Guinea in preparation for combat operations. An advance party of one officer and eleven enlisted men flew to Port Moresby, New Guinea, on 15 August. The next day, the Second Battalion and components of other units of the regiment followed. The First and Third Battalions sailed from Cairns on 20 August on the liberty ship SS *Duntroon* and arrived in Port Moresby Harbor on the afternoon of the twenty-second in time to see a P-38 fighter pilot lose control of his plane and crash into the bay between the ship and the shore. Upon going ashore, the men were loaded aboard trucks and taken to Rigo Valley. Our camp was just across the road from Fifth Fighter Command Headquarters. Poor sanitation facilities, and fly infestation sent a third of the troopers to the hospital in short time with dysentery, or as the men called it, "the GI's." Additional jungle warfare training exercises were executed in the old Pack Mule encampment area. At this season south of the Owen-Stanley Mountain range, there was little or no rainfall, and water was scarce. The troopers learned to ration their canteen water supplies carefully. Training was a very serious matter because the Japanese army was just north of the mountain range that ran west to east across the large island of New Guinea. On a map, this island resembles a huge oriental dragon; it has a land mass equal to that of the state of Texas. While the 503d was conditioning its troops at Port Moresby, General MacArthur conceived the idea of "leapfrogging" the well-fortified areas held by the Japs and conquering weakly held but strategically important enemy positions. At this time there were relatively few Allied armed forces in the SWPA because the Allied leaders had decided to commit the bulk of the effort to the European theater of operations. General MacArthur had included the 503d Parachute Infantry Regiment in his leapfrog strategy.

Red alert sounded for our regiment on 1 September 1943. Quickly an air of stern, sober, and dedicated seriousness encompassed the 503d troopers' attitude. There were hurried ordnance checks, equipment shortage checks, parachute and parachute harness assembly checks, sand table studies, map studies, unit assignments, sharpening of jump knives, machetes, and trench knives, and final zeroing in of weapons. There were jump site objectives to be studied, areas to secure, and patrol area

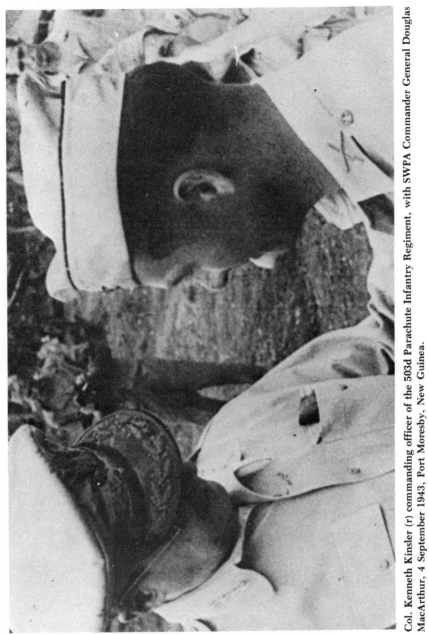

Col. Kenneth Kinsler (r) commanding officer of the 503d Parachute Infantry Regiment, with SWPA Commander General Douglas MacArthur, 4 September 1943, Port Moresby, New Guinea.

Photo Courtesy John Pratt

designations. Finally, by the evening of 4 September, all the physical requirements for combat preparedness had been completed. There was a last but not least preparation to be made — spiritual. Church call sounded as darkness fell. Protestant Chaplain Probert E. Herb and Father John J. Powers of the Roman Catholic faith reported very good attendance.

In Port Moresby, Papuan New Guinea, on the Saturday evening of 4 September 1943, in canvass-enclosed churches, we observed proud, straight-backed but humble paratroopers, now with bowed heads and bended knees, in baggy paratrooper jump suits, partaking of holy communion. At dawn tomorrow their mettle would be tested.

3
The Markham Valley Operation

An early Allied plan, termed Elkton III, listed three military objectives: (1) the invasion and reduction of Rabaul on the east end of New Britain; (2) the seizure of the Markham Valley of Papuan New Guinea; and (3) establishment of air control of the shipping lanes of the Huon Peninsula, Vitiaz, and Dampier Straits of New Guinea. Units for this undertaking were to be under the command of the New Guinea force commander, General Sir Thomas Blamey, commander in chief of the Australian military forces, Southwest Pacific Area. Headquarters at this time was at Brisbane, Australia. Lt. Gen. Walter Kreuger was commander of the newly organized U.S. Sixth Army, which had arrived in the SWPA in February 1943. General Kreuger created the U.S. Army First Corps under command of Lt. Gen. Robert L. Eichelberger with the attached 503d Parachute Infantry Regiment.

The second objective — seizure and control of the Markham Valley — was to be accomplished first to facilitate the accomplishment of the other two. The enemy was well entrenched in the Markham Valley. The Allies had too few ships to launch an entirely amphibious assault and too few aircraft for a strictly airborne attack. Nevertheless, General MacArthur ordered that the valley be seized. All available assault forces would be needed: parachute, overland, and shore-to-shore.

The Markham Valley extends northwestward from Lae toward the Ramu River. The trough of the valley varies up to twenty-five miles in width. It is bounded by jungle and mountains on either side. The prevailing winds run parallel with the Markham and Ramu river valleys. The grassy soil is well drained, and the extensive flat area would provide excellent airfield sites to accommodate the planned home of the Second Air Task Force with eight runways and adequate dispersal areas.

In September 1943 Japanese land combat forces of the Lae sector were under command of Maj. Gen. Ryoichi Shoge of the *Forty-first Division Infantry Group*. Many of his command were replacements passing through to Salamaua. Patrolling the Markham Valley and the Finschafen areas also fell under his command. The overall Japanese Lae zone commander was Lt. Gen. Hatazo Adachi, commander of the *Eighteenth Army*. General Shoge's troops consisted of *a naval guard unit*, and elements of the *Twenty-first, 102d*, and *115th infantry regiments*, with attached artillery and engineer supports. They totalled about ten thousand Japanese troops, including men of the *Fifty-first Division*, and a battalion of the *Special Naval Landing Forces*, better known as the Imperial Marines (hereafter designated as the SNLF).

The Allied base of operations for the Markham Valley, Lae, and Finschafen assaults was at Port Moresby, New Guinea. Allied attack plans included an air assault by paratroopers — the first tactical use of airborne troops in the Pacific theater of operations. The overland phase of operations involved the 2/2d Australian Pioneer Battalion, the 2/6th Field Company (AIF), and one company of the Papuan Infantry Battalion. Six days before the parachute attack, the units were to begin their trek from Tsili-Tsili and traverse the Watut River to the Nadzab area. The shore-to-shore invasion involved the Ninth Australian Division, commanded by Maj. Gen. G. F. Wooten, which was to land in the Bula River area east of Lae of 4 September. Following the parachute drop and seizure of the Nadzab airfield, airborne engineers and the Seventh Australian Army Division, commanded by Maj. Gen. E. A. Vasey, would be transported to the captured airfield by air transport, as soon as it was secured and runway repairs were made so aircraft could land.

For nearly three weeks before the Lae operation, U.S. and Anzac airman had made shambles of threatening enemy airfields at Wewak, Hansa Bay, Alexishafen, and Madang. At Wewak, more than 250 enemy planes were destroyed on the ground and in aerial dogfights. The Third Australian Division and the U.S. Forty-first Division were executing diversionary attacks in the Salamaua area, which, coincident with the assaults overland and shore-to-shore and the parachute drop in the Huon Gulf, were intended to confuse the enemy.

Lt. Gen. George C. Kenney, commanding general of the Allied air forces and commander of the Fifth U.S. Army Air Force, would provide the transport planes, preassault bombardment, and fighter protection for the airborne operation. September 1943 found the SWPA air force with 14 squadrons of transport planes, 197 heavy bombers, and 598 fighters. Many planes were old, subject to casualties, and difficult to keep in flying condition. The 348th Fighter Group had P-47s, the 475th Fighter Group flew P-38s, and the 380th Heavy Bombardment Group was made up of B-25s, B-17s, and A-20s. The USAAF would provide the heavy artillery for the 503d paratroopers for the duration of the war. These various air groups were dispersed in eight different airfields in the Port Moresby, Dobadura, Tsili-Tsili, and Marilinan areas.

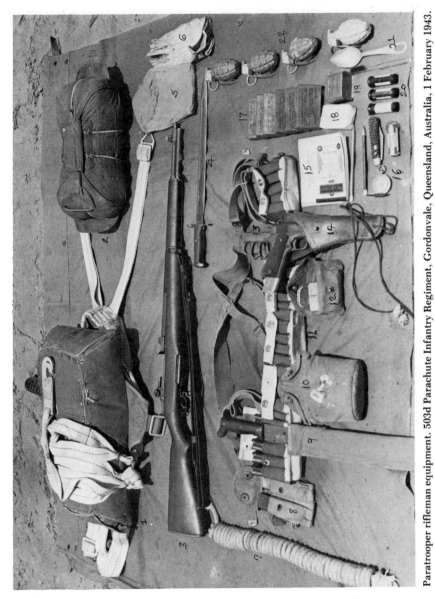

Paratrooper rifleman equipment. 503d Parachute Infantry Regiment, Gordonvale, Queensland, Australia, 1 February 1943.

47

Key to photo on page 47 (Paratrooper Rifleman Equipment)

1. Main parachute (back)
2. Reserve parachute (chest)
3. M-1 Garand rifle with eight-round clip
4. Bayonet
5. Mosquito head net
6. Leather gloves
7. Jump rope used for descending from trees
8. Extra ammunition clips for .45 caliber pistol
9. Machete
10. Water canteen
11. 200-round ammunition belt
12. First-aid kit
13. Trench knife with brass knuckles
14. .45 caliber pistol
15. Notebook with pencils
16. Switchblade jump knife, compass, match container
17. Dehydrated food rations (type K)
18. Bandage
19. Oil and cleaning patches for weapon
20. Halozone tablets for water treatment, salt tablets, foot powder
21. Spoon
22. Hand grenades

In addition, the paratrooper had a steel helmet, binoculars, maps, tobacco, extra socks, and poncho, and most troopers jumped with extra mortar, machine gun ammunition, and bandoleers of rifle ammunition. Total combat jump loads weighed about eighty pounds.

Predawn reveille on Sunday morning 5 September 1943, exploded to the shrill whistles of the noncom charge of quarters. The troopers of the 503d Parachute Infantry Regiment rapidly assembled in their battalion areas and nervously nibbled at a hastily prepared but unappetizing breakfast. Men and equipment were loaded aboard two-and-one-half-ton trucks (lorries) for the trip to the assigned airstrip. Here the troopers donned their preadjusted chutes. The padded equipment bundles, with company and battalion codes stenciled on their covers, were loaded aboard the appropriate airplanes by the squads or platoons that would use their contents.

Individual weapons were disassembled and placed in their "fiddle cases," which were held secure during jumps by the belly band of the parachute harness assembly. These padded cases had a wire inserted through grommets, which if pulled sharply, would open the weapon container. A later innovation by the thoughtful paratroopers made the "fiddle cases" obsolete. A rifle-bore cleaning patch was partially inserted into the bore of the weapon. Even though the weapon barrel plunged into earth upon landing, the patch could be quickly removed and the weapon was ready to fire. This idea eliminated having to assemble weapons while under enemy fire.

The troopers rubbed a skin-darkening dermaflage onto their faces and hands. Each man carried the popular mosquito repellent oil of citronelle in his first aid kit, which also held bandages, sulfa drugs, a needle-equipped tube of morphine, and Halozone tablets for water purification. The baggy jump suits were stiflingly hot. After this operation, they would never be used again in the SWPA but would be replaced by green herringbone twill coveralls.

Ninety-six C-47 troop transport planes were lined up alongside the runway. They were part of the Fifty-fourth Troop Carrier Wing, commanded by Col. Paul H. Prentiss. Seventy-nine of them would carry the seventeen hundred paratroopers of the 503d PIR. All companies were understrength because of illness, deaths, and the lack of replacements since the 503d had been sent overseas. Five of the C-47s would carry four officers and twenty-eight enlisted men of the Australian Imperial Forces of the 2/4th Field Regiment with their twenty-five-pounder field artillery pieces. The twenty-five-pound artillery piece was standard for the Australian army at this time. It had a bore of about three and one-half inches and a nearly eight-feet-long barrel, and its projectile weighed nearly twenty-five pounds. These volunteers, who had never made a parachute jump before, would jump into the Nadzab area two hours after the initial 503d PIR assault. The Australian artillerymen of the 2/4th were all volunteers. They were instructed in the basics of plane exits, prelanding and fall techniques, and other paratrooper skills by Lt. Robert W. Armstrong, First Battalion Headquarters Company of the 503d. These brave Aussies, who possessed a minimum of training in airborne technicalities but a maximum of intestinal fortitude, had disassembled and packed their field pieces. Tying their bundles together to parachutes in chain formation, they were prepared to go.

The remaining twelve C-47s were loaded with essential equipment for the operation, such as radios, stretchers, tents, medical supplies, and ammunition. Seizure of the trail from Lae to Nadzab to Salamaua would prevent the Japanese from reinforcing their positions to the south.

503d Paratroopers heading for planes on Port Moresby, New Guinea, airstrip for their first combat jump at Nadzab, 5 September 1943.

Photo Courtesy John Pratt

As preparations were finalized for takeoff, a rain began falling and the airstrip was closed in. After daybreak, the rain ceased, but a heavy blanket of fog enclosed the area and threatened to abort the mission. At 0800 hours, the fog lifted and a weather plane surveying the "saddle" of the Owen-Stanley Mountain range gave an all-clear signal. Command was given to start the engines. At 0825 the first C-47 rolled down the runway. Within fifteen minutes, three flights of C-47s, totaling seventy-nine planes, were airborne carrying the 503d PIR. The first part of the fighter escort group, one hundred fighter planes, joined the paratroopers over Thirty-Mile Airdrome. We crossed the Owen-Stanley Mountains through the "saddle" (the lowest point in the range) at an altitude of nine thousand feet. The cargo doors of the C-47s had been removed, and the irregular edges of the door frames had been heavily taped with masking tape to prevent the snagging of troopers or their equipment on exit. At this altitude, it was very cold.

Having crossed the "saddle," our transport planes regrouped and descended to thirty-five hundred feet as we approached Marilinan. Above Marilinan, our troop transport convoy maneuvered into six-plane elements in step-upright echelon with all three flights abreast. Each flight carried a battalion of paratroopers to the designated drop zones. Additional fighter plane protection was obtained from the fields at Marilinan, Tsili-Tsili, and Dobadura. The transport planes dropped to treetop level as we hedgehopped toward our drop zones. It now became very hot and humid in our planes at this low altitude. The heavy equipment each man carried and the tight parachute harness added to the discomfort. The maneuvers of the plane and the bumpiness of the flight as the planes hit air pockets produced some air sickness. "Honey buckets" were called for and were soon filled. Some staid and healthy troopers became ill after smelling the foul odor as the buckets were passed to the next needy troopers.

The 302 airplanes from eight airfields in the Port Moresby-Dobadura-Marilinan areas followed a flight path along the Watut River from Tsili-Tsili, then turned right where the Watut joined the Markham. Six squadrons of B-25 strafers were flying at a thousand feet; each had eight .50-caliber machine guns in its nose and sixty fragmentation bombs in each bomb bay. Immediately behind, at fifteen hundred feet altitude, were six A-20s, in pairs, three pairs abreast, to lay smoke as the last fragmentation bomb exploded. Behind the A-20s came our C-47s in three columns of three-plane elements on course for the separate battalions' drop zones. Flying on each side of our transports and a thousand feet above were the close cover fighter planes. Another group of fighters flew

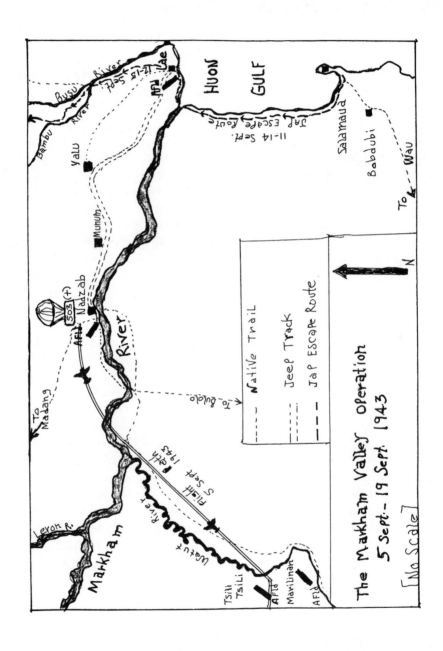

The Markham Valley Operation
5 Sept.– 19 Sept. 1943

[No Scale]

Legend:
- — — Native Trail
- –·–·– Jeep Track
- ▬ ▬ Jap Escape Route

at seven thousand feet, and a third group was up in the sun at fifteen to twenty thousand feet, staggered in formation.

At 0948 the troopers were alerted. Final equipment checks were made, helmets donned, and chin straps buckled. Inasmuch as we were jumping at such a low altitude, a great many troopers removed their reserve parachutes and shoved them under their seats. The seats were like a bench running fore to aft on either side of the plane's interior so the troopers faced each other in flight. The transport planes now ascended to the ordered four-to-five hundred foot jump altitude. At 1009 hours, we were given the red light from our flight leader. The men were standing, their anchor line snap fasteners hooked up. They had finished the equipment check, and the lead jumper was standing in the door. It was very hot, crowded, and uncomfortable. Everyone wanted to get the hell out of the old "flying coffins" and into fresh air.

Green lights flashed and troopers began leaping into space at 1022 hours. All seventy-nine troop transports were emptied in four and one-half minutes. One trooper, who fainted during equipment check, failed to jump but returned the following day on the first transport to land on the captured airstrip. Two men fell to their deaths when their parachutes malfunctioned. Another trooper landed atop a very tall teakwood tree. After sliding down his jump rope, he fell an additional sixty to seventy feet to earth and succumbed shortly thereafter to internal injuries. By 1204 all the C-47 transports had returned to Port Moresby. The additional five transports of Australian artillerymen and the twelve C-47 cargo planes of equipment had emptied over Nadzab airfield by 1230 hours and returned safely to their base.

Fortunately, the enemy offered resistance from neither air nor land. The troopers greatest foe was the suffocating heat, high humidity, and razor-sharp leaf edges of the eight-foot-tall Kunai grass through which they had to fight to reach their assembly areas. The noise of crunching bombs and the deafening staccato of the .50 caliber machine guns of our friendly B-25s as they blasted the trails leading from our jump areas informed us of the seriousness of this operation. The troopers were elated that these "fly boys" were on their side! Three B-17s, flying high above, carried the "brass hats" who witnessed the unfolding melodrama far below. General Kenney was in one bomber, General MacArthur in a second, and the third was protecting these two. General Kenney later wrote to General Arnold that MacArthur was jumping up and down like a kid. MacArthur told his aide that this parachute airborne assault was the greatest example of combat efficiency he had ever witnessed.

A Markham Valley drop zone near Nadzab, Sunday 5 September 1943.

U.S. Army Photo

54

The First Battalion of the 503d seized the Nadzab airstrip and began to prepare it to receive the C-47s, which were to bring in the Australian Seventh Division. The Second Battalion blocked the approach to the west and Salamaua while the Third Battalion blocked the approach from Lae. The preassigned battalion, company, and platoon responsibilities were rapidly and vigorously carried out. Patrols were immediately sent out to reconnoiter the trails and the riverbed area. By nightfall the perimeters were secured. During the day, five B-17s, loaded with supplies attached to parachutes, flew over Nadzab. They dropped fifteen tons of supplies on ground panels laid out by the 503d troopers.

The 2/2d Australian Pioneer Battalion, the 2/6th Field Company (AIF), and a company of the Papuan Infantry Battalion, which had traveled the Watut River from Tsili-Tsili to the Nadzab area in a week, observed the show from across the south bend of the Markham River. Contact was made between the paratroopers and the Aussies in late afternoon. The Australians forded the Markham River on folding boat bridges. Paratroopers of the First Battalion secured the airstrip and dug in. The Aussie engineers worked through the night of 5 September to prepare the seized airfield for the C-47s, which were to bring in the Australian Seventh Division. Grass fires, started by flame throwers to burn off the airstrip area, got out of control and burned several hundred parachutes that had not been reclaimed after the morning jump, but no Allied casualties resulted.

A news reporter asked Father Powers, the regimental Catholic Chaplain, how he felt about the troopers going into combat on the Sabbath. He replied, "The better the day, the better the deed." He was proved correct. Early in the morning of 6 September, the first flight of C-47s arrived carrying the advanced echelon of the U.S. 871st Airborne Engineer Battalion. Additional flights that day brought in elements of the Seventh Australian Division from Tsili-Tsili with General Vasey's headquarters, engineer equipment, and an air liaison company. Soon afterward, the Twenty-fifth Australian Infantry Brigade arrived from Port Moresby via Marilinan. By 10 September, the Seventh Australian Division had relieved the 503d PIR of its defensive status. Construction of new airfields had begun as planned, and by 14 September, Nadzab had two parallel runways six thousand feet long. As early as 11 September, 333 planeloads from Tsili-Tsili and 87 from the more southerly bases had landed.

When the 503d PIR jumped, each man was carrying three days' rations. These were K rations, and they contained small cans of potted ham and cheese, pressure-cooked eggs, hardtack biscuit crackers, jelly, and a substance that resembled butter but would not melt upon being heated. A small package containing four cigarettes was in each K ration box. The cigarettes were the cheapest brands available and tasted like the biscuit crackers. When the Australian division arrived, under command of Gen. Sir Thomas Blamey, the Yanks began drawing Aussie rations of canned and corned beef, termed "bully beef," dehydrated onions, and tasteless British tobacco. Tea rather than coffee was a startling breakfast adventure for the Yank paratroopers. The salty, greasy beef was a change from the American rations, but it created a greater demand for drinking water. The juice of green coconuts was used in great amounts in lieu of potable drinking water. The innovative, imaginative, and experienced Aussies issued small boxes of matches. The body and head of each match was covered with wax, which had to be scraped off before the match head would ignite when rubbed against an abrasive material. The wax on the match stem facilitated burning. High humidity, tropical downpours, or perspiration caused American matches to get damp and fall apart unless kept in small vials with cotton to absorb the moisture.

By evening of 8 September, the Twenty-fifth Australian Brigade had arrived and had replaced the Third Battalion of the 503d, which had been guarding the forward approaches of Lae. The Third Battalion was withdrawn to the vicinity of the airstrip. Bad weather set in at this time, and the remainder of the Seventh Australian Division could not be flown in, nor could the troopers be evacuated. The skies cleared slowly as the aggressive Aussies of the Twenty-fifth Brigade continued their push down the valley toward Lae. On 14 September, the Third Battalion of the 503d was sent forward to protect the Aussies' line of communication and to prevent enemy infiltration to their rear. On this same date, the First Battalion was evacuated to Port Moresby by air to prepare for its next mission.

The Third Battalion of the 503d, now under the direct command of General Vasey, was ordered to the Yalu village area, about halfway between Nadzab and Lae. Here a base of operations was established and numerous patrols were dispatched, resulting in several encounters with small enemy groups. Japanese General Adachi, sensing his predicament, ordered his forces to withdraw from Lae and Salamaua to the north coast of the Huon Peninsula. General Vasey became aware of the withdrawal through captured enemy documents and a Japanese prisoner of war, and he anxiously sought the enemy escape route.

On 14 September, Lt. Col. Tolson ordered Company I, commanded by Capt. John N. Davis, to reconnoiter the village of Log Crossing on

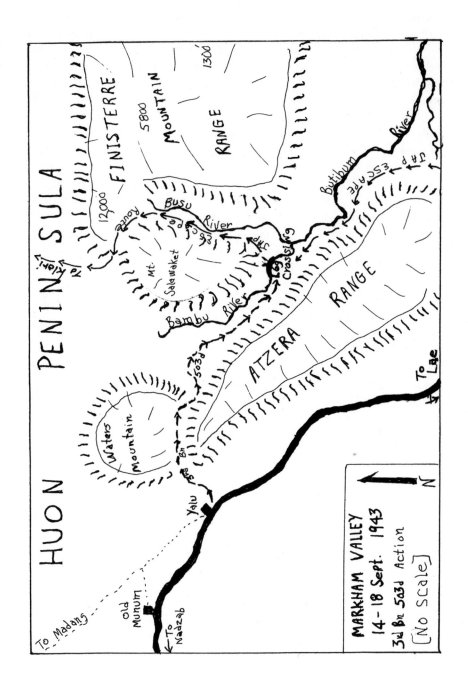

HUON PENINSULA

FINISTERRE MOUNTAIN RANGE

12000

1300

5800

Rouge Escape 93

Busu River

Mt. Salawaket

Bambu River

Jap

Log Crossing

Butibum River

Jap Escape

ATZERA RANGE

Waters Mountain

503d

Bn

Yalu

To Lae

N

MARKHAM VALLEY
14-18 Sept. 1943
3d Bn 503d Action
[No Scale]

To Madang

Old Munum

To Nadzab

57

the Bambu River, some six miles northeast of Yalu. Upon reaching the village in later afternoon, Company I discovered signs of recent enemy occupancy and a well-beaten trail indicating heavy foot traffic. The trail led north from the village. Darkness overcame the company on its return trip to the battalion perimeter, so the troops bedded down a few yards off the trail until dawn. Field radio communications were practically non existent in the damp tropical jungle mountains, but when the company reported to its commander, Tolson, on the early morning of 15 September, it learned that General Vasey had ordered the entire battalion to Log Crossing to intercept the Japanese troops escaping from Lae. Taking advantage of the knowledge gained from the reconnoiter, Tolson ordered Company I to lead the way. Because the track was single file, the battalion marched strung out for nearly a mile.

At approximately 1600 hours and about 200 yards north of Log Crossing village, the lead (point) squad of Company I surprised a four-man machine gun outpost on the west bank of the Bambu River. Three of the enemy soldiers were killed and one escaped downstream. Their heavy NAMBU machine gun was captured. Lt. Lyle Murphy, leading his second platoon downstream, ran into a large Japanese detachment moving upstream. A fierce firefight developed that lasted almost until dark. Lt. Col. Tolson, marching between elements of Companies I and H, hurried to the front and immediately dispatched troopers to secure the area. The battalion dug in for the night. A few Japanese stragglers entrapped within the village were slain. First Sergeant Frank Boganski of Headquarters Company, on a hasty reconnaissance of the riverbed near the battalion command post, killed a hiding Japanese who turned out to be a medical officer. The high quality medical instruments he carried in his ornately inscribed leather bags were presented to Capt. Thomas Stevens, Third Battalion surgeon.

The Japanese troops intercepted by the Third Battalion troopers were those of the *Imperial Fifty-first Division*, who had escaped the Salamaua encirclement and were following retreating Lae forces through the forbidding Finisterre Mountains toward distant Madang. In the predawn hours of 16 September, a severe earthquake jolted the sleepy but alert troopers out of their foxholes. Large trees fell to the ground, causing tension, anxiety, and confusion. Around midmorning, a forward patrol of Australian infantrymen charged across the stream below Company H outposts. The Japanese had apparently fled the area under cover of darkness. By noon, the Third Battalion had been relieved and ordered to return to Nadzab. The dead paratroopers were buried in the village of Log Crossing. The wounded were carried back to Yalu

503d cemetery at Nadzab, New Guinea, September 1943

Photo Courtesy Mike Matievich

village, where jeep ambulances transported them to Nadzab airfield for evacuation to the general hospital at Port Moresby.

The Third Battalion paratroopers were withdrawn to the Nadzab airstrip for evacuation to rejoin their mother regiment, which had earlier been flown back to the base camp. Marching along a jeep track trail leading from Nadzab to Lae, the troopers came upon an Australian Salvation Army officer passing out Chiclet gumdrops. Armed enemy troops could not have been far away. An alarmed paratrooper asked the Salvation Army officer why he was so close to the front. The trooper received the counterquery: "What are *you* doing here, Yank?" The Third Battalion of the 503d was flown back to Port Moresby and its base camp on the evening of 19 September 1943.

The Second Battalion and Regimental Headquarters had already been evacuated, so by 19 September, all sections of the 503d PIR were back at their base camp at Port Moresby. The 503d had accomplished its first airborne mission with skill and determination. The Japanese began their retreat from the Lae sector with a ten-day food supply, which they rapidly consumed. Soon, they were suffering from starvation, dysentery, malaria, and other tropical diseases. Early in their trek across the mountains they abandoned their heavy weapons. Later, they began discarding rifles, helmets, packs, and other items. Of the ten thousand Japanese troops in the Lae area, twenty-six hundred were killed and six hundred more became casualties on the retreat march.

The Markham Valley operation had cost the 503d three men killed in the initial jump, thirty-three injured jumping, twenty-six ill and listed as nonbattle casualties, eight killed in action with the enemy, and twelve wounded. By the end of December 1943, the Allied air force had three airdromes in operation in the Markham and Ramu river valleys: one at Nadzab, one at Lae, and one at the junction of the Ramu and Gusap rivers. The second and third phases of the Elkton III plan had been accomplished at a surprisingly low cost to the SWPA forces. The 503d Parachute Infantry Regiment had announced its presence in the war and had passed the acid test of battle.

4
Critique

Following the return of the 503d Parachute Infantry Regiment to the base camp at Port Moresby, the men licked their wounds and thought about what they had learned. They had performed their assigned missions flawlessly but they saw the need for additional equipment. Telescopic rifles would be useful for sniper purposes. The 1903 Springfield rifles with 10X telescopes mounted were obtained and issued to selected expert marksmen. Ironically, before the next mission, the "brass" decided that the telescopes would be jarred off true aim by the shock of the parachute opening or on impact of landing and took away the rifles. This decision would prove fatal in later campaigns when the men came under enemy sniper fire that they were unable to counter.

In the Nadzab campaign, the Japanese were found to be using smokeless powder. In the hushed stillness of the forbidding jungle, the sound of a single shot fired by an enemy rifleman would reverberate and confuse us about its origin. The sound would make it seem as though the bullet exploded at its target the same instant the weapon was fired. Rumors became rampant that the Nips were using dum-dum bullets, wooden bullets, and bullets with the ends cut off so they would spread upon impact. The Japs were masters at camouflage, and their riflemen were very difficult to locate in the darkened jungle. For these reasons, the American soldiers erroneously termed each Japanese rifleman a sniper. The true Jap sniper did use a telescopic rifle, as we shall see in later chapters.

The Port Moresby encampment was dull, muddy, and generally unhealthy. Numerous troopers were suffering from tropical diseases, some of which had been acquired at Nadzab. The more common ailments were jungle rot (a fungus infection of the skin, especially the feet and legs), malaria, scrub typhus, Japanese river fever (the ague), and dysentery. Colonel Kinsler called an assembly of the regiment to award medals for gallantry, valor, or having been wounded. Recipients who were hospitalized had their medals pinned onto their pajama tops in the base hospital. Colonel Jones related that one trooper who was given the Order of the Purple Heart was found to be hospitalized for

ADVANCED ECHELON
GENERAL HEADQUARTERS

CS: prr
(Office)

18 September 1943
(Date)

BY COURIER

COLONEL KINSLER
NOW THAT THE FALL OF LAE IS AN ACCOMPLISHED FACT
I WISH TO MAKE OF RECORD THE SPLENDID AND IMPOR-
TANT PART TAKEN BY FIVE NOUGHT THREE PARACHUTE IN-
FANTRY REGIMENT STOP UNDER YOUR ABLE LEADERSHIP
CMA OFFICERS AND MEN EXHIBITED THE HIGHEST ORDER
OF COMBAT EFFICIENCY STOP PLEASE EXPRESS TO ALL
RANKS MY GRATIFICATION AND DEEP PRIDE

MACARTHUR

OFFICIAL:

H./S./W. ALLEN
Lt. Col., AGD
Asst. Adjutant General

The 503rd Parachute Infantry

Combat Mission

This Certifies that *Frank D Hanks* jumped in the parachute attack against the Japanese Garrison at Lae, New Guinea, on September the Fifth, Nineteen Hundred and Forty-three.

Kenneth H. Kinsler

Kenneth H. Kinsler
Colonel, 503rd Parachute Infantry
Commanding

Combat Jump Certificates issued each Paratrooper of the Nadzab Operation. Col. Kinsler failed to sign all of them prior to his demise. The above is an authentic copy showing his signature.

Courtesy Frank D. Hanks

63

a venereal disease. The award was quickly retrieved, much to the embarrassment of the presenting officer and the temporary recipient.

A detachment of men and officers was dispatched from each company back to Gordonvale to train some four hundred newly arrived paratroopers, the first replacements for the 503d since it had left the United States a year before. These men were sent in anticipation of battle casualties at Nadzab, but because the casualties were lighter than expected, the men were used to expand standard seven-man squads to eleven men and to additional squads or platoons. After some low-altitude jumps, these men were flown to Port Moresby to be assigned to various companies for additional jungle training.

In late afternoon of 22 October 1943, Colonel Kinsler summoned his lieutenant colonels to his tent. He shared a bottle of whiskey with them in a cordial and apparently normal social interaction. That night, Colonel Kinsler and an Australian nurse travelled to a nearby gravel pit. Later, the nurse reported that Colonel Kinsler had committed suicide. No note was ever found to indicate why he took his life. He was buried at 0900 hours next day in the American sector of the Port Moresby Cemetery. (His body was later reinterred in the U.S. Military Cemetery in Honolulu, Hawaii; space A-78.) Lt. Col. Joe Lawrie, the regimental executive officer, summoned Lt. Col. George Jones, the commanding officer of the Second Battalion, to the regimental command post from a training exercise he was conducting in the field. As the senior officer of the 503d PIR, Jones was immediately ordered to assume command.

Col. George M. Jones led the troopers until 10 August 1945. Jones was a native of and had been educated in Memphis, Tennessee. He obtained an appointment to West Point Military Academy and graduated in the Class of 1935. He entered flight training in September of that year. In February 1936, he was transferred to the Sixth Infantry Regiment as commander of a machine gun company. In 1937 he was assigned to the Fourteenth Infantry in the Canal Zone and later to the Military Police unit, Atlantic Sector. Jones returned to the States in 1939 and attended the basic infantry officers course at the Infantry School. This course was cut short because of gathering war clouds in Europe. After graduating in 1940, Jones sought adventure and volunteered for the newly organized 501st Parachute Battalion. When the battalion completed training in March 1941, he became the thirty-first officer in the U.S. Army parachute troops. Jones was promoted to commanding officer of

Col. George M. Jones, commander of the 503d Regimental Combat Team from October 1943 to August 1945. The shoulder patch is not that of the 503d.

Headquarters Company and returned with the 501st Parachute Battalion to Panama. He rapidly advanced to the position of battalion executive officer, which he held until the battalion commander, Kinsler, was reassigned to the States in early July 1942. Jones then served as the 501st Parachute Battalion commander until the 501st Battalion joined the First and Third Battalions of the 503d Parachute Infantry Regiment en route to its overseas assignments. Jones was the regimental executive officer during the voyage and commander of troops aboard the ship.

In Australia, he served as regimental executive officer for several months and then was reassigned to his old battalion, now designated the Second Battalion of the 503d. After the death of Colonel Kinsler, he was promoted to full colonel and commander of the 503d Parachute Infantry Regiment. Jones stated in a recent letter: "My philosophy of command was to put out as few orders as possible. To simplify the task of seeing that they were carried out; ascertain by roll call that everyone got the word. After 48 hours had passed, find an officer who was not obeying the order and promptly Court Martial him for disobedience to orders. I found after doing this a couple of times, that I got excellent responses and compliance to my few orders. I never had to worry about the Enlisted Men complying with my orders."

Meanwhile, plans for Operation III of the Elkton Plan were well under way. Gen. Walter Kreuger, commander of the U.S. Sixth Army; called the "Alamo Force," prepared his plan, "Dexterity," and submitted it to General MacArthur for approval. This operation — the capture of Rabaul on New Britain Island — was placed under command of the U.S. Sixth Army. Units assigned to the operation were the First Marine Division, tried and tested veterans of Guadalcanal, the Thirty-second U.S. Army Division, veterans of the Buna-Gona campaign, the 632d Tank Destroyer Battalion, and the 503d Parachute Infantry Regiment. The troopers were to be used only to capture the Cape Gloucester airfield.

The date 26 December 1943 was set for the operation, but problems arose. The weather was too bad for a parachute jump over the Cape Gloucester airfield. Both General Krueger and the First Marine Division commander, Maj. Gen. William Rupertus, disliked the plan. Where transport planes to carry the 503d would have to be ferried to dobadura, insufficient room would necessitate the removal of a heavy bombardment squadron back to Port Moresby. The jump would have to be piecemeal. The main problem seemed to be that General MacArthur had released the 503d to the Sixth Army, and following standard operation procedure, General Krueger felt compelled to use the

503d. He later learned that he was not compelled to use these airborne troops needlessly, and the 503d's participation in the operation was abandoned.

Beefed up by replacements, well-trained, and battle-tested, the paratroopers were languishing at Port Moresby. Colonel Jones believed that the troopers would get stale without recreation, better food, whiskey, and, as he put it, "other things young men like." He asked General Krueger either to give the 503d a mission or return it to Australia for rest and rehabilitation (R and R). General Krueger conceded to the latter request. On 25 January 1944, company details of selected officers and men were flown back to Cairns and transported to the old Gordonvale encampment area to prepare for the return of the entire regiment on board the SS *John Carroll* and a British liner. The convoy reached Cairns, Australia, on the afternoon of 27 January. Because many men had malaria and Gordonvale was an indigenous area, the regiment was ordered to Brisbane. It arrived at Camp Cable, about thirty miles outside Brisbane, on 2 February 1944. This relatively pleasant campsite had been constructed and used as a jungle warfare training facility by the U.S. Thirty-second and several Australian division groups.

The men were granted furloughs to the larger cities to the south and liberal weekend leaves to the nearby towns and hamlets. The furloughs were usually for about two weeks. While the regiment was at Camp Cable, an American Red Cross volunteer and a qualified parachutist, Harold M. Templeman, joined the 503d.

After R and R, and because the progress of the island-hopping campaign to the north was accelerating, the 503d Parachute Infantry Regiment left Camp Cable on 8 April 1944. The regiment boarded another Dutch Inter island ocean liner, the SS *Van Der Lijn*. Again the officers were Dutchmen and the crew Javanese. Sailing north, the regiment arrived at Milne Bay, New Guinea, in the early morning of 15 April 1944. Confusion as to our destination became apparent, and the ship left on 16 April, docking the following day at Oro Bay in the Dobadura area. An amusing incident event occurred while the ship was being offloaded. A DUKW (known in GI vernacular as a "duck"), loaded with the officers' club booze supply and driven by a couple of Negro soldiers, headed up the coast rather than toward the designated landing area. The "Warden" was on the bridge and commanded the guard to fire on them. The guard missed two shots, perhaps intentionally. The Warden grabbed the M-1 rifle and emptied the clip at the disappearing ocean craft. The colonel also failed to score a hit but apparently frightened

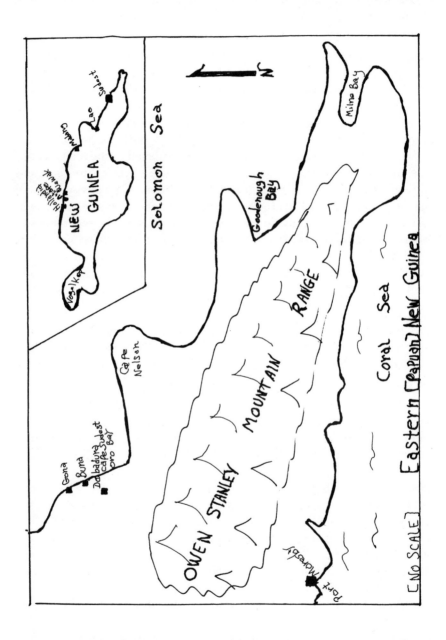

Eastern (Papuan) New Guinea

[No SCALE]

68

the pirates to turn back and put in to the designated landing area. A camp was established at Cape Sudest, near the ocean bay, where the troopers remained for the next six weeks, finding the area very hot, humid, wet, and boring.

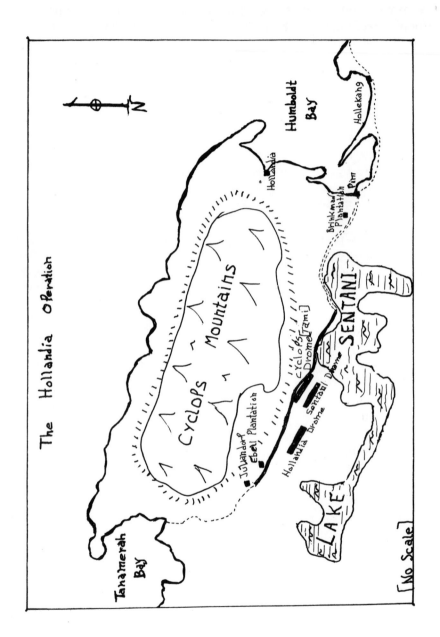

The Hollandia Operation

Tanamerah Bay

Cyclops Mountains

Humboldt Bay

Hollandia

Hollekang

Pim

Brinkman Plantation

SENTANI

Juliandorp Ebel Plantation

Cyclops Drome [Tami]

Sentani Drome

Hollandia Drome

LAKE SENTANI

[No Scale]

5
The Hollandia Operation

There was an urgent reason for moving the 503d Parachute Infantry Regiment from the relative paradise of Camp Cable to the disagreeable rear-base encampment near Dobadura. An early plan of General Headquarters called for an assault landing in the Hansa Bay area, approximately halfway between Madang and Wewak, two of the major enemy strongholds in New Guinea. With the rapid conclusion of the Admiralties campaign, the Bismarck Archepelago was all but neutralized. General Headquarters discarded the proposed Hansa Bay assault and submitted a more daring plan — an assault on the area near Hollandia, more than 200 miles northwest of the great Japanese bastion of Wewak, and a simultaneous attack against Aitape, about 125 miles east-southeast of Hollandia between the Driniumor and Esim rivers.

Aitape was important to the Nippons because of its airfields, which were used for staging planes from Hollandia to Wewak, Aitape was in Papuan New Guinea, an area that before the war was under British control. Hollandia was in the territory of New Guinea mandated by the Netherlands government. Hollandia is a wet tropical rain forest area, where annual rainfall exceeds one hundred inches. The Cyclops Mountain range parallels the coastal area with deep indentations at each end of the range forming Tanahmerah Bay in the west and Humboldt Bay to the east. A deep inland depression in the land mass south of the Cyclops range formed the large freshwater Lake Sentani. The Japanese had built the Hollandia, Sentani, and Cyclops airfields just north of the lake. Hollandia was the New Guinea terminus of Japanese shipping from Japan via the Philippine Islands, serving as a supply base for transshipment of troops, planes, and freight to points down the New Guinea coast. The Japs had amassed huge stocks of supplies here. Humboldt Bay was the only anchorage between Wewak and Geelvink Bay to the west that afforded a good shelter for ships in all seasons. The Allies desired these areas so as to develop major air, naval, and supply bases.

In the SWPA at this time, all combat operations were conducted through four headquarters groups, each under the direct control of

General Douglas MacArthur. Allied air forces, consisting of the U.S. Fifth Air Force and the Royal Australian Air Force (under Air-Vice Marshal William D. Bostock, RAAF), were commanded by Lt. Gen. George C. Kenney (USA). Allied naval forces was the U.S. Seventh Fleet, commanded by Vice-Admiral Thomas C. Kinkaid (USN). This fleet consisted of the Seventh Amphibious Force, commanded by Rear Admiral Daniel E. Barbey (USN), and assigned ships of the Royal Australian and Royal Netherlands fleet. Allied land forces were under command of Gen. Sir Thomas Blamey (AIF). The U.S. Sixth Army, commanded by Lt. Gen. Walter Krueger, was subordinate to General Blamey. The separate operations of the U.S. Sixth Army referred to as Alamo Force were under direct command of General Krueger. In most instances, Australian commanders controlled operations in which predominantly Australian troops were used and the U.S. Sixth Army controlled operations that used primarily American troops.

Allied aircraft began bombardment of the proposed landing sites on 30 March 1944. The heavier and more numerous air attacks were against Madang and Wewak; these were land-based air attacks from the Nadzab airdromes, captured six months earlier by the 503d, and almost five hundred miles southeast of Hollandia. Fighter planes on these missions had to carry spare wing tanks because this distance was beyond their range. They strafed the Wewak, Aitape, and Hollandia areas and escorted Allied bombers on their flights to soften up the assault areas.

D-Day for the attack on the Aitape, Humboldt Bay, and Tanahmerah Bay areas was set for 22 April 1944. The plan was termed Operation Reckless. Because of Japanese airfields in the Caroline Island group, the Geelvink Bay area, and the Wakde and Noemfoor Island areas, all of which wre out of range of Allied land-based aircraft, this daring bypass operation could be accomplished only with the support of carrier-based aircraft of the United States Navy. GHQ of the SWPA had considered using paratroopers to seize the airfields north of Lake Sentani but dropped the plan when no assurance was given that sufficient men and equipment could be flown to the area in time to construct a fighter strip before the Fifth Fleet Carrier Task Force 58 was scheduled to be withdrawn. Carrier Task Force 58, under Vice-Admiral Marc A. Mitscher, had patrolled the western Caroline Islands, destroyed 150 Japanese aircraft, sunk several enemy naval vessels, and scattered numerous other enemy ships, thus removing any threat from enemy naval units and land-based aircraft from that region to the Allied landing forces in the Aitape and Hollandia areas.

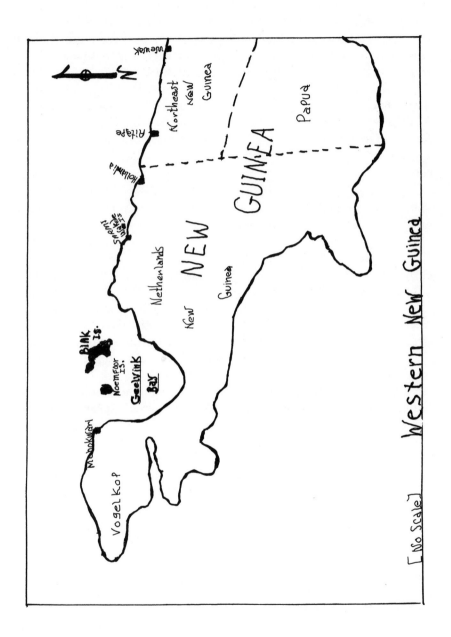

Western New Guinea

[No Scale]

73

After preparatory bombardment by Naval Task Force 77, under command of Admiral Barbey, troops of the Forty-first U.S. Division began landing at Aitape and Humboldt Bay. The Twenty-fourth U.S. Division stormed ashore at Tanahmerah Bay where the main effort to move rapidly inland to seize the enemy airfields was to be made. This was the first operation in the SWPA in which U.S. Navy carrier planes were used as close support in U.S. Army troop landings. All three of the enemy airfields had been taken by April 26. Two days later, Cyclops Airfield was being used by some Allied aircraft. GHQ reserves for the Reckless Operation were the U.S. Sixth Infantry Division at Milne Bay and the 503d Parachute Infantry Regiment based at Oro Bay, Papuan New Guinea.

The assault on Hollandia routed some fifteen thousand enemy defenders who fled to the hills, hoping to escape overland to the west and safety. The fleeing Japanese were pursued relentlessly. The 503d boarded C-47s of the 54th Troop Carrier Wing at Oro Bay on 2 June 1944, at 0600 hours. The flight to Hollandia took the troopers over their earlier prize, Nadzab airdrome. They landed at Cyclops Field at 1000 hours. The men of the 503d moved out and assembled about seven miles south of Hollandia, where they established a bivouac. For the next month, they patrolled the plains, Lake Sentani, the mountains, and the streams. The 503d had relieved and taken over the sector assigned to the Thirty-fourth Infantry when the latter was dispatched to another operational area. The mission of the 503d was to secure Tami airstrip, located approximately twelve miles east of Hollandia, with one battalion. One rifle company was to effect a perimeter defense around Advance Echelon Alamo Force (U.S. Sixth Army HQ) at Hollekang. Another rifle company was to guard a large Japanese supply dump located at Sawmill Jetty. One platoon of troopers was assigned to guard an engineer landing boat maintenance shop located at Waab village.

At this time the 503d consisted of 1,994 enlisted men and 152 officers. The troopers patrolled extensively east of their assigned area to Bouganville Bay area thence south to include the area about ten miles south of the Tami River. One patrol of the 503d ranged as far as Aitape, approximately 160 miles east of Hollandia. The main purpose of these patrol activities was to keep the Japanese forces encircled in the Wewak area and prevent their escape overland to the Sarmi area, where they would have access to the food and supply dumps captured during the Hollandia operation. As in all jungle operations, the troopers found that transport of heavy weapons and equipment was difficult. It was often impossible to maintain or move sufficient ammunition for the mortars to warrant carrying these weapons. The thickly matted canopies of the huge trees in the tropical rain forests presented serious problems for the mortarmen, who had to try to fire high-angle trajectory rounds without their being deflected or causing a tree burst.

The patrolling troopers generally met a demoralized and weakened enemy, though occasionally they met fanatic resistance. Mostly, the enemy moved in groups of three to ten men, sometimes including officers, and carried scanty arms, equipment, and food. Eleven prisoners of war the troopers captured were Formosan laborers. One captured Japanese was a member of the Japanese merchant marine, a survivor of a ship that had been sunk off Aitape, In the course of their month-long Hollandia assignment, the troopers of the 503d had killed 56 Japanese, captured 12, and found 185 bodies along the trails.

The 503d had been placed on alert as U.S. Sixth Army reserve for the Noemfoor Island operation. Its contribution to Operation Reckless was to serve as air-mobile infantry reserve, available on a few hours' notice, to facilitate the mopping-up operations of the Hollandia area (incidentally providing invaluable experience for the trooper replacements), and to assist in the envelopment and isolation of sixty thousand Japanese troops of the Eighteenth Army between Madang, Hansa Bay, Wewak, and Hollandia. Alamo Force had lost 565 men killed in action as compared to 13,000 Japanese by the end of June 1944. The 503d had one enlisted man slightly wounded, not requiring hospitalization, and twenty cases of dengue fever, which resulted in a loss of duty days.

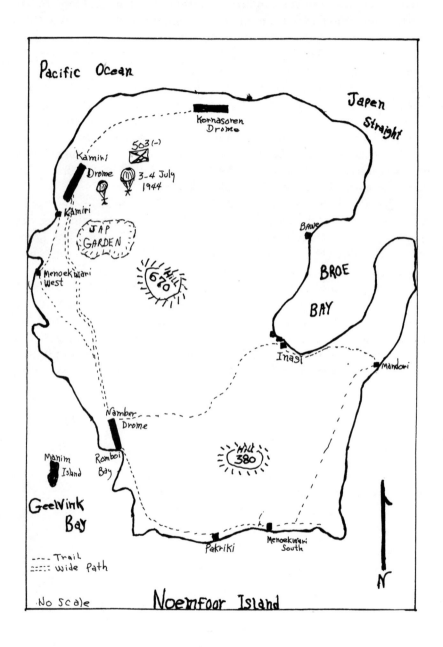

Pacific Ocean

Japen Straight

Kornasoren Drome

Kamiri Drome

503 (-)

3-4 July 1944

Kamiri

Bawe

JAP GARDEN

Menoekwari West

BROE BAY

HILL 670

Inasi

Mandori

Namber Drome

Romboi Bay

HILL 380

Manim Island

Geelvink Bay

Pakriki

Menoekwari South

- - - - Trail
::::: Wide Path

No Scale

N

Noemfoor Island

76

6
The Noemfoor Operation

A rapid surge of forward thrusts by MacArthur's forces following the victorious Hollandia campaign found U.S. Army forces on Wakde and Biak islands as well as on Sarmi, located on the Netherlands New Guinea coast of the Vogelkop Peninsula in the Geelvink Bay area. (Vogelkop is Dutch for "Bird's Head.") Biak Island is nearly 325 miles and Sarmi nearly 145 miles northwest of Hollandia. The Wakde Islands lie approximately 20 miles east and two miles offshore from Sarmi. A GHQ radiogram of 5 June 1944 alerted General Krueger that it might be necessary to seize Noemfoor Island to insure success at Biak. This warning proved to be correct, for, early in the Biak campaign, it was discovered the Japanese were using Noemfoor as a staging area to supply fresh troops for their beleaguered Biak detachment. Japanese barges were transporting troops from Manokwari on the Vogelkop Peninsula to Noemfoor (a distance of about 60 nautical miles) during the hours of darkness, then making another overnight run of approximately 75 miles to Biak.

The planning for Operation Noemfoor (code named Tabletennis) was begun at Camp Cretin (the U.S. Sixth Army headquarters base just offshore from Finschafen, Papuan New Guinea) in early June 1944. There were three reasons for securing this Japanese-held island: to deny the Japanese of the Vogelkop area an overnight staging position for reinforcements to their troops on Biak; to stop Japanese construction of three airdromes on the island; and to deny the Japanese a base from which they could threaten the sea lanes of western Biak.

For several weeks, planes of the Fifth U.S. Army Air Force, under command of Maj. Gen. Ennis C. Whitehead, had neutralized the Noemfoor, Owi, and Biak airdromes, as well as those at Manokwari and others in the Geelvink Bay area, thus reducing or eliminating possible Japanese air response to the proposed Allied invasion of Noemfoor Island. The U.S. Sixth Army Field Order No. 19 of 21 June 1944 gave the Noemfoor Task Force the code name CYCLONE. The Cyclone Force was composed of the 158th Infantry Regimental Combat Team, reinforced. Brig. Gen. Edwin D. Patrick was designated as the task force commander; he was the former chief of staff of the Sixth Army and Alamo

Force. He had doggedly prevailed upon General Krueger to give him a field command, until finally, on 10 May 1944, Krueger conceded. General Patrick enjoyed his first field command in combat in the Wakde-Sarmi area from 21 May until late June 1944.

Field Order No. 19, defining the Cyclone Task Force, listed the assigned units. The force consisted of 8,069 combat personnel, of which 5,495 were service troops, and about 10,000 air force personnel, for a total invasion force of approximately 23,000 men. The 158th Infantry Regiment was commanded by Col. Erle O. Sandlin and accompanied by the 147th Field Artillery Battalion, which had 105mm howitzers. Other major combat units were the 116th Antiaircraft Artillery Group (two battalions plus three batteries), a platoon of the 603d Tank Company, a 4.2-inch mortar company of the 641st Tank Destroyer Battalion, the Twenty-seventh Engineers, the 593d Battalion Engineer Shore and Boat Regiment, one company of the 543d Engineer Boat and Shore Regiment, and a support battery of the Second Engineer Special Brigade. The Thirty-fourth Infantry Regiment of the Twenty-fourth Division on Biak and the 503d Parachute Infantry Regiment located at Hollandia would be in reserve.

The 503d PIR received its order regarding the Tabletennis operation on 28 June 1944 and was assigned the U.S. Sixth Army reserve code name Escalator. By 30 June the 503d Regiment had moved from Hollekang to the vicinity of the Ebeli plantation near Hollandia. Twenty-two hundred freshly packed parachutes were ordered to be sent by air from the rear base at Gordonvale, Queensland, Australia. They arrived at Hollandia on 1 July 1944.

Noemfoor Island is roughly circular in shape. Geologically it is a series of limestone and coral terraces. The highest elevation is about 670 feet above sea level. The north-south length is almost 15 miles, and the width is approximately 13 miles. About five thousand natives inhabit coastal villages. Dense rain forest persists except along beaches or tidal inlets, where there are mangrove swamps. The northern half of the island is generally low and flat, whereas the southern part is rugged. The Japanese had partially built three airfields: Kornasoren, Kamiri, and Namber. Kornasoren had a 5,250-foot runway and was 155 feet wide. It ran east to west on the northern coastal plain. It could be lengthened an additional 3,500 feet. Kamiri, 5,000 by 200 feet, was near the shore on the northwest coast. Namber, on the southwest part of the island, was 4,000 feet long by 320 feet wide. It had cleared approaches of 1,000 feet at each end.

A prelanding reconnaissance was accomplished by a party of Alamo Force scouts, who landed on Noemfoor via PT boats on 21 June. They remained on the island two days before the Japs discovered them. They confirmed that the main enemy defenses were at Kamiri drome and that the trail from Kamiri to Namber could not accommodate heavy vehicles or equipment. Sixth Army Headquarters decided to make a landing on the beach at Kamiri. If successful, they would separate the enemy forces between Namber and Kornasoren dromes. Alamo Force G-2 Section estimated the Japanese garrison on Noemfoor at more than three thousand troops. Later, however, it was discovered that no more than two thousand enemy troops were on the island, including about a thousand infantry effectives and another thousand service personnel. In addition, there were more than six hundred Formosan (Taiwanese) and five hundred Javanese slave laborers. The enemy combat troops were the *Third Battalion, 219th Infantry Regiment* plus another two hundred men of the *Second Battalion, 219th Infantry*, and a like number of personnel of the *222d Infantry*, of the *Thirty-Sixth Division*, who had been unable to reach Biak. The Japanese forces on Noemfoor were commanded by one Colonel Shimizu. The service personnel were under direct command of a Major Mori but under Colonel Shimizu's overall control. The first names of Shimizu and Mori cannot be found in references.

Cyclone Task Force was to seize the airdromes and develop the sites for support operations west of Noemfoor. It was also to prepare facilities for two groups of fighter planes and a half squadron of night fighters and later for an additional fighter group, two squadrons of medium bombers, and two squadrons of light bombers. To facilitate these objectives, Cyclone Task Force included two American engineer aviation battalions and the Royal Australian Air Force No. 62 Works Wing, under control of a famous and distinguished Australian engineer of Aitape fame, Group Captain W.A.C. Dale (RAAF). Service unit personnel numbered about fifty-five hundred men, of whom about three thousand were engaged on the airfield projects. The remainder were in medical, quartermaster, ordnance, and signal units and other noncombatants.

The amphibious phase of the Noemfoor campaign was directed by Rear Admiral William M. Fechteler and was designated Attack Force 77. The covering force, commanded by Rear Admiral Russell S. Berkey, contained one heavy cruiser, two light cruisers, and ten destroyers. The main force contained fifteen destroyers, eight LST's, four patrol craft, one tug, and fourteen LCIs (including three rocket-equipped LCIs carrying demolition experts and equipment) to prepare the landing approaches through the reefs.

D-Day, 2 July 1944, dawned bright and clear. Because Kamiri was the strongest Japanese defense area, the heaviest naval bombardment yet delivered in the SWPA was undertaken by Allied naval forces and bomber squadrons from H hour minus 80 minutes to H minus 15 minutes. Two fighter squadrons secured the airspace above to protect shipping and the assault forces. There was no opposition to the landing at 0800 hours. Because of the heavy preliminary bombardment, Cyclone Task Force losses at day's end were three men killed in action (one accidentally), nineteen wounded in action, and two injured.

By D-Day evening, more than seven thousand men had come ashore, including thirty-three hundred troops of the 158th Infantry Regiment. A Japanese prisoner, stunned and captured near Kamiri Drome, disclosed that he had heard that three thousand Japanese replacements had arrived on Noemfoor a week earlier, but he had not seen any of them. This testimony led General Patrick to conclude that there were probably at least five thousand enemy effectives on the island. Because he was relatively inexperienced in combat leadership, General Patrick radioed General Krueger late on D-Day to request that the 503d Parachute Infantry Regiment be sent to Noemfoor to reinforce him. General Patrick wanted to gain possession of the Namber and Kornasoren airdromes without jeopardizing his newly won Kamiri perimeter. General Krueger immediately ordered the 503d Parachute Infantry Regiment to proceed to Noemfoor.

Preparations for the parachute drop were completed by 1 July. All troops and equipment were inspected and all equipment shortages were replaced. Sand tables, maps, photographs, and lectures were used to inform the troopers about the drop zone. Four reconnaissance flights were flown over the drop zone carrying Colonel Jones, Maj. Cameron Knox, the First Battalion commander, Lt. Col. John W. Britten, the Second Battalion commander, Major John R. Erickson, the third Battalion commander, and Captains Harris T. Mitchell, John B. Pratt, John R. Richmond, and First Lt. William T. Bossert.

Not enough C-47 transport planes were available to lift the entire regiment, so arrangements were made to lift each battalion separately. The Fifty-fourth Troop Carrier Wing units had been so busy since the Markham Valley operation of September 1943 supplying fighter and bomber squadrons with fuel, food, and ammunition that training for parachute troop drops in combat operations had been tabled. Pilots had all but forgotten formation flying.

Thirty-eight C-47 airplanes of the Fifty-fourth Troop Carrier Wing were assigned to lift the 503d Parachute Infantry Regiment. These planes arrived at Hollandia, Dutch New Guinea, on the afternoon of 30 June 1944. The following day, a practice flight was held stressing formation flying, airspeed, and altitude. Each plane carried the jumpmaster for that plane's load on the first day of the jump. Parking for the planes was arranged, cargo doors removed, doorways taped, and the planes otherwise put in jumping condition by U.S. Army Air Force personnel under the direction of 1st Lt. Lawrence S. Browne, the regimental operations officer. Arrangements were made to have thirty-eight trucks at the regimental command post at 0300 hours on 3 July 1944; each truck was numbered to correspond with a similarly numbered plane. Take off from Cyclops drome was scheduled for 0630 hours. The First Battalion, plus elements of the Regimental Headquarters and service companies, were to jump on 3 July. The Third Battalion and the remainder of Regimental Headquarters and service companies were to jump on 4 July and the Second Battalion on 5 July. The destination was Kamiri airstrip.

The first of the 503d paratroopers to be airlifted were at Cyclops drome at 0505 hours and had enplaned by 0615 hours. The first airplane was airborne at 0630 hours; the remaining thirty-seven planes followed at thirty-second intervals. The planes rendezvoused over Humboldt Bay until the flight formations had been accomplished. A series of errors was to haunt this jump. Kornasoren airstrip had been the initial jump site. At the last moment, the destination was changed to Kamiri airstrip, where engineers were already at work with dozens of pieces of construction equipment. The planes of the Fifty-fourth Troop Carrier Wing were to fly from Hollandia to Noemfoor in "V" formation columns of twelve flights. Upon reaching the drop zone, the formations were to change to two planes abreast, echeloned to right rear. The distance between flights was to have been 600 feet; the first flight was to be at 400 feet altitude with alternate flights at 450 feet altitude.

A Canadian paratroop officer attached to Cyclone Task Force advised General Patrick on 2 July that the troop-carrying aircraft should fly over Kamiri airstrip in single file. At 0600 hours on 3 July, nearly twenty hours after receiving this advice, General Patrick radioed Alamo Force of the recommendation. The radiogram was received at 0740 hours, but it was not delivered to G-3 Section until 0915 hours. By the time the Alamo message center relayed the request to the Fifth Air Force,

Kamiri Airstrip 3 July 1945. Note two planes abreast and military equipment on the field, both of which contributed to casualties.

Photo Courtesy George Brown

Company A moving out on Noemfoor on 3 July after the jump. Steel helmets presented problems in the jungle, and men often left them behind.

83

the 503d paratroopers were well on their way to Noemfoor. Because the first two planes had erroneously set altimeters troopers started jumping at 175 feet altitude. The following planes were below 400 feet altitude. A smoke screen laid down near the airstrip added to the confusion of the pilots, who were hard-pressed to find their way. Exit jumping began at 1010 hours. There were 72 jump casualties among the 739 men who dropped on 3 July. Thirty-one troopers suffered severe fractures that would prohibit them from ever making another parachute jump. Nine men in the lead plane suffered severe injuries, including Colonel Jones's radio operator. Major Knox, the First Battalion commander, suffered a broken foot. The two-planes abreast flight formation and low-altitude jumping from the first ten planes resulted in numerous troopers landing off the runway of the airstrip, in areas littered with vehicles, supply dumps, wrecked Japanese aircraft, splintered trees from the preassault bombardment, and antiaircraft emplacements. Troopers who unluckily landed astride one of these hazards were likely to be injured. Having been made aware of these heavy casualties on the first day, General Krueger ordered General Patrick to be sure the edges of the runway were clear of vehicles. He also instructed the Fifty-fourth Troop Carrier Wing commander to fly the next airlift over Kamiri in single-file formation. By the evening of 3 July, the First Battalion of the 503d had relieved the First Battalion of the 158th Infantry and assumed defense around Kamiri airstrip. Regimental and First Battalion command posts of the 503d were established at Kamiri drome.

The Third Battalion of the 503d Regiment began jumping onto Kamiri airstrip along with the remainder of Regimental Headquarters and service companies men at 0955 hours on 4 July. By 1025 hours, the 685 men of this echelon were on the ground. Even with the precautions, however, there were 56 jump casualties, mostly from landing on the hard, packed, and newly rolled coral runway. Thus far, 1,424 paratroopers had jumped; their casualty rate was 9 percent; and they had not received any enemy fire. Among the 128 trooper casualties suffered during the two airlifts, 59 were severe factures. The paratroopers had lost the services of a battalion commander, three company commanders, the regimental communications officer, and numerous key noncommissioned officers. The Third Battalion of the 503d was given the mission of relieving units of the Second Battalion of the 158th Infantry on the east end of Kamiri airstrip. The men were in perimeter position by 1730 hours of 4 July.

Alarmed by the high casualty rates on both the drops, Colonel Jones, the commander of the paratroopers, requested that the Second Battalion

The Second Battalion, 503d Parachute Infantry Regiment on the beach at Biak Island awaiting overwater transportation to Noemfoor Island, 10 July, 1944.

be flown to Noemfoor as soon as Kamiri strip was operational for the landing of C-47 airplanes. In the meantime, a Japanese prisoner reported that Namber drome was practically abandoned. General Patrick dispatched a force to secure that airfield. On 6 July, three destroyers, a rocket LCI, and landing support vessels saw the Second Battalion of the 158th Infantry go ashore to capture Namber airfield, while at the same time, a detachment of the 503d Paratroopers landed on Manim Island, three miles west of Namber in Romboi Bay, and installed a radar unit there. Because of heavy rains, equipment shortages, and the need for an early end to the campaign, General Krueger ordered the Second Battalion of the 503d flown from Hollandia to Biak and thence to Noemfoor by LCIs. While at Biak and awaiting transport to Noemfoor Island, two paratroopers of the Second Battalion ventured to the front lines near Mokmer drome and were killed in action after joining other U.S. Army forces in an assault on an enemy position. The Second Battalion of the 503d landed in Romboi Bay, near Namber drome, on 11 July at 0930 hours and was immediately ordered to proceed overland to Inasi, a native village on the east side of the island, and initiate patrols in that area. The men reached Inasi on 13 July 1944.

The snafus experienced by the 503d paratroopers could have been avoided had the Cyclone Task Force commander and Alamo Force headquarters not made numerous faulty plans and calculations. The alternate Alamo Force reserve for Noemfoor, the Thirty-fourth Infantry Regiment of the Twenty-fourth Division, had been assembled on the beach at Biak since 30 June and could have loaded for overwater transportation to Noemfoor in less than twenty-four hours. LCIs could have made the seventy-five to eighty mile trip from Biak to Noemfoor in less than ten hours. After General Patrick's request for reinforcements at 1115 hours 2 July, the men of the Thirty-fourth Infantry could have been on Noemfoor by the following evening. Only one battalion of troopers was on the island by that time, and it had suffered extraordinary and unnecessary jump casualties.

The First and Third Battalions of the 503d vigorously patrolled to the south and southwest of their Kamiri perimeter from the third through the tenth of July. The First Battalion of the 158th Infantry, less Company A, met opposition and established a night perimeter around a large Japanese garden area near Kamiri village on the night of 4 July. The 600-by-350-yard area was largely overgrown with papaya, taro, and casava. An incline, designated Hill 201, and its approaches were bombarded by heavy machine guns, 81mm mortars, a platoon of 4.2-inch mortars of the 641st Tank Destroyer Battalion, and a battery of 105mm howitzers of the 147th Field Artillery Battalion. The only Japanese offensive operation of the campaign occurred early in the morning of 5 July. It was met by heavy counteroffensive fire that decimated the Japanese. The body count taken the next day and the dead and wounded found along trails on following days indicated nearly four hundred enemy casualties. But then contact with the enemy was lost. Vigorous patrolling by both the paratroopers and 158th Infantrymen confirmed that the main Japanese forces had evacuated the northern section of Noemfoor Island.

As the bastard regiment of Cyclone Task Force, the 503d Parachute Infantry was assigned to patrol and consolidate in the southern half of Noemfoor. The 503d vigorously carried out this assignment. On 14 July, Battery B of the 147th Field Artillery Battalion was assigned to the 503d Regiment. Compared with their counterparts in the 158th Infantry, the paratroopers were lightly equipped. They were assigned only one battery of artillery; the other batteries of the 147th Field Artillery remained with the 158th Infantry. The 158th Infantry had vehicles for transportation of food, ammunition, and casualties as well as tanks and weapons carriers for assault. Artillery, the greatest killer on the battlefield, was used to the maximum by the 158th Infantry and saved the lives of countless Infantrymen. Its patrols were accompanied by artillery observers.

Throughout the two-month campaign the 503d parachute infantrymen were deficient in most supportive attachments. Whether the failure to provide these deserved supports was the fault of General Krueger, General Patrick, or Colonel Jones, or to be shared equally, is not indicated either in records or memories.

On 13 July, Company C of the 503d was dispatched on patrol with the mission of contacting the main enemy body and forcing it towards the Second Battalion at Inasi. Contact was made at 1400 hours. A sharp firefight developed between Company C and the enemy force, estimated at four hundred men with numerous heavy machine guns, and mortars. A prisoner later reported that the enemy force actually numbered twelve hundred troops and was commanded by Colonel Shimizu. The Japanese were entrenched on Hill 670 with a strong screen of riflemen (commonly called snipers). All their automatic weapons were sited. Following a three-and-a-half-hour firefight, Company C withdrew three hundred yards to the north, dug in for the night, and awaited reinforcements. Companies A and B joined their sister company by 1845

87

hours. Harrassing fire was directed at Hill 670 by Battery B, 147th Field Artillery Battalion.

On 14 July, patrols went forward from the First Battalion to determine the profile of the enemy on Hill 670. Intense rifle and machine gun fire forced them to withdraw, and an artillery barrage was mounted against the hill. Patrol activities then resumed for the remainder of the day to determine the enemy flanks. At this time, Battery B of the 147th Field Artillery Battalion was replaced by Battery A and attached to the 503d. Battery A was located at Namber drome. At 0700 hours on 15 July, after an artillery barrage, Company B moved onto Hill 670. These troopers encountered light opposition but discovered that the main body of the Japanese had withdrawn from their positions during the night. A perimeter defense was established on Hill 670, and far-ranging patrols were dispatched to try to relocate the main body of the enemy forces.

Jungle warfare in the dense tropical rain forest posed problems that had no answers in existing U.S. Army field manuals. Communications ranged from poor to bad. The field telephone was useless at a distance greater than eight or ten miles. The maximum range of supporting artillery was surpassed by numerous patrols. Artillery forward observers did not accompany patrols smaller than company strength. The artillerymen were exceptionally accurate, but the 503d paratroop officers, either through ignorance or indifference, failed to use them to maximum effectiveness. The lives of innumerable troopers could have been saved had more reconnaissance by fire preceded reconnaissance by force. There were no roads connecting the areas patrolled by the 503d troopers and their bases of supply and hospital facilities at Kamiri, ten or twelve miles away. The evacuation of wounded and dead required carrying parties and accompanying riflemen. Native parties were used whenever feasible. The heavy GI litters were soon discarded in favor of trooper-invented poncho litters, which could be hastily made by interlacing a poncho between light poles. A single casualty required two four-man carrying teams plus the accompanying riflemen. Because several hours usually elapsed before a casualty reached a hospital, loss of life from blood loss or trauma resulted too frequently. To facilitate a carry and relieve exhausted troopers, the dead were usually transported by tying their hands and feet to each end of a pole. Two men, supporting the ends of the pole on their shoulders, could carry their swinging but cumbersome deceased comrade to collecting points with a minimum of difficulty. Medical doctors accompanied patrols of company strength or greater. First aid men went with smaller patrols. When battle casualties were heavy, the heroics of the brave and exceptionally well-trained medics matched those of the physicians. The medics were assigned to the various companies from battalion medical headquarters; the various medical personnel were under control of the regimental surgeon.

In addition to losses inflicted by the enemy, the troopers were plagued by malaria, tropical fungal diseases, scrub typhus, and dysentery. In combination, these maladies sorely sapped the strength of the combatants. Resupply of food, water, and ammunition in the jungle was very difficult. Aerial drops were feasible, but obtaining even one transport plane for a short time each day was difficult. Dead and wounded troopers usually had to be carried for hours from the battleground where they had fallen to the nearest shore for evacuation to the field hospital or the Graves Registration Unit at Kamiri. The boat ride required additional hours.

The communication of Intelligence information from the regimental command down to the squad members of the various companies was poor to nonexistent. Many patrols failed their missions because they were not informed whether their purpose was combat or reconnaissance or whether they were seeking stragglers or a main enemy force. Even the latter confused the battalion commanders, for they usually had little or no information about the number or capabilities of the enemy. Colonel Jones located his troops in the jungle by observing colored smoke released by grenades at specified hours as he flew overhead in a field artillery liaison plane. This plane was also used to carry forward-area drops of blood plasma, telephone wire, messages, and limited quantities of food.

During the period from 15 to 23 July 1944, the First Battalion of the 503d was patrolling to the south and southeast of Hill 670, attempting to locate the main body of the Japanese forces. The Second Battalion, located in Inasi, patrolled to the north and northwest with the same mission. On 23 July, patrols of Companies D and E operating about four miles north of Inasi, finally encountered the enemy. For heroic action and outstanding combat leadership, Sgt. Ray E. Eubanks, a Company D squad leader, was awarded the Congressional Medal of Honor, posthumously (see appendix C). The Japanese withdrew, using as a delaying action a strong screen of rifle fire. The Second Battalion troopers broke off the engagement on 25 July to return to their base for supplies. Although patrols were again sent out, contact with the enemy had been lost. Patrol activities from 27 July to 8 August continued in all directions from the various battalion command posts at Inasi, Menoekwari, and Namber. The dense jungle and tropical rains made it extremely difficult to conduct patrols for any significant duration. Several small

Sgt. Ray E. Eubanks, posthumously awarded the Congressional Medal of Honor for heroism on Noemfoor Island. The medal was presented to his father, Ezekiel Eubanks, at Fort Bragg, North Carolina.

enemy groups were encountered, mostly near Inasi, and the aggressive troopers inflicted heavy losses on them.

On 10 August 1944, a Company G patrol of the 503d found a trail about two miles south-southwest of Inasi, which looked as though a large force had recently traveled it. This information was given to Major Erickson, Third Battalion commander, who immediately dispatched Company G to contact the enemy force, which it did the following day, near Hill 380, about two and one-half miles south-southwest of Inasi. The Japanese troops under Colonel Shimizu were entrenched along a flattened ridge. There were about 360 of them, armed with a variety of small weapons, mortars, and machine guns. A fierce firefight lasted all afternoon, with G Company suffering several casualties before withdrawing so that artillery fire from the 147th Field Artillery Battalion and air strikes by B-25 bombers of the 309th Bomb Wing, operating out of Kornasoran drome, could be laid on the enemy positions. Company H of the 503d, relieving Company G, then moved into the area. Many enemy dead and wounded were found, but the main enemy body had once again retreated. The area was secured for the night. The following day, 12 August, Company H trailed the withdrawing enemy forces, finding them in late afternoon. Another fierce battle ensued. Company H, suffering numerous casualties, withdrew to the crest of Hill 380 and dug in. Artillery fire was again directed against the enemy during the night. At 0700 hours, 13 August, Company H moved down from Hill 380 and secured the battleground of the previous evening. Heavy losses had been inflicted on the Japanese force. Several mortars and light and heavy machine guns were captured. In the early morning jungle light, the horrible discovery was made that three H Company men, whose bodies could not be recovered during the previous evening's battle, had been cannibalized by the Japanese during the night.

As early as 1 August 1944, patrols on Noemfoor began finding bodies from which fleshy portions had been carved. Later, prisoners confirmed cannibalism among the Japanese troops; the usual victims were freshly slain Formosan laborers accompanying the enemy forces as slaves. The men of Company H, enraged at finding the mutilated bodies of their fallen comrades, gave no quarter as they hotly pursued the enemy. During the day of 13 August, numerous Japanese soldiers were killed during their retreat. Several of them had knapsacks filled with human flesh, and others were slain while eating human flesh.

While the Third Battalion forces of the 503d were pursuing the remnants of Colonel Shimizu's troops, the First Battalion began moving to block the enemy to the south and west. Company A contacted units

The starving Japanese forces on Noemfoor resorted to cannibalism rather than surrender. This enemy soldier's fleshy thighs have been cut away for food.

Photo Courtesy Mike Mattevich

92

of the Japanese main body at 1730 hours on 14 August. For two days clashes with the enemy forces were numerous; at the same time, the Third Battalion was mopping up stragglers and engaging the rear of the fleeing enemy. Finally, on 17 August, the remnants of Shimizu's men were driven into a pocket, with the paratroopers on three sides and the ocean on the fourth. This final engagement was near the village of Pakriki. About twenty of the enemy escaped, including the elusive Colonel Shimizu.

The Third Battalion was transported back to Inasi by boat while the First Battalion patrolled the Pakriki area until 22 August, when it proceeded, less one company, overland to Namber drome. The commanding general of Cyclone Task Force directed that the 503d Parachute Infantry Regiment, less three companies, be moved to a newly cleared campsite near Kamiri airstrip. This move was completed on 23 August 1944. The three companies remaining in the southern part of the island were Company D at Namber drome, Company I at Inasi, and Company C at Menoekwari south. These units continued patrolling until relieved by the First Battalion of the 158th Infantry on 27 August 1944, when they rejoined their regiment in its new rest quarters. On the same date, a platoon of Company E of the 503d was detailed to relieve a platoon of Company F of the 158th Infantry at Menoekwari west, guarding a radar unit located there. Neither the colors of the Japanese 219th Infantry nor Colonel Shimizu with his three-hundred-year-old saber was ever found, though intense and vigorous patrolling continued until the Noemfoor combatants were ordered to the Philippines. Sixth Army Headquarters officially declared Noemfoor Island secure on 31 August 1944.

To the end of August of 1944, the 158th Infantry Regiment had killed 611 Japanese, captured 179 (mostly from artillery fire at Hill 201), and liberated 209 Javanese slave laborers. The 158th Infantry Regiment had lost only 6 men killed in action and 41 wounded in action. From 3 July to 31 August 1944, the 503d Parachute Infantry Regiment had counted 1,087 dead Japanese and had captured 82 prisoners and liberated 312 Formosans and 9 Javanese natives. After an initial loss of 128 jump casualties, the 503d lost an additional 39 men killed in action, 72 wounded in action, and more than 400 sick who were rendered combat-ineffective. In retrospect, it is clear that neither the Thirty-fourth Infantry nor the 503d Parachute Infantry Regiment was needed to secure the island. A squadron of Australian P-40s arrived at Kamiri drome on 6 July. Two fighter groups were based there by 9 September. Construction at Namber drome was abandoned in favor of Kornasoren, where two 7,000-foot runways were completed and fifty P-38s and a squadron of B-24s were eventually based. The runway had to be lengthened to seven thousand feet to accommodate the heavily laden B-24s. The high trees on the approaches to Kornasoren drome were cleared by Company C of the 161st Parachute Engineer Battalion, recently arrived on Noemfoor Island, which formed an integral part of the 503d Parachute Infantry Regimental Combat Team formed thereafter. Company C, 161st Parachute Engineer Battalion, prepared a clean, well-drained, new campsite near Kamiri drome for the 503d troopers.

The gains of the Noemfoor Island campaign provided additional air cover for the upcoming invasion of the Vogelkop Peninsula and Morotai Island and the first large-scale bombing of Japanese petroleum resources on Borneo. Although the 503d had originally been ordered to Hollandia as a mobile reserve force for Biak, it was used in a less classical campaign. Nevertheless, the paratroopers had once again surpassed the demands made of them and had become hardened as tempered steel in their latest acid test of battle.

7
Formation of the 503d Parachute Infantry Regimental Combat Team

By the end of the Noemfoor campaign, the troopers of the 503d Parachute Infantry Regiment had been overseas nearly two years. Some men of the Second Battalion, who had served in the Panama Canal Zone, had been away from their motherland almost three years. Being a bastard regiment, the 503d was under direct command of General MacArthur's headquarters. He, in turn, would relinquish command of the regiment to the U.S. Sixth Army, which would assign the troopers to various commands, both American and Australian, as necessity demanded and GHQ approved.

The paratroopers of the 503d were lightly armed and were basically to be used as shock troops. The regiment was entirely dependent on units to which it was attached for supplies, artillery support, evacuation of casualties, and transportation. Being very mobile on foot and quite aggressive, the troopers often outdistanced their supply lines and supporting forces. The paratroopers' heavy artillery support for the entirety of the war was provided by the United States Army Air Force, with explosive and napalm bombs, multimounted .50-caliber machine guns, and 20mm guns for strafing. The chief disadvantage of relying on the USAAF was that sometimes it was necessary to wait long periods of time for an air strike if another target had priority. The troopers of the 503d enjoyed their first taste of American artillery support in their offensive operations on Noemfoor. We must not forget the Australian artillerymen and their twenty-five-pounders who jumped with us in Markham Valley on 5 September 1943, but the Aussie artillerymen fired no shots in support of the Third Battalion infantrymen at Log Crossing, the paratroopers' only combat encounter with Japanese forces during the Nadzab campaign. In the Noemfoor operation, artillery support was not used to maximum effectiveness because the officers of the 503d did not know how to use it. In rest camp at the end of the Noemfoor campaign, a major structural change in the composition of the 503d was made.

Engineering services are a necessity in all field operations — bridge building, road improvement, tank trap elimination, construction of special fortifications, water purification, special demolitions, and other support activities. The 503d paratroopers acquired the first company of parachute troop engineers formed in the U.S. Army.

In August 1943, volunteers were sought to form an engineer battalion of airborne troops at Camp Carson, Colorado. The resulting 161st Airborne Engineer Battalion consisted of Headquarters, A, B, and C companies, with Company C designated as the paratroop company. The remaining battalion members were to be glider troops. Company C was detached from the rest of the battalion and sent to Laurinburg-Maxton Army Air Force Base at Laurinburg, North Carolina, where engineer training was accomplished as well as Stage A of paratrooper jump training. When Company C was sent to the parachute jump school at Fort Benning, Georgia, the men immediately began Stage B training. Their qualifying jump occurred in Alabama on New Years Eve 1944. Proudly sporting their silver wings, the men, of Company C, 161st Parachute Engineers, returned to Laurinburg-Maxton and thence to Camp Mackall, where their paratroop engineer training was refined. They were sent to California, boarded ship on 26 April 1944, and sailed for the South Pacific the following day. Their home for the next two weeks was the converted luxury liner SS *America*, which had been renamed USS *West Point*. They sailed unescorted to Sydney, Australia. Aboard the same ship were fifteen hundred nurses and members of the Women's Army Corps (unfortunately, the women were on separate decks, the approaches to which were well guarded by a detachment of U.S. Marines). A couple of days were spent in Sydney harbor offloading personnel and supplies before sailing north for Milne Bay, Papuan New Guinea, and the war zone.

The day of arrival in Milne Bay in late May 1944, was anything but pleasant. A tropical downpour welcomed these newcomers to the SWPA. Billeted in floorless tents the first night, the men and all their equipment became soaked and muddy. After drying out, the men built a camp on a hillside where they managed to stay fairly dry. While at Milne Bay, these troopers constructed warehouses, unloaded ships, constructed roads, and established supply dump areas. They were alerted to jump with the 503d on Noemfoor but were held in reserve and landed three days after D-Day by boat. The men of Company C went on patrols with the infantry, built innumerable latrines, cleared timber for the approaches to the Kornasoren airstrip, built new roads, and repaired old ones around the airfields. They also cleared off the jungle and constructed campsites for both the 158th and 503d infantry regiments. They established a water point (a water purification center) from which all units on the island received their fresh water supply.

The distinguished, talented, diversified trained paratrooper engineers of Company C, 161st Engineer Battalion, consisted of 128 men and 10 officers. The company consisted of three platoons of three squads each. Their weapons were those of the parachute infantry. Among their troops were headquarters personnel, cooks, heavy equipment operators, and medical personnel. Company C was commanded by Capt. James Byer of Sarasota, Florida. These talented paratroop engineers were as welcome to the weary infantry battalions as Santa Claus would have been in August. The bedraggled men of the 503d, viewing their clean campsite and facilities, expressed their gratitude and compliments to their new comrades-in-arms, Company C, 161st Parachute Engineers.

At about the same time, a battalion of Red Legs appeared on the scene. Near the end of the Noemfoor campaign, some 503d troopers received additional fire support from 75mm pack howitzers belonging to the newly arrived 462d Parachute Field Artillery Battalion. Artillery has long been known to be the greatest killer on the battlefield. It was not until the summer of 1942, however, that a parachute was placed on a cannon. Parachute artillery battalions had their genesis with the activation of the parachute test battery in July 1942 at Fort Benning, Georgia, under command of 2d Lt. Joseph D. Harris. (Lieutenant Harris was later killed in action in Italy while serving with the Eighty-second Airborne Division.) The standard artillery piece of the U.S. Army was (and is) the 105mm howitzer. It has a range of 12,330 yards and weighs 4,980 pounds. Because of the size, weight, and inability of the 105mm howitzer to be disassembled into "jumping" segments, the lightweight 75mm pack howitzer was selected for airborne use. It weighed 1,268 pounds but had a maximum range of only 9,475 yards.

The 462d Parachute Field Artillery Battalion was activated at Camp MacKall on 16 June 1943 under command of Lt. Col. Forrest Armstrong. Early problems of "scatter" with the artillery "coffin" bombs were solved by old-timers in the parachuting business such as Harry "Tug" Wilson, of test platoon fame, "Buzz" Campbell, rigging officer of the test platoon, and Col. John B. Shinberger, who devised a heavy-duty webbing to interconnect all of the airplanes' exterior loads to form a "daisy chain." 1st Lt. C. W. Plemmons emerged as the 462d Parachute Field Artillery Battalion rigging officer.

The 75mm pack howitzers of the 462d Parachute Field Artillery Battalion were packaged into seven loads for parachute drops. In addition, two ammunition loads were rigged, making a total of nine loads per gun. Six of the nine loads were belly-mounted on the transport plane, while the other three were door loads, which were to be shoved out of the transport plane by the jumping artillerymen as they exited. Each battery consisted of 91 men and six howitzers (four on line with two in reserve to cover drop or combat losses). Nine men were assigned to each gun. A .50-caliber machine gun section was assigned to each 75mm howitzer battery. These troopers also possessed small arms and rocket launchers (bazookas) for unit protection. The 462d Parachute Field Artillery Battalion consisted of a Headquarters and Service Battery plus Batteries A, B, C, and D for a total complement of 621 men and officers.

The pack howitzer batteries were A, B, and C, as described above. The nucleus of the 462d was the Headquarters and Service Battery with a strength of 129 men and officers. This battery consisted of various sections to assume the following duties. The battalion Executive Section (S-1) was responsible for administrative detail, movement orders, and liaison with battery, battalion, and regimental combat team commanders. The Intelligence Section (S-2) was responsible for area reconnaissance, assigning battalion survey parties to provide target area surveys by triangulating target locations and the tie-back baseline survey to the firing battery locations. The S-2 officer was also responsible for local battalion security.

The Plans and Training Section (S-3) was to operate the battalion Fire Direction Center during combat. In the Fire Direction Center, personnel from each of the firing batteries as well as from headquarters maintained firing charts on which each target was plotted. Each battery was represented, along with the fire direction plotter, so as to read off commands relayed to the firing batteries in an effort to avoid firing on friendly troops. The S-3 section also directed communications from headquarters. The Supply and Service Section (S-4) was responsible for all supplies and resupplies, including ammunition, rations, and other essential items. This group coordinated battery supply sections and mess. The battalion motor officer and the Parachute Maintenance Section operated through S-4. There were two medical officers and seventeen medics under control of the regimental medical officer. The 462d Red Legs also brought along Chaplin Kermit White, a native of West Virginia. The 462d Parachute Artillery Battalion had its own air force of two LC-5 spotter planes, two pilots, and airplane mechanics.

Battery D, with a strength of two hundred men and officers, was conceived as an antiaircraft-antitank unit to protect the 462d Artillery Battalion batteries. It was composed of two antitank and two antiaircraft platoons. Each antiaircraft platoon had five squads of five men each, plus squad leaders. The antitank platoons consisted of a crew chief and nine cannoneers for each of the two guns assigned. All platoons had a platoon leader, a platoon sergeant, and the section chiefs mentioned above for the antitank platoons. Twelve .50-caliber machine guns were available to Battery D, ten on line with two in reserve to cover drop or combat losses. Rocket launchers were also assigned to Battery D. The .50-caliber machine guns were belly loads on the transport planes. The disassembled parts were wrapped in padded canvas containers, the barrel, receiver, and tripod all in one package and ammunition and grenades in other containers placed in nacelles beneath the plane.

The 462d Parachute Field Artillery Battalion sailed from San Francisco on 11 March 1944 aboard the U.S. Army transport *Seacat*. After arriving in Brisbane on 25 March 1944, they proceeded directly to Camp Cable, where they spent the next three months. During this time, they made parachute jumps to maintain pay status, received jungle training, and employed battery firing practice. In early July, the 462d boarded the Dutch freighter *Van Hoitz* for a long voyage. The transport made stops at Milne Bay, Lae, and other ports to drop off Aussie servicemen returning to their units from leave. Upon arrival on Noemfoor, men of the 462d were assigned immediate fire support missions. During one such assignment, while sound ranging high-angle fire, Lt. Col. Donald F. Madigan, who had succeeded Lieutenant Colonel Armstrong, was seriously wounded by a tree burst. He was evacuated back to the United States shortly afterward. Command of the 462d was then given to Maj. Arlis E. Kline, senior officer of the battalion and of S-3.

In the closing days of August 1944, the troopers of the 462d joined their "older" brothers awaiting further orders. Up until that time, there were three parachute trooper entities: Company C, 161st Parachute Engineer Battalion, the 462d Parachute Field Artillery Battalion, and the 503d Parachute Infantry Regiment. These three units now blended organizationally and as comrades in arms for the remainder of World War II. The three parachute entities coalesced as three winds of death. These pioneers in airborne history are hereafter referred to as members of the 503d Parachute Infantry Regimental Combat Team.

Between the time of the 503d parachute attack at Nabzab on 5 September 1943 and the end of August 1944, the Allied forces had traversed the length of the giant island of New Guinea. In the leap-frogging offensive tactics adopted to achieve this end, 135,000 Japanese troops had been cut off beyond all hope of rescue and with little hope for survival. The enemy dead are enumerated in the army histories of the various New Guinea campaigns by the Allied forces. The far-reaching western areas, which a few months before could be penetrated only by Allied submarines could now be bombed at will. These targets were the Macassar Strait, the Molucca Passage, and, to the northwest, the Halmaheras. Beyond these, an ocean leap away, lay the Philippine Islands!

8
Return to the Philippines

In late summer and early autumn 1944, the paratroopers of the 503d Regimental Combat Team (RCT) took advantage of the opportunity to rest and relax. There were months-old motion pictures to be appreciated, swimming, sunning on the nearby beaches, equipment to be cleaned, normal garrison duties, and letters to be written. During this brief period of serenity, an outstanding United Service Organization troupe, The Bob Hope Show, arrived. The traveling artists included the popular Bob Hope, vocalist Frances Langford, comedian Jerry Colonna, accomplished dancer Kay Thompson, and a big band of the era, Les Brown and His Band of Reknown. During one performance, a security patrol member, deep in the nearby jungle, accidentally discharged his weapon. The honorable Bob Hope still maintains that a Jap shot at him.

At the rest camp on the hillside near Kamiri drome, the troopers received long overdue money paid in guldens, the monetary standard unit of the Netherlands government and its possessions. Stud poker games were soon underway and the noise of "galloping dominoes" (dice) was heard. Nearby air force personnel, especially the Aussies, who had established supply routes to "spirits" in Australia, soon began traversing the campsite, plying their wares. In the early trading, a bottle of "hootch" could be bartered for captured Japanese artifacts such as flags, sabers, and other contraband. A flooded market, however, soon found the "sly grog" merchants accepting only money. The equivalent of ten to twenty pounds (Australian) per bottle was paid in guldens.

Men of the 503d were frequently detailed to unload cargo supply ships in the harbor. They naturally acquired innumerable cases of beer and liquor despite the watchful eyes of guards. The contraband "spirits" ferried out by "moonlight requisition" supplemented the scant beer rations issued at the end of the Noemfoor campaign. Stealing beer and whiskey was the troopers' way of obtaining what they deemed was rightfully theirs. Beer rations were regularly issued in combat zones but not to men on the firing line. As a result, noncombatants usually got more than their share. To maintain an esprit de corps, some of the "hillbilly moonshiners" of the 503d attempted to promote a tropical version of their former mountain trade. They stole sugar, canned fruits, and yeast from the battalion mess supplies, placed mixtures of these ingredients in galvanized buckets, hid them in the nearby undergrowth, and awaited fermentation. The end product was terrible to smell and dangerous to imbibe.

Not to be outdone, the island natives used a hollowed-out bamboo trunk in a unique way. They would climb a coconut tree, pluck a flower blossom from the canopy of the tree, then hang the bamboo tube underneath the exuding stem until the tube filled with sap of the plant. After a few days of natural fermentation, one had a native drink called "tuba." This distillate guaranteed to produce a dark brown taste in the mouth next day, a kaleidoscopic hangover, and diarrhea.

At this time, the troopers were engaged in extensive combat training on Noemfoor Island. Parachute jumps were accomplished both to maintain pay status and for practice. At assigned intervals, troopers of the various companies marched to the United States Military Cemetery on the island and paid their final respects to fallen comrades. Each company fired three volleys of shots over the place of interment. With "Taps" ringing in their ears, the somber but proud troopers silently returned to their encampment, heavy at heart over the loss of their buddies.

An enterprising trooper of Company E, impressed with the Japanese knee mortar, which could fire a nearly flat trajectory, began experiments to convert the U.S. 60mm mortar to such capabilities. After several trips to the nearby U.S. Army ordnance shop and junk pile, Cpl. Norman Petzelt of Woodstock, Georgia, had assembled the parts needed. Using ordnance tools, he soon had an operable 60mm mortar that could be fired at a nearly flat trajectory, but it never had a chance for mass production and use during World War II. The patent rights were abrogated by the U.S. Army because the inventor and parts were government property.

In June 1944, GHQ had issued a broad general plan to liberate the Philippine Islands. The U.S. Sixth Army was directed to prepare to seize Morotai in the Halmahera Island group on 15 September. Morotai lay about halfway between Noemfoor and Mindanao in the southern Philippines. On 20 October 1944 Salebaboe Island of the Talaud group was to be captured. Airfields on Salebaboe were to be used for an airborne assault on Misamis Oriental in northwestern Mindanao at the same time that an assault landing in Saranganu Bay of southern Mindanao was to be made. This campaign was to be followed by an offensive against Leyte.

A GHQ warning instruction reached the Sixth Army commander on 2 September 1944, and set a target date for the airborne operation of 15 November. The seizure and control of the Leyte-Samar Island area was to be accomplished on 7 and 20 December. To free the Sixth Army for these missions, GHQ transferred all its missions in Netherlands New Guinea, New Britain, Admiralties, and Morotai to the newly organized U.S. Eighth Army. The latter was activated under command of Lt. Gen. Robert L. Eichelberger on 25 September, 1944. The Australian army was to assume the missions of the Sixth Army on Papuan New Guinea as well as those of the Fourteenth Corps in the Solomon Island group.

A GHQ radiogram of 15 September canceled the Talaud and Mindanao operations because of the successes of the naval carrier forces of the U.S. Third Fleet. They had caused such tremendous damage to Japanese air forces and naval shipping that the liberation plans for the Philippines could be accelerated. The revised target date for the Leyte operation was scheduled for 20 October. The paratroopers of the 503d were placed on alert on 21 September to prepare for overwater movement to Leyte, Philippine Islands, for staging for a new assault.

The assault movement on Leyte began with the departure of minesweepers from Seeadler Harbor in the Admiralties on 11 October. The U.S. Army's historical accounts of the invasion of Leyte, Samar, and the early battle engagements by army and naval units appear elsewhere. Heavy casualties and supply shortages were affecting the engaging forces of the four U.S. Army divisions, the First Cavalry and the Twenty-fourth Infantry divisions of the Tenth Corps and the Seventh and Ninety-sixth Infantry divisions of the Twenty-fourth Corps. On 23 October, Col. George M. Jones, commander of the 503d Regimental Combat Team, Maj. E. C. Clark of section S-3, Lt. M. L. Smith, assistant of section S-2, and Maj. Arlis E. Kline, the 462d Parachute Field Artillery Battalion commander, left Noemfoor Island for Leyte to receive information and instructions for preliminary planning on the RCT's proposed involvement in the Love III (Mindoro) operation and to prepare the staging area.

By 11 November, these divisions, less two regiments, covered a fifty-mile front in northern Leyte. GHQ had already ordered the SWPA to make replacements to the Sixth Army to cover combat losses. Simultaneously, several combat units had been ordered forward to Leyte Island; those of the U.S. Army Eleventh Corps, the Thirty-second Infantry Division, and the 112th Cavalry RCT, reached Leyte on 14 November. The 503d Parachute Infantry Regimental Combat Team sailed from Noemfoor Island on 13 November, aboard the USS *Comet* and the USS *Knox*. These troopships joined a very large convoy bearing needed supplies from rear New Guinea, American, and Australian bases plus a newcomer to the SWPA, the Eleventh Airborne Division, which had been in training for the past five months at the old campsite of the 503d near Dobadura, Papuan New Guinea.

The convoy reached Leyte safely on 19 November. The 503d RCT disembarked south of Dulag. The Burauen airfields developed by the Japs and improved by the USAAF were ten miles to the northwest. Foxholes were dug and gun emplacements installed, although they rapidly filled with water seeping beneath the sandy beaches at sea level and from the torrential rain that seemed never to cease. The troopers of the 503d established beach defenses as best they could. The 462d Parachute Field Artillery Battalion directed its guns toward a possible counterinvasion by sea and enemy aircraft. Company C, 161st Parachute Engineer Battalion, installed several miles of double-apron barbed-wire fence. Other men of Company C helped erect a tent city, a hospital, and innumerable latrines. It also provided troopers to ride "shotgun" on barges bringing supplies from the offshore freighters to the food, supply, and ammunition dumps near Tacloban, a few miles to the north.

Leyte is approximately 115 miles long north to south and varies from 15 to 43 miles wide east to west. The rugged and heavily forested Cordillera Mountains extend from Carigara Bay in the north to Cabalion and Sogod bays in the south. This 4,000-foot-high barrier divides the island into two distinct areas and exerts a marked influence on the weather. The eastern half has no dry season; it rains there about two out of three days per month from October through January, then one day out of three the remainder of the year. The weather on the western side of the mountain range has neither a distinct nor regular pattern of rainfall.

The troopers were depressed by the constant rain and cloud cover. The weather plus the ability of sound to travel rapidly across water enabled the troopers to hear the magnified rumblings of the artillery battles raging in the mountains of Leyte and on Samar to the east. The booms of heavy artillery bursts, fired in support of infantry troops on Leyte and Samar, were somber reminders of the seriousness of war. Training activities of the men of the 503d RCT were limited because the area to their immediate rear was marshy. Limited training sessions, maintenance of equipment procedures, and essential company duties were performed daily, generally in the morning. Afternoon activities were limited to sunbathing and swimming. Motion pictures were

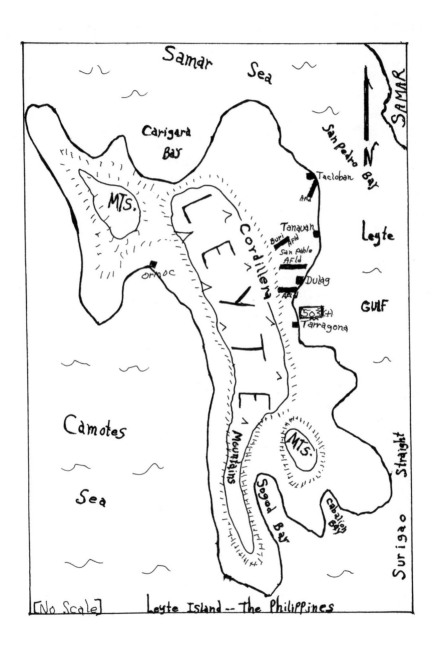

Samar Sea

Carigara
Bay

SAMAR

San Pedro Bay

N

Tacloban
AFd

Tanauan
Buri AFd
San Pablo AFld

Leyte

Dulag
AFU

GULF

503 (H)
Tarragona

MTS.

Ormoc

Cordillera

L E Y T E

Camotes

Sea

Mountains

MTS.

Sogod Bay

Cabalian Bay

Surigao Straight

[No Scale]   Leyte Island -- The Philippines

sometimes shown after nightfall unless torrential rainfall with accompanying lightning discharges interferred or mandatory blackouts were imposed because of the frequent enemy air raids on Allied shipping in the harbor and the airfields at Burauen, Dulag, and Tacloban.

Progress on the Tacloban airstrip had been hindered by rain squalls and mud. It could accommodate too few fighter planes to protect airstrips or shipping, let alone provide aerial support to the fighting troops in the mountains. Japanese bombers from Luzon constantly harassed our airstrips and naval shipping. The U.S. fighter planes had a limited flying range for retaliatory strikes. No bombers were yet stationed on Leyte. Admiral Halsey, realizing that MacArthur was unable to protect shipping, retained seven aircraft carriers to lend him support. All ships of his fleet, leaving for rest and resupply at Ulithi, were stripped of all but self-defense ammunition. The touchy Leyte situation resulted in no rest for Halsey's sailors, only resupply with battle loads and a turn-around at the Ulithi supply base.

On the stormy late afternoon and night of 26 November 1944, a fleet of Japanese bombers, accompanied by fighter planes, attacked shipping in the Dulag-Tacloban harbor area. Aerial dogfights and antiaircraft fire from shore batteries as well as from ships at anchor provided excitement for the 503d troopers. They watched as one USAAF P-38 fighter plane was hit by enemy fire. The pilot bailed out and was floating to earth in his parachute when a Japanese fighter plane attacked and machine-gunned him. Troopers saw the arms of the Yank pilot drop from his parachute risers and go limp. This brutal murder was committed by an inhuman Japanese individual in violation of the Geneva Conference. As twilight fell, a wave of Japanese troop transport planes arrived with their fighter escort. Three of the transport planes were shot down and crash-landed on shore in the 503d area. Most of the Japanese paratroopers and demolition personnel on board were killed on impact or by the Yankee paratroopers near the crash scene. Some three dozen Japanese escaped into the nearby marshes, only to be hunted down and killed the following morning.

By 1 December 1944, work on the Buri and San Pablo airstrips were abandoned. The Dulag airstrip was partly usable, but both the Dulag and Tacloban airstrips were inadequate to provide the USAAF with sufficient facilities to counter the Japanese menace and relieve the flat tops of Admiral Halsey's fleet. Thirty-five inches of rain had fallen in the past forty days. The enemy airforce, the rain and mud of Leyte, and the reinforcements that were trickling in to bolster the Japanese land forces all contributed to slow down the recapture of Leyte. The

USAAF needed dry airfields and clear flying weather to counter the Japanese aerial and naval threat to our invasion forces. Mindoro Island, to the west and north of Leyte, possessed the desired weather conditions. The need to seize Mindoro Island was the primary reason the 503d Parachute Infantry Regimental Combat Team had been ordered to the Philippines.

9
The Mindoro Island Campaign

Because of the incessant rainfall and resulting mud on the Allied airfields that were being constructed, enlarged, or renovated in the Dulag-Tacloban areas of Leyte, inadequate space was available to accommodate the troop transport planes needed to lift the 503d Parachute Infantry Regimental Combat Team. These troopers were scheduled to jump on Mindoro Island to seize and secure existing and potential airfield development sites in the San José area. GHQ had been planning the capture of Mindoro Island since 6 October, 1944. Its seizure would have a dual benefit: airdromes constructed there would provide dry airstrips under clear skies for Allied planes to intercept Japanese shipping to Leyte and other islands of the southern Philippines and, more important, to provide direct air support for planned operations in the Manila-Central Plains area on the island of Luzon to the north. The Mindoro target date was set for 5 December 1944.

Slow development of the Leyte airstrips, with resultant lack of land-based aircraft to support and protect the Allied supply lanes, resulted in the cancellation of the airborne assault. Instead, the troopers were alerted to prepare for a shore-to-shore assault on Mindoro alongside the Nineteenth Infantry RCT of the Twenty-fourth Division, now in Sixth Army reserve in the Cavite area of Leyte. Because the USAAF was unable to provide an adequate fighter plane umbrella for the assault shipping from Leyte to Mindoro, MacArthur relied on the U.S. Navy for protection. To make proper preparations for naval escort carrier-based planes to protect the assaulting troops, Admiral Kincaid obtained a ten-day delay for the invasion of Mindoro.

GHQ issued a directive on 1 December 1944, to postpone the Mindoro operation to 15 December. Rear Admiral Arthur D. Struble was to command the Mindoro attack force. The U.S. Navy Third Fleet was arranged into three task force groups. Their mission was to keep enemy aircraft on the more than one-hundred airfields on Luzon from launching attacks against the Mindoro Invasion force during three vital days — 14, 15, and 16 December — the approach, beach assault, and unloading stages of the invasion.

General MacArthur assigned responsibility for the operation to General Krueger's Sixth Army; he delegated the order to an especially created headquarters group designated the Western Visayan Task force and commanded by Brig. Gen. William C. Dunckel. The amended Sixth Army Field Order No. 33 issued 5 December 1944 assigned the Nineteenth RCT, the 503d Parachute Infantry RCT, one battalion of the Twenty-first Infantry Regiment (Task Force Reserve), numerous antiaircraft units, engineer groups, and various service units to the task force. Nearly eighteen thousand assault troops were involved. An additional ninety-five hundred Air Force personnel brought the total to over twenty-seven thousand troops. The Twenty-first Infantry RCT on Leyte (less one battalion) of the Twenty-fourth Division was designated Sixth Army Reserve.

Field Order No. 2, Western Visayan Task Force, was received at 503d RCT Headquarters on 9 December. The subsequent Field Order No. 8, 503d RCT, was issued the same date. The embarkation date was set for 11 December 1944. The troopers of the 503d RCT, alerted for a combat mission, undertook the usual precombat preparations: replacement of essential equipment, study of plans for assault, assignments to small units, ordnance checks to ensure that individual weapons were satisfactory, and finally, "the banquet." Assaults, whether by water or air, were preceded by the replacement of the monotonous field rations with a feast. Before boarding their assigned assault boats, the troopers gorged on turkey and dressing with all the accompaniments. A farm-reared trooper, recalling that back home livestock were always fed choice grains before slaughter, referred to these banquets as "fattening us up for the kill."

After embarking at 0830 hours on 11 December 1944, the 503d RCT troopers made a practice landing, reembarked immediately, and joined the forming assault convoy in San Pedro Bay. The attack force consisted of one light cruiser, twelve destroyers, nine destroyer transports, thirty LSTs, twelve LSMs, thirty-one LCI(L)s, sixteen minesweepers, and several smaller craft. A close covering group under Rear Admiral Russell S. Berkey included three cruisers, seven destroyers, and a motor torpedo boat group with twenty-three PT boats. The assembled convoy departed from San Pedro Bay at 0130 hours on 12 December 1944.

The island of Mindoro is just south of Luzon and separated from it by a narrow channel. Rather ovoid in outline, Mindoro is about 110 miles long and 60 miles wide. The island is just slightly larger than Leyte. Philippine weather is peculiar. While it is the wet season on one side of the archipelago, it is dry on the other. During October, November, and December, the northeast monsoons swept the Pacific-facing islands while the western islands were dry. General MacArthur wanted only a toehold on Mindoro, not the entire island. The desired spot was on the southwest coast of the island near the village of San José.

To confuse Japanese intelligence, Rear Admiral Berkey's flotilla headed east while Struble's transport group headed southeast, as though headed to Hollandia or Manus, until darkness fell. Then Berkey's force reversed course, reentered Leyte Gulf at high speed, and assumed a position ahead of the transport group now winding its way down Surigao Strait. The moonless night gave an aura of false serenity to the seaborne troopers of the 503d RCT. Precautions had been taken to impress the Japanese that Mindoro was of no consequence to the Allies. Even the Mindoro Filipino guerrillas were told to lie low and do nothing to alert the Japanese forces stationed there. The ruse worked; by December 1944 Japanese forces on Mindoro had been reduced to fewer than one thousand troops, distributed in small detachments in and around the coastal villages. At San José, there were eighty soldiers. The Japanese had not developed or improved any airdromes in the San José area.

During the night of 12 December the convoys traveled through the Surigao Strait south of Leyte and headed westward into the Mindanao Sea. When morning of 13 December dawned, Japanese aircraft had the three task force groups under surveillance as they sailed across the Mindanao Sea. The most westerly was the heavy covering and carrier group of Rear Admiral Theodore D. Ruddock, Jr., with six escort carriers, three battleships, three light cruisers, and eighteen destroyers. Its mission was to provide air cover over the convoy once it had sailed across the confining Mindanao Sea. The USAAF had been providing security up to this point. The main convoy consisted of three rows of LSTs, ten to a row, flanked by the thirty-one LCIs and the twelve LSMs. In a formation outside these ships were the protective cruisers and destroyers and the twenty-three PT boats, idling along at half-throttle in the rear. The third group, far in the rear, sailing at four knots, was the slow-tow convoy of small craft, barges, yard oilers, and tugs, all protected by four screening escorts.

The operation seemed perfect until 1500 hours on 13 December, when the convoy was off the southern tip of Negros Island and about to enter the Sulu Sea. Suddenly, a single black enemy plane appeared mast high over the convoy, approaching from Negros. Neither radar nor lookouts had discerned its approach. The plane banked sharply and crashed into the flagship cruiser *Nashville*. In less time than a heartbeat, 325 casualties resulted from the flames and explosions; 135 dead were counted. General Dunckel was painfully burned and wounded. Nearly all his staff were killed, including Col. Bruce C. Hill, his chief of staff. Admiral Struble, unhurt, lost his chief of staff, Capt. Everett W. Abdill. The Army Air Force's commanding officer of the 310th Bombardment Wing, Col. John T. Murtha, was critically wounded and succumbed shortly thereafter. The fire was quickly extinguished, but the *Nashville* was so badly damaged that she reversed course to return to Leyte Gulf, screened by a destroyer. Admiral Struble, the wounded General Dunckel, and the remainder of their staffs transferred to the destroyer *Dashiell*. A short time thereafter, at dusk, as the convoy steamed into the relatively open waters of the Sulu Sea, the first large kamikaze attack began. Fifteen enemy planes were intercepted thirteen miles away. Only two escaped to dive on the Allied convoy. One plane was splashed but the second hit the aft part of a destroyer, killing or wounding most of the men in the bridge area. Disabled, this destroyer returned to Leyte Gulf. A later attack brought more action but no damage because of poor visibility and accurate antiaircraft fire by the protective screening ships.

That night Admiral Ruddock deliberately made a feint attack against Puerto Princesa, hoping the Japanese would guess that Palawan, and not Mindoro, was the objective. The ruse succeeded. Regrettably, one of the most gruesome of Japanese atrocities in the Asiatic war resulted. Believing the U.S. naval attack convoy was headed toward this island, the Japanese at Puerto Princesa drove 150 American soldier prisoners of war into two air raid tunnels. These men had been used as slave laborers on nearby airfield construction sites. The Japs soaked the prisoners with gasoline and set them afire. The POWS who tried to escape were machine-gunned to death. Four Yanks escaped through the opposite end of one tunnel only to face a high cliff overhanging the sea. The long leap to the beach below resulted in the death of one of these escapees. American troops found the charred remains of the dead in the air raid shelters when they occupied Palawan later in the southern Philippine operation.

Few "suicide" Jap planes had been witnessed between Pearl Harbor and the Leyte campaign. After the huge air and naval losses suffered by the enemy from the Marianas invasion and in the Philippine naval battles, however, the Japanese leaders organized kamikaze units. Use of kamikaze (divine wind) planes ensured nearly a 100 percent chance of a bulls-eye for every bomb-laden plane that was pilot-directed toward Allied naval forces. Before the war's end, they caused tremendous losses to Allied forces in both material and men.

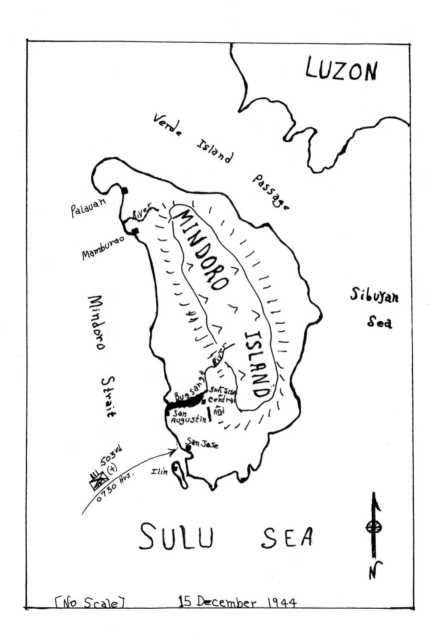

LUZON

Verde Island Passage

Palauan

River

Mamburao

MINDORO

Mindoro Strait

Sibuyan Sea

ISLAND

River

Bug Sanga

San Jose Cendral

A⊞d

San Augustin

San Jose

503rd
(†)
0730 Hrs.

Ilin

SULU SEA

N

[No Scale]   15 December 1944

D-Day minus one, 14 December, was relatively quiet. A 40-plane enemy raid was intercepted at about 1100 hours by 106 Allied fighter planes. Eight enemy planes got through to plot the convoy but were shot down by antiaircraft fire of the screening ships. That night, as the troop convoy steamed steadily northward, Admiral Ruddock again turned toward Puerto Princesa. This second diversionary raid proved rewarding because at dawn on D-Day, the Japanese had not the slightest hint as to where the convoy was or where the Allied assault might occur.

The San José area of Mindoro is flat land surrounded by hills. The smooth alluvial plain extends about thirty-odd miles along the southwest coast and about six miles inland. The village of San José is about four miles from the beach. No roads and few native trails penetrated the mountains to the north and east. The area could be sealed off by establishing a well-defended perimeter without capturing the entire island. Allied forces wanted dry airfields, and the San José region offered an ideal location to construct them. There was an old U.S. Army airstrip south of San José that had been used before the war, which the Japanese had not developed. They probably had little need to, for Manila was only 130 miles to the north. The area had once been a rich producer of sugar, but no crops had been planted in more than two years, and the fields were badly overgrown.

H-hour on 15 December 1944 was originally set at 0720 hours but had to be delayed ten minutes. Filipinos began streaming to the beaches with their belongings and water buffalo and waving flags. Because shore bombardment was necessary to flush out the Japanese, some destroyers fired a few airbursts to warn the natives to get clear of the assault area. It succeeded. The U.S. Navy carriers' fighter planes were over the beach assault areas at daybreak. Navy and air force fighter planes launched a dawn raid on all enemy airfields within striking distance of Mindoro and found numerous enemy planes warming up. Most of these were destroyed on the ground. A ten-minute preassault bombardment caused the Japanese to flee to the hills. The landing was unopposed. The Nineteenth Infantry RCT landed on White Beach north of Caminawit Point, where a PT boat base was later established. The 503d Parachute RCT landed two battalions abreast on either side of the mouth of the Bugsanga River at Green and Blue beaches. By noon, units were near San José village. Early evening found the old airstrip captured and a sound perimeter established.

Allied air force P-38s from Leyte and the naval convoy fighter planes were engaged in ferocious air battles with enemy kamikazes all morning. Two LSTs were lost to these suicide bombers on D-Day. Engineers

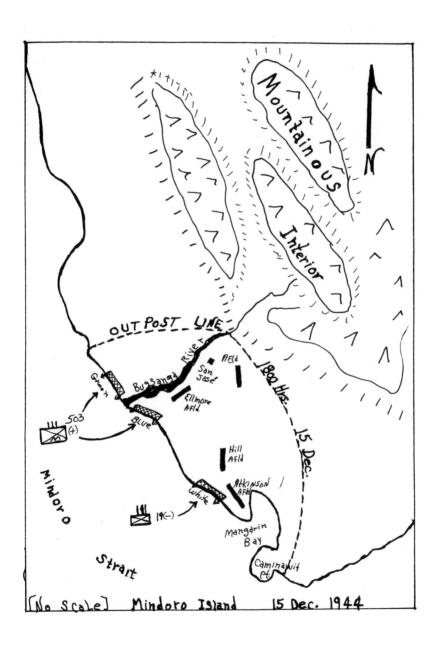

Mountainous Interior

OUTPOST LINE

Bugsanga River

AFld
San Jose
Ellmore AFld

Green

503 (+)

BLUE

1800 Hrs. 15 Dec.

Hill AFld

Atkinson AFld

White

19(-)

Mindoro

Strait

Mangarin Bay

Caminawit Pt.

[No Scale]   Mindoro Island   15 Dec. 1944

quickly set to work surveying the much needed airdrome sites. Some twelve hundred troops of the U.S. Seventy-seventh Division on Leyte, brought along as stevedores, had all the ships unloaded by nightfall of D-Day, which pleased the naval personnel because they did not relish being grounded ashore during kamikaze attacks. These empty ships sailed south through the Sulu Sea a day earlier than planned on their return trip to Leyte. Late that evening Admiral Kincaid ordered the retiring fleet to return to Mindoro to protect the beachhead because the Leyte-based airstrips were closed in by bad weather. Ironically, the Third Fleet to the north of Luzon, which was keeping Luzon's airfields neutralized, was devastated by a furious typhoon and lost three destroyers and 790 lives. Mindoro, so far, was not a cheap prize.

During the sixteen days following D-Day, the troopers of the 503d RCT consolidated their assigned defense lines. Adjacent and supported units within their sector were issued instructions on what to do in case of an enemy counterattack. A ten-mile perimeter was established and patrolled. The 462d Parachute Field Artillery Battalion dug in along the tree line of the beach. These troopers were assigned to support the infantry troopers and establish counterlanding defenses. The firing A, B, and C batteries were each assigned to an infantry battalion. Battery D, with its antiaircraft and antitank sections, was assigned to establish a beach defense and to bring initial fire on landing vessels should the Japs attempt a counterlanding. The .50-caliber machine guns were provided with both antiaircraft and ground gun mounts. Antiaircraft mounts were used during daylight hours, the ground mounts at night. The machine gun squads at the mouth of the Bugsanga River were credited with shooting down one Japanese plane during an air raid. Later, they relieved a Japanese sailor of his head as he swam ashore from his sunken ship right in front of a .50-caliber machine gun. He was buried where he fell.

Company C, 161st Parachute Engineer Battalion, assisted in strengthening the infantry positions by erecting miles of double-apron barbed-wire fence, prepared special demolitions, then booby-trapped the wire with mines and bangalore torpedoes. The men of C Company did such an excellent job that they later feasted on two water buffalo that strayed into their booby-trapped area. The Filipino owners did not hold the 161st troopers in high esteem after that, but the fresh meat was a welcome reprieve from the monotonous C and K field rations. The engineer troopers also erected several buildings within the 503d perimeter and improved others. Colonel Jones, the RCT commander, later commended the Company C engineers as a versatile, hardworking, efficient unit, which usually exceeded all expectations despite limited personnel and only adequate engineering equipment.

Work on the Mindoro airdromes proceeded smoothly. The six thousand service troops of the 1974th Engineer Aviation Battalion and the Australian Third Airborne Construction Squadron worked around the clock. Within five days, the Hill strip was ready to receive fighter planes and the San José strip, being built to accommodate bombers, was ahead of schedule. From two to twelve Japanese aircraft flew over the Mindoro perimeter each day and night to make harassing raids. Their attention centered on the PT boat base at Caminawit Point. The last enemy bombing run before dawn usually flew over the entrenched troopers on the outpost line of defense releasing fragmentation bombs with delayed-action fuses. They used both ordinary bombs and parachute bombs. The Japanese hoped that the delayed-action fuses on the bombs would catch careless troopers away from the shelter of their foxholes after the noise of the planes' engines had died away in the distance. Once in a while, the enemy dropped phosphorous "cluster" bombs, which usually only started a few grass fires or set a native hut afire.

Christmas Eve saw numerous air alerts on Mindoro. Since the invasion, the troopers of the 503d RCT had dug alternate and supplementary positions to cover and counter any naval or airborne counteroffensive the Japanese might possibly employ. On Christmas Day, the troopers enjoyed roast turkey and all the trimmings, flown in from Leyte. The feast was shared with the nearly two thousand Filipinos within the perimeter. The following day at 1615 hours, a navy PB4Y patrol plane reported a Japanese task force consisting of one battleship, one cruiser, and six destroyers steaming toward Mindoro from the South China Sea at twenty knots. Late in the day, USAAF planes sighted and bombed a large force of transports and cargo ships, with their escorts, sailing south from the Subic Bay area of Luzon. The troopers hurried to prepare to counter both amphibious landings and a paratroop drop.

Thirteen Mindoro-based army B-25s, loaded with five-hundred-pound bombs, rose to attack the rapidly approaching enemy naval force. The various fighter planes — P-47s, P-38s, P-51s, anything with wings — took to the air. The only U.S. naval forces available were the twenty-two PT boats. Sadly, only eleven of these gallant small craft were operational. In addition to preparing to attack the oncoming enemy, the PT boats had to shepherd to safety four Liberty ships that were lying off the beachhead unloading supplies. The Japanese began their attack as darkness fell. The furiously wild scene was as bitter and dazzling as any the defenders ever saw. The antiaircraft fire of the enemy ships spewed fiery red streams through the night sky at the Allied planes. Exploding bombs fell in crazy-quilt patterns. The Allied planes switched on their running lights to distinguish themselves from several Japanese planes that had entered the fray. The scene was chaotic, mad, and swirling, as though from Dante's *Inferno*. The Army Air Force lost four B-25s, four P-38s, seven P-47s, and five P-40s. Bomb stocks were low because LSM's bringing these crucial supplies to Mindoro had been sunk in recent kamikaze attacks. Because it was very hazardous for the bomb-laden fighter planes to take off at night on the rough airstrips, most of them were armed only for strafing; and low-level attacks on ships are often fatal. With gasoline in short supply, many pilots made a final attack and headed for Leyte — a night flight through bad weather that was even more hazardous than the fight.

Even though no beach landing or paratroop attack materialized, the hectic activities of the evening were sufficient to inspire the task force command post personnel to board any vehicle that would run and flee to the hills and the outpost line of defense. The navy lost one PBM patrol bomber that evening. In the meanwhile, Allied planes and four PT boats began attacking the enemy force bearing down on Mindoro a scant forty miles to the north. Colonel Jones, who had gone to the beach with a skeleton staff to make a rapid appraisal of defenses, squeezed into the 161st Engineers' dugouts as the Japanese fleet steamed north and worked over the San José airfield and the perimeter defenses. Shelling of Allied shore installations continued until about 0045 hours on 27 December, when the Japanese ships retired to the west at high speed. They had all received considerable damage from the Allied counterattacks from navy PT boats and the Allied air force.

On 1 January 1945, the 503d RCT passed from Sixth Army Command to that of the U.S. Eighth Army. At this time, the remainder of the Twenty-first Infantry reserve from Leyte arrived on Mindoro to reinforce the beachhead. General Krueger had feared that Japanese reinforcements might be moved from Luzon immediately after the enemy naval raid. Extensive patrolling was maintained and outposts established at some distances away. The troopers on the outpost line of defense did considerable night patrolling to their immediate rear, where the air force, navy, and service troops had their supply dumps. The stealthy troopers returned to their positions at dawn with such captured delicacies as canned roast beef with gravy, canned chicken, canned fruit and vegetables, and other treasured condiments to supplement their meager field rations.

Company B securing Palauan as natives move back in. Japanese dead are in the foreground.

Regimental patrols were dispatched to several small adjacent islands but with no results. One notable exception was that of a Philippine scout company commanded by Lt. L. M. Dean, 503d Parachute Infantry, which was sent to patrol the northwest section of Mindoro. It discovered a garrison of sixty Japanese at the barrio of Palauan on 1 January 1945. Company B (reinforced) of the 503d RCT was dispatched by boat to Mamburao, thence overland to Palauan to destroy the Japanese outpost. As the troopers disembarked from the LCI in shallow waters on 2 January, an unidentified plane buzzed the ship. The LCI began to move in reverse. The troopers still on board unloading equipment began jumping overbaord and swimming and wading to shore. In the confusion of the pitch-black night, Staff Sergeant Bernard O'Boyle shed his gear and stripped naked. He swan out to the disoriented and floundering troopers and directed some to shore, then swam several yards further out to sea and towed ashore a nonswimming fellow trooper. For saving several lives, Sergeant O'Boyle was awarded the Soldiers Medal. Unfortunately, two troopers drowned as the result of the unnecessarily rapid exit of the LCI.

Shortly after sunrise, the troopers of Company B began a demanding twenty-mile march to Palauan. En route, the men crossed a crocodile-infested stream in a small boat, two men at a time. Around noon, a young Filipino lad warned them of an advancing thirteen-man Japanese patrol. The troopers sprang an ambush at 1400 hours, killing nine of the enemy. They marched at night so as to reach Palauan as soon as possible, arriving in the predawn hours of 3 January. They assumed preplanned positions around the barrio. A day-long sniping battle ensued; the forewarned enemy was in fortified positions. Company B suffered four men killed in action and fourteen wounded. Twenty-six enemy dead were tallied. The following day was spent in mopping up and securing all native buildings. The Stars and Stripes replaced the Japanese flag over the village. The Filipino official insisted that the Filipino colors should be hoisted above the American flag because the Yanks were on Filipino soil. Platoon Sergeant Mike Matievich of Milwaukee, Wisconsin, led the B Company troopers in "one hell of a roar." Sergeant Matievich addressed two-well selected Yankee words at the local official, and the Filipino colors flew below the Stars and Stripes.

Local natives reported that the escaping enemy included eleven wounded. Company B was withdrawn to Mamburao on 5 January while the Philippine scouts pursued the fleeing enemy force into the mountains. The troopers of Company B were ordered to return to their San

Photo Courtesy: Mike Matievich

At Palauan, Mindoro, 5 January 1945, and the Stars and Stripes fly above the Filipino colors after a short confrontation with a local official as to which flag should be uppermost.

José base on 15 January 1945. Boarding the same ship that had brought them to Mamburao, the tired, exasperated, and saddened troopers called the sailors "chicken" because of their behavior during the landing on 2 January. Heated words between the troopers and sailors resulted in a close-quarters battle aboard ship. The men of Company B arrived at their San José campsite at dark the same day. This encampment had been constructed by the troopers of Company C, 161st Parachute Engineer Battalion, just before the end of the Mindoro operation.

This model campsite was just across the Bugsanga River from the other task force units. The troopers wanted, and Colonel Jones ensured that the 503d Parachute RCT be separated from and have a better campsite than the other task force group members. A bridge across the Bugsanga River, desired by General Dunckel, was constructed by the engineers of Company C after the general had been assigned to Sixth Army Headquarters. Colonel Jones had once again fulfilled a commission to separate "straight legs" from the men wearing paratrooper boots. The bridge constructed by Company C was devastated in subsequent monsoon flood waters.

By the end of January 1945, the Western Visayan Task Force ground operations on Mindoro had cost 16 men killed in action, 71 wounded, and four missing. Establishing the base on Mindoro had cost Allied forces nearly 500 men killed and 400 wounded in action. The Japanese had lost 170 troops killed in action and 15 prisoners of war. The most visible result of the Mindoro operation was saving the Lingayen Gulf invasion passage from being a mass slaughter. The Mindoro bases also proved to be useful staging points for the several expeditions in the liberation of the southern Philippines. The Mindoro operation ended on 31 January 1945. The men of the 503d had been alerted on 25 January to prepare for another combat mission.

10
The Airborne Assault on Fortress Corregidor

On 6 May 1942, Lt. Gen. Jonathan M. "Skinny" Wainwright, commander of U.S. forces in the Philippines, dispatched a radio message to Pres. Franklin D. Roosevelt and Gen. Douglas MacArthur. It read: *"With broken heart and head bowed in sadness but not in shame, I report that today I must arrange terms for the surrender of the fortified islands of Manila Bay. Please say to the Nation that my troops and I have accomplished all that is humanly possible and that we have upheld the best traditions of the United States and its Army. With profound regret and with continued pride in my gallant troops, I go to meet the Japanese Commander."* This terse, heartbreaking communique was sent from Malinta Tunnel, the operational bowels of Corregidor, while Japanese troops stormed toward the east entrance. The brave men on the rock had given their ultimate and set a standard of duty for all members of the American armed forces.

In late January 1945, the troopers of the 503d Parachute Regimental Combat Team bathed in the splendor of a scenic view of the Bugsanga River near San José, Mindoro Island, Philippines. This grass-filled, sun-drenched, wind-swept valley provided quarters for the nearly three thousand paratroopers in pyramidal tents. An alert on 25 January to prepare for another mission caused the adrenalin to start flowing in the placidly resting troopers, who had completed their assigned combat mission here and had been languishing in rest camp for nearly two weeks. Excitement increased and rumors flourished when, on 2 February, the 511th Parachute Infantry Regiment of the Eleventh Airborne Division arrived nearby and began filling equipment shortages and checking out parachutes. (When the Eleventh Airborne Division arrived at Dobadura, New Guinea, General Krueger was anxious to integrate the 503d into that command structure. It was only through the efforts of Lt. Col. John J. Tolson, former Third Battalion commander, that an order to do so was rescinded.) Morale sagged next dawn when the 503d troopers observed the junior 511th Parachute Regiment winging overhead for a jump

---

*Jonathan M. Wainwright, *General Wainwright's Story*, pp. 122-23.

Enemy photograph obtained on Corregidor depicts Japanese troops lowering the American flag on or about 6 May 1942.

on Tangaytay Ridge, south of Manila. As the planes carrying the 511th disappeared to the northeast, the 503d again was placed on alert for a possible jump onto Nichols Field, south of Manila, in conjunction with the 511th's drive toward that city. This alert was canceled on February 5.

A radio message from Gen. Douglas MacArthur outlining plans to clear Manila Bay was received by Lt. Gen. Walter Krueger's Sixth Army Headquarters on 3 February. MacArthur envisioned securing Bataan, including Mariveles, and capturing Corregidor and the south coast of Manila Bay in the Ternate area. Corregidor was to be captured by shore-to-shore assault, parachute drop, or both. The Sixth Army was to conduct ground operations, the navy was to sweep the harbor for obstructions, and the supply services were to develop the port of Manila.

Krueger, an exceptionally shrewd military strategist, had anticipated MacArthur's move and had the plan of attack already drawn up. He submitted it to the commander in chief on 4 February. MacArthur hastily approved General Krueger's plan and designed 12 February as the target date. Combat mission alerts were issued the assigned army, navy, and air force unit commanders on 6 February.

General Krueger requested that the airborne assault be made by the veteran 503d Parachute Infantry Regimental Combat Team. These paratroopers were to be mounted in Mindoro by the Eighth Army, transported to the objective area by Fifth Army Air Force, and pass to the control of the commanding general of the Eleventh Corps upon completion of their drop onto Corregidor. After alerting the 503d on 6 February, Genearl Krueger requested Colonel Jones to make a personal reconnaissance over the island and recommend a suitable drop zone. Colonel Jones reconnoitered Corregidor in a B-25 bomber and radioed Krueger and MacArthur late that day that Kindley Field, on the eastern tip of the island, was the only suitable jump site. General Krueger hastily vetoed this proposal, believing that a drop there would expose the paratroopers to devastating fire from Malinta Hill and Topside. Krueger preferred that the drop be made on Topside itself, where the Japs were least likely to expect it. General Krueger's decision undoubtedly prevented a disaster, for the Japanese commander on Corregidor had heavily mined Kindley Field, had heavy weapons zeroed in on it in anticipation of a possible parachute attack, and had more than three thousand troops in Malinta Tunnel plus an additional three thousand marines on Middleside and on Topside. Aerial photographs and reconnaissance indicated only two practicable drop areas on Topside: the parade ground and the golf course. Each of these areas was little over three hundred yards long and a couple of hundred yards wide—extremely small for a parachute drop. To make matters worse, they were strewn with concrete blocks, rocks, and corrugated roofing, pitted with bomb craters, surrounded by shattered trees, tangled brush, and demolished buildings, and bounded by the sea and sheer cliffs. Nevertheless, since they were the only available sites on Topside, their disadvantages were accepted by Sixth Army planners and jump plans were formulated.

The troopers of the 503d RCT soon began receiving "confidential" rumors that Corregidor was to be their prize. They sensed that this mission would be hazardous, but naturally they betrayed no visible signs of tenseness. Instead, the men became busy, quiet, and determined—their normal behavioral pattern before a combat operation. They went about the usual oiling, cleaning, adjusting, and caring for weapons and equipment. When he is preparing for combat, a trooper's weapon becomes more than a mechanical device—it is a comrade who must not fail him in a crisis. Jump bundles were laid out and packed with all equipment too bulky to be carried out the door of the plane. Ammunition for the initial drop plus resupply had to be packed. Additional bundles contained communication wire reels, radios, field telephones, switchboards, explosives, and other essential accoutrements needed by paratroopers in combat. The medics were to jump with blood plasma, aid kits, and basic essential supplies on their persons, but only enough to meet initial needs. A normal supplement of six bundles of medical supplies was prepared for each battalion. These included full sets of surgical instruments, essential drugs, quantities of dressings, adhesives, and other necessary items. All bundles were painted with identifying symbols or numbers.

On 8 February, the rumor became a confirmed fact. Colonel Jones made the official announcement that Corregidor indeed would be the next target objective of the 503d Regimental Combat Team. A carefully guarded tent in the S-2 (Intelligence) section was finally opened for viewing and study by all units of the command. Because Corregidor was a particularly hazardous and difficult target, the Sixth U.S. Army Command had prepared a special relief model of the rock on a large sand table. The model was accompanied by photographs, diagrams, and maps. The maps were issued to all unit leaders along with battle assignments. After all officers had been oriented and orders issued, each squad of each company and battery visited the exhibit and studied its assignments. They were reviewed with all men in the squads, for among paratroopers especially, it is vital that each man comprehends the full plan of an operation because many will be called upon to act alone or in isolated groups in adverse circumstances.

In the ensuing days, squads and companies spent the morning on the firing range for final target practice and adjustment of their weapons. The hot, bored, healthy, and physically splendid young paratroopers spent the afternoons swimming in the Bugsanga River or visiting with local natives, some of whom had done mending or laundering of their clothing. On 10 February there were selected practice parachute jumps onto small drop zones. These low-altitude jumps were scheduled for all officers and enlisted men who were to jumpmaster on the Corregidor attack. On 12 February, all battalion and company commanders studied the target area from the noses of B-25 bombers. The troopers of the 503d RCT were as varied as the ingredients in a tossed salad; each additive contributes its individual color and zest to the dish. Some troopers were pure adventure-seekers; while others were egotists, who wanted to get rid of inferiority complexes through extraordinary performance. Some of them exhibited fearlessness, recklessness, and thoughtlessness yet yearned for excitement. A few possessed very stable personalities but cherished a secret desire to accomplish heroic feats. Yet the attitude of each paratrooper of the 503d displayed his feeling as expressed in the regimental march: "I'm proud I'm allowed to be one of the crowd."

General Krueger's timetable was upset when the securing of Bataan fell behind schedule and it became clear that Mariveles would not be seized before the assault on Corregidor. General Krueger recommended to the commander in chief that the target date for Mariveles-Corregidor operations be changed to 15 February. MacArthur concurred. General Krueger's final attack plan provided for securing Bataan, followed by an amphibious assault in Mariveles Bay by the 151st Infantry Regimental Combat Team and reinforced by the Third Battalion, Thirty-fourth Infantry Regiment, Twenty-fourth Division. The 503d would make an airborne assault on Topside of Corregidor beginning at 0830, 16 February. This action was to be coupled with an amphibious assault movement by the Third Battalion, Thirty-fourth Infantry Regiment, reinforced, mounted at Mariveles, and launched at 1030 on 16 February against the beach at San José Bay on the south coast of Corregidor at the foot of Malinta Hill, designated Black Beach.

Colonel Jones called a regimental team formation on the afternoon of 14 February. All troopers of all the units in the combat team were present. The men wore coveralls, web belts, jump boots, and weapons. Formal gatherings such as this were rare, but the sight of these splendid fighting paratroopers all together was memorable. These were quiet,

Corregidor, looking west. Kindley Field is in the foreground, Malinta Hill in the middle, and Topside in the background.

Col. Jones and his staff study a sand table model of the Rock on 8 February 1945. Left to right: Major Kline, Lieutenant Lewis, Col. Jones, Maj. Clark, Capt. Donavan, Lt. Col. Erickson, Maj. Caskey, and Lt. Berado. The officer to the right rear of Maj. Clark is unidentified.

129

determined, undemonstrative, "go to hell and do it" paratroopers. The call of "ATTENTION" sounded, followed by the command "At ease!" Colonel Jones read a brief message from MacArthur commending the past contributions of the RCT to the Pacific war and wishing the troopers good luck in their new challenge. A few common-sense remarks from Colonel Jones followed. The formation ended with the bugling of "Retreat" and "To the Colors." Proudly erect, the troopers marched off the field. This was the last regimental formation this unexcelled group of 503d RCT troopers would ever hold together during World War II. Hundreds of these paratroopers were about to march into the abyss of the "valley of the shadow of death," never to emerge. A beer ration was issued at 1800 hours, with each trooper receiving six hot cans of the beverage. Pulses quickened and tongues wagged.

Dawn on 15 February 1945 was bright and clear. Somber, silent, serious troopers completed packing and piling equipment bundles. Individual parachutes were drawn and fitted. Tents were struck except for the supply tents, which were left standing to protect stores of supplies and individual duffel bags left with supplies. Valuables were removed, however, because experience had taught that personal property would be stolen from duffel bags by careless, inefficient, untrustworthy, and thieving men assigned to guard and protect their contents. The stockade was emptied by order of the "warden," Colonel Jones. The garrison prisoners would not jump with their units but would be assigned to special labor details for seaborne movement of supplies from Mindoro to Corregidor, once the initial assault objectives had been attained. As Gen. John J. "Black Jack" Pershing remarked during World War I, "If you want a good soldier, you'll find him in the brig!" These 503d troopers would later exhibit the highest order of combat efficiency as they delivered supplies from the beach at Bottomside to the Topside of Corregidor under heavy enemy fire. Evening of 15 February found most of the troopers attending a movie on the parade ground. Dawn of the next day would usher in the most daring, challenging, and hazardous parachute attack attempted during World War II. The crack troops of the 503d Parachute Regimental Combat Team were ready to make that attack.

The decision of General Krueger and General MacArthur to employ paratroopers to assault such a small objective as Corregidor Island with its rugged terrain, unpredictable winds, and estimated 850 defenders merits attention. Fortress Corregidor was shaped somewhat like a tadpole. The large, rounded, headlike portion pointed westerly toward the South China Sea. The maximum width of this "head" was about one and one-half miles, and the overall length of the entire island was approximately three and one-half miles. The "tail" (eastern) section was sandy and wooded. It sloped downhill eastward from Malinta Hill, whose elevation was some 350 feet, to East Point, which was at sea level. A small islet, Hooker Point, off the East Point, could be reached at ebbtide. To the west of Malinta Hill, the ground fell away steeply and abruptly to a 500-yard-wide waist of land called Bottomside. Immediately west of this sandy area lay a gradually elevated area termed Middleside, which gave way on the west to steep slopes leading to Topside, as the larger land mass of the tadpole's "head" was called. Overall, the total land mass of Corregidor covers less than one square mile.

Fortress Corregidor was the key to the defense of Manila Bay, one of the finest natural harbors in the Far East. This excellent anchorage was greatly desired by the U.S. Navy. The U.S. Army also needed it to support its forces that were still engaged in a raging battle on Luzon. There were several reasons for the desire to recapture Corregidor. First, the island was of little significance in the Japanese defense plans for Luzon. In addition, intelligence estimates indicated that only about eight hundred to a thousand Japanese defenders were on the island. This underestimate was a major error by U.S. Sixth Army Intelligence, which General Krueger later publicly acknowledged. The error was the result of information obtained from four men of the Fifty-ninth and Sixtieth Coast Artillery, who had escaped from Fort Frank (Carabao) in May 1944, and of aerial photographic evidence of enemy troops on the island. The aerial photographs missed the thousands of Japanese who were living underground on the island fortress.

Thus despite fairly good sources of information and the U.S. Army's skill at photographic interpretation, the Nippon forces on Corregidor exceeded U.S. Army estimates by over sixfold. They had been reinforced by Japanese troops escaping U.S. Eleventh Corps thrusts on Bataan, and a shipment of Japanese Imperial (SNLF) troops had recently arrived undetected.

There were several reasons for the plan to recapture Corregidor through an airborne assault on a particularly small and rough area that previously would have been ill suited for such an undertaking. There was a challenge of successfully coordinating a simultaneous parachute and amphibious attack for the first time since the Lae-Markham Valley operation of Papuan New Guinea in September 1943. Another important motivation for using paratroopers to retake Corregidor was to attain an element of surprise. Finally, the overriding reason was that

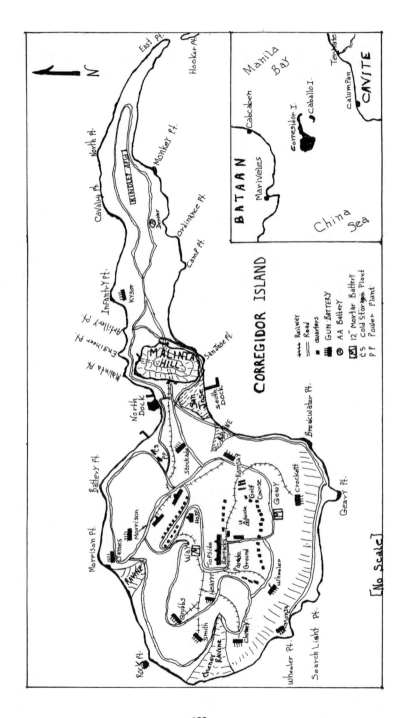

CORREGIDOR ISLAND

Railway
Road
Quarters
GUN BATTERY
AA Battery
12" Mortar Battery
CS Cold Storage Plant
PP Power Plant

N

[No Scale]

East Pt.
Hooker Pt.
North Pt.
Monkey Pt.
Cavalry Pt.
KINDLEY AFLD
Denver
Ordinance Pt.
Camp Pt.
Infantry Pt.
Kysor
Artillery Pt.
San Jose Pt.
Engineer Pt.
Malinta Pt.
MALINTA HILL
San Jose
North Dock
South Dock
RAVINE
Breakwater Pt.
Battery Pt.
Crockett
Stockade
Geary Pt.
Morrison Pt.
Ramsay
Golf Course
Geary
Hospital
Idaho
Morrison
James
Topside
Barracks
Wheeler
Parade Ground
Way
Crubbs
Cheney Ravine
Smith
Cheney
Monja
Wheeler Pt.
Rock Pt.
RAVINE
Search Light Pt.

Mariveles
Cabcaben
BATAAN
MANILA BAY
Corregidor I.
Caballo I.
CalumPan
Ternate
CAVITE
China Sea

132

numerous officers of GHQ of the SWPA had long awaited the recapture of Corregidor. For public relations purposes, its recapture in a dramatic way such as a parachute attack would be ideal. Sentimental reasons for desiring its recpature had persisted in the hearts of American troops for nearly three years, along with an inner desire for revenge.

Preparations for the attack had to be laid by the United States Army Air Force and the United States Navy. In late January, B-24s of the 307th Bomb Group concentrated their heavy demolition bomb loads on Topside and Malinta Hill. On 22 January, they dropped nearly one hundred tons of bombs. This rate was maintained each day until 7 February, when the daily tonnage doubled. By 15 February, the Fifth and Thirteenth Air Force planes had dropped more than three thousand one-hundred tons of bombs on Corregidor. The fortress was garrisoned by troops of the *Manila Bay Entrance Force*, commanded by Capt. Akira Itagaki of the *Imperial Japanese Navy*. The majority of the more than six thousand troops on Corregidor were SNLF. (They were sometimes referred to as "tiger" marines because of a curious 1,000-stitched cloth waistband that depicted a tiger in outline.) Other troops under Itagaki's command were *three army provisional companies of infantry* and *two provisional army artillery batteries*, all of which had assigned sectors to defend, mostly around the perimeter of the island. Having been alerted of the possibility of an airborne attack, Captain Itagaki determined that only Kindley Field, on the tip end of the island, could be considered a jump site. He had Kindley Field mined and his heavy artillery defenses on Malinta Hill and Topside aimed toward the site. Anticipating an amphibious attack, Captain Itagaki had made James, Cheney, and Ramsay ravines his strongest positions with more than three thousand troops and an excess of three thousand more in reserve in the Malinta tunnels or on the tail of the island.

Before amphibious troops could be landed at San José, the waters through which the assault ships had to pass would have to be cleared of mines. Naval bombardment, supplementing that of the USAAF, began on 13 February. Minesweeping of the channel in preparation for the seizure of Mariveles and Corregidor began simultaneously. Most of the naval gunfire was directed toward the north side of the island, where Japanese defenses appeared strongest. Admiral Berkey failed to silence all the menacing guns of the enemy, however, for on 14 February, fire from Corregidor's guns damaged a minesweeper and two destroyers. Admiral Berkey requested additional firepower. Admiral Kincaid complied by dispatching three heavy cruisers and five destroyers from

Lingayen Gulf to lend support to the five light cruisers and nine destroyers Berkey already had under his command.

At 0700 hours on 16 February, Berkey's cruisers and destroyers moved in close again and started shelling Corregidor's defenses. From the sky came P-38s, A-20s, B-25s, and the heavy bombers of the arsenal of the USAAF. The naval fire was generally directed toward Bottomside, where the Thirty-fourth Infantry's Third Battalion was to land, and toward the harassing batteries of Caballo Island to the south. PT boats were ordered into position to rescue any paratroopers who might miss their drop zones and splash down into Manila Bay. Reveille for the first lift of paratroopers was at 0530 hours on this memorable day, Thursday, 16 February 1945. Breakfast was a spoonful of dehydrated eggs and coffee, eaten by the flickering light of a gasoline torch in the predawn breeze. Troopers carrying their cumbersome equipment then climbed aboard waiting trucks for the trip to the airdrome. The motor column arrived on schedule among the black forms of C-47 transport planes lined up alongside the runways. Just as daylight dawned in the east, Col. John Lackey, commanding officer of the 317th Troop Carrier Group, issued orders to enplane. Before harnessing up in their parachutes, the troopers donned their "Mae West" life preservers, which were a safety measure in case of an inadvertent landing in the sea. Assembled troopers, lined up in single file beside their assigned planes and waddled (the only adequate description of the gait of a fully equipped and harnessed paratrooper) toward and up the four steps into their planes. Engines were started, and the planes jerked and bounced as they assumed position and taxied for the takeoff point. Thundering down the airstrips, the troop transports lifted into the cool air of the Mindoro dawn. Once aloft, the air armada circled once as the planes jockeyed into attack combat formation. Then, the lead plane headed north to Corregidor. The time was 0700 hours.

This initial assault force of paratroopers was designated the Third Battalion Combat Team. It consisted of the Third Battalion, 503d Parachute Infantry Regiment, commanded by Lt. Col. John R. Erickson of Cheyenne, Wyoming. Erickson had firmly established himself among the regimental command as a paratroop leader. He had been wounded by Japanese rifle fire in the waning days of battle on Noemfoor Island in August 1944. Assault units under his command for the first lift included Battery A, 462d Parachute Field Artillery Battalion; Company C, 161st Parachute Engineer Battalion; elements of the Regimental Headquarters Company; a detachment of Headquarters Battery of the

On the way to the Rock, 16 February 1945. The second trooper from the left wears the standard infantry boot.

The parade ground drop zone (center); Malinta Hill (background); Cheney Ravine (bottom left foreground). Notice the effects of wind drift on the paratroopers' positions.

136

462d; and a platoon of .50-caliber machine guns of Battery D, 462d Parachute Field Artillery Battalion.

The Thirty-one C-47s carrying the first lift of paratroops hedge-hopped low over mountains and the ocean surface on their approach to the drop zones atop Corregidor, whose elevation was approximately 538 feet. Colonel Jones was in the lead plane with Colonel Lackey. The size of the jump fields mandated that the troopers would have to jump in abbreviated "sticks" of six to eight men each. They would have to exit almost en masse over the drop zones. A premature or delayed jump could result in troopers landing outside either extremity of the drop zones. The planes approached in two columns of single planes in train, one column for the golf course, the other for the old parade ground. On the first pass, the planes were at 550 feet altitude — too high for the sudden twenty-mile-per-hour wind gusts from the northeast — which caused most troopers to miss the drop zones and others to drift over the cliffs south of the golf course. Erickson was the first man to jump, followed by T/5 Arthur O. Smithback of Stoughton, Wisconsin. Colonel Jones quickly directed the pilots to come in at 400 feet and the jumpmasters to delay their counts by eight to ten seconds before jumping their men. This order resulted in more troopers landing in their drop zones and fewer casualties. Erickson was on the ground at 0833, three minutes behind schedule.

Each troop-carrying plane had to make three or more passes over the drop zones. The column of planes for the two separate drop zones executed counterrotating orbits to avoid collisions in the air and to facilitate a more rapid approach and discharge of the remaining cargo over their prescribed jump areas in succeeding passes. Smoke screens were laid by mission support planes to keep observers on Malinta Hill blind about the events unfolding on Topside and offshore. Enemy antiaircraft fire struck a few planes, wounding a number of troopers, including Father John J. Powers, who was shot in the leg. He was again seriously injured on his landing. The final pass by the trailing C-47 was at 0932. No planes had been lost to enemy fire, but one plane was because of engine trouble forced to disgorge the demolition section of the Third Battalion Combat Team in the vicinity of Castillejos, Luzon, near San Marcelino Airfield, Bataan. These troopers would come ashore the following day with the First Battalion. Colonel Jones jumped on the final pass of the command transport plane. He missed the parade ground drop zone and landed astride the splintered trunk of a small tree, receiving painful injuries.

A short stick of 503d paratroopers descending onto Corregidor in the golf course drop zone area. Officers empty swimming pool in foreground. February 16, 1945.

U.S. Army Photo SC 263635

138

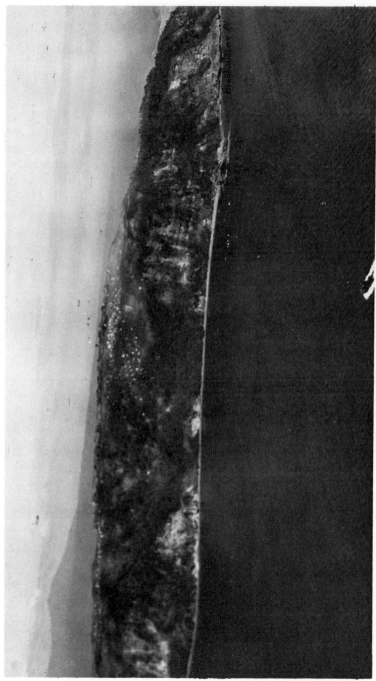

Drop zone onto the golf course mid-photo; parade ground drop zone upper left, 16 February 1945. Note the PT boat in the foreground heading for shore to rescue troopers who drifted seaward.

U.S. Army Photo SC 202594

139

The numerous successive passes each troop transport made to disgorge its contents had a negative psychological effect on the Japanese defenders. A Japanese prisoner later reported that enemy officers estimated there were eight thousand attacking paratroopers. This overestimate may have been a blessing for the Japanese hesitated too long before launching their first counterattacks, and by then their efforts were suicidal because the troopers were well organized and prepared.

In less than three hours, the troopers of the 503d RCT had been passed about in chains of command. Lieutenant General Eichelberger's Eighth Army mounted the troopers. Once aloft, they were under control of the commanding general of the Fifth Air Force. Upon reaching Corregidor's soil, the troopers passed to control of Lieutenant General Krueger's Sixth Army and his Eleventh Corps, commanded by Lt. Gen. Charles P. Hall. General Hall, who had organized the task force for recapture of Corregidor, gave the name "Rock Force" to the organization. The latter command was to become effective when Colonel Jones alighted on Topside of Corregidor. The task force commander, Col. George M. Jones, quickly assumed control on the ground and ensured that the mission's assignments for the initial drop were being executed per plan.

To naval and Thirty-fourth Infantry observers, the sight of hundreds of varicolored parachutes blossoming in the morning breeze was spectacular. There were white, red, green, yellow, and camouflaged parachutes. Several men and chutes were "holed" by enemy riflemen and machine gunners hidden in small isolated groups near the drop zones. On the first lift, seven troopers who were blown too far southward over the cliffs were rescued by PT boat 376, skippered by Lt. John A. Mapp. As the first lift of paratroopers began the airborne assault on Topside, the Third Battalion, Thirty-fourth Infantry, of the veteran Twenty-fourth Division sailed from Mariveles aboard twenty-five LCMs of the 592d Engineer Boat and Shore Regiment. This infantry combat team (reinforced) was led by Lt. Col. Edward M. Postelthwait (West Point, Class of 1937).* They employed a circuitous route around the west end of Corregidor. Captain Itagaki, watching the amphibious fleet but neglecting the air, had taken his aides-de-camp to the southern edge

---

*Lt. Col. Edward M. Postelthwait, commander of the infamous Third Battalion, Thirty-fourth Infantry, on Corregidor, was apparently impressed by the paratroopers. After the war, Colonel Postelthwait went to jump school at Fort Benning, obtained his "wings," and eventually became regimental commander of the 503d in Germany in 1957.

of Topside, near Breakwater Point, to observe the movement of the American amphibious assault forces. Suddenly, a couple of dozen paratroopers began pelting the area in and around his observation point. These aggressive troopers attacked, killing Captain Itagaki and most of his entourage, and captured his wounded aide.

Simultaneously, on the golf course and the old parade ground, the first lift of troopers carried out their assigned missions. A perimeter was established to protect the second lift of paratroopers, scheduled to drop at 1240 hours, all nearby barracks and officers' quarters were cleared of enemy troops, and fire support positions for the assault by the Third Battalion, Thirty-fourth Infantry, at Bottomside were established. By 1000 hours, assigned missions had been accomplished. Company H had killed some enemy riflemen in the enlisted mens' barracks and had placed a platoon of men atop Morrison Hill, the highest point on the island. Company G secured the area adjacent to Ramsey Ravine, while Battery D of the 462d positioned fire of two .50-caliber machine guns on the Bottomside beach area in support of the rapidly approaching amphibious landing. Company I meanwhile was securing the jump sites for the next lift. Two men of I Company, Pfc. Donald E. Rich and Pvt. Earl J. Williams, who had drifted past the drop zone and landed amid the enemy, each killed two Japs before they got out of their harnesses. Overhead, seventy A-20s of the USAAF were bombing and strafing targets on Corregidor and Caballo Island to the south. Promptly at 0930 hours, the naval vessels commenced their concentrated fire on Malinta Hill and the San José Black Beach area preparatory to the Third Battalion, Thirty-fourth Infantry's amphibious assault scheduled for 1030. Several support aircraft controllers had jumped with the troopers. Others hovered overhead in a B-25 bomber directing close support fire missions.

Sixth Army planners had decided on an amphibious assault on Bottomside for several reasons. The paratroopers would need a secure overwater supply and evacuation route such as was offered by Bottomside beaches. They hoped that Malinta Hill could be occupied and secured before the Japanese garrison recovered from the shock of the bombardment laid down by Allied forces. Also, Malinta Hill would have to be taken before American forces could secure the tail of Corregidor, Bottomside, and the eastern slopes of Middleside. Without the amphibious assault, the 503d paratroopers would later have had to attack across the open area of Bottomside, which could have been a costly move. An early blessing, in addition to the slaying of Corregidors' commanding officer, Captain Itagaki, was the paratroopers' capture of the island's communications center on Topside. Japanese wire communications from

Old Glory being hoisted to the top of a lone Signal Corps pole by Pfc. Clyde I. Bates and T/5 Frank G. Arrigo of RHQ. This flag flew day and night until the Rock was secure.

the tail, Malinta Hill, the enemy's ravine defenses, and all other strong points led to a central location on Topside but were not connected with each other. The Trooper's destruction of both this nerve center and the Japanese commander totally disrupted control among the defenders.

The Third Battalion of the Thirty-fourth Infantry stormed ashore on the south side of Bottomside at 1028 hours, two minutes ahead of schedule. The first four waves reached shore safely, but as the fifth wave neared the beach, heavy machine gun fire broke out from Ramsay Ravine, Breakwater Point, and the southwest edge of Malinta Hill at San José Point. As the LSMs discharged their cargo, the mines on the beaches began taking their toll. In rapid succession, a medium tank of the 603d Tank Company, an M-7 self-propelled gun of Cannon Company of the Thirty-fourth Infantry, and a 37mm antitank gun of the Thirty-fourth Infantry's Antitank Company were destroyed. Moving aggressively, Companies K and L pushed to the top of Malinta Hill and had it secured by 1100 hours. Surprise and the preassault bombardment had paid lush dividends. The landing had cost the amphibious forces two men killed in action and six wounded.

By the time the Japanese defenders had regained their senses, the initial assault objectives had been secured with far fewer combat losses than anticipated. Colonel Jones had predicted a possible 50 percent jump casualty rate. The rate for the first lift was approximately 25 percent. As the troopers of the Third Battalion secured the drop zones for the second lift, some of the first drop officers decided that conditions were too hazardous to risk dropping the Second Battalion and suggested postponing the next lift. In the haste of early combat, command action broke down, so the second lift began dropping at 1240 hours, nearly half an hour behind schedule. The second lift, transported by fifty-one C-47s, consisted of a detachment of Regimental Headquarters, the Second Battalion of the 503d Parachute Infantry, Service Company, Battery B of the 462d Parachute Field Artillery Battalion, and a .50-caliber machine gun platoon of Battery D of the 462d. Jumping with those troopers was Lt. Col. John J. "Smiling Jack" Tolson III, former Third Battalion commander and now assigned to the Sixth Army G-3 Section. It was he who had prevailed on General Krueger to employ the 503d RCT on the Corregidor mission. Tolson had jumped with the 503d Parachute Infantry on Noemfoor Island as liaison officer from the Sixth Army. Now this old trooper was the appointed deputy Rock Force commander and Sixth Army Liaison officer. Lieutenant Colonel Tolson broke his foot landing in a shell hole but had it splinted and remained in action with the Rock Force.

The flight path to the jump sites looking to the northwest. Golf course middle right, Parade ground upper left. Note the sheer cliffs in the foreground.

144

The crew of this 75mm howitzer of the 462d Parachute Battalion has just completed assembling the weapon. Here the men hug the ground as they come under enemy rifle and machine gun fire.

145

503d Paratroopers on Corregidor moving forward to a new assignment. The searing heat, dust, flies, and scenery were all very depressing.

146

On the second lift, an additonal ten troopers slipped over the nearby seaside cliffs to be rescued by the navy's PT boat 376. Two trips to shore in rubber rafts by Lt. Raymond P. Shafer and Lt. Charles Adam of PT 376 saved seventeen troopers. These heroic rescues were accomplished while enemy fire splashed the sea around the raft. With two reinforced parachute infantry battalion combat teams on the ground on Topside, the troopers aggressively moved to the attack. Lieutenant Colonel Erickson's Third Battalion spent the remainder of the day securing the northern half of Topside and the upper slopes of Middleside. Major Lawton B. Caskey and his Second Battalion, leaving a small defense force to secure the jump sites, began clearing the southern half of Topside of the enemy.

By the time the Second Battalion Combat Team was on the ground, the enemy had recovered from the initial shock and began placing heavily concentrated rifle and machine gun fire on the parade ground and the old enlisted men's barracks area. Attempts to recover supply bundles had to be abandoned. For some reason, airborne assault planning had left the western end of the drop zones undefended. Most of the enemy fire came from the direction of Batteries Cheney, Crockett, and Wheeler. To get into a better firing position, Capt. Henry W. Gibson of Battery B of the 462d had a howitzer disassembled, toted to the second floor of a ruined officer's quarters building, then reassembled. A dangling parachute obscured the line of fire, so Pfc. John P. Prettyman attempted to remove it. While accomplishing this feat, Prettyman was killed by machine gun fire. He was awarded the Silver Star posthumously. The howitzer was then able to fire and effectively silence several enemy gun positions. The original Sixth Army Order No. 48 of 7 February was for only the 503d Parachute Infantry Regiment to make the jump on Corredgidor. Fortunately, an amendment of 11 February made the entire RCT available, thereby assuring the assault force of artillery and engineer support. The 462d Parachute Artillery Battalion Commander, Maj. Arlis E. Kline, suffered a jawbone separation on landing. This condition is similar to a lockjaw. Despite his injury, Kline remained in command until conditions permitted his evacuation a few days later. Major Kline was succeeded by Maj. Melvin Knudson, the S-3 officer of the 462d. Major Knudson retained command of the 462d Parachute Artillery Battalion until war's end.

Of the 2,022 paratroopers who dropped this date, seventeen were blown over the crest of Topside and were rescued by the United States Navy. Some less fortunate men had to hide overnight before being rescued. Others made their way to friendly lines the next day. Several

Paratroopers of the 462d Artillery Battalion salvage 75mm ammunition from a shell crater on the parade ground drop zone, Corregidor, 17 February 1945.

U.S. Army Photo SC 263671

wounded or injured troopers hid alone or were guarded by their buddies overnight in isolated ravines and cliffsides. Many troopers who undershot or overshot the drop zones and landed in the midst of the enemy defenders were shot or bayoneted upon landing. A great number of bodies of such ill-fated men were recovered in the ensuing days and their horrible fate was revealed.

In the first two airlifts, two men refused to jump. The United States Army *Articles of War* decreed that these men could have been shot by their jumpmasters for "misconduct in the face of the enemy." To avoid struggles within the planes and a disastrous delay, these two men were placed under arrest in the custody of the crew chiefs of the planes. They were subsequently used in resupply of their former comrades by boat, but after their court-martial they would never again be associated with the paratroopers. A temperamental prerequisite for a paratrooper who will jump in combat is a carefree, self-reliant disposition and the ability to make instantaneous decisions when one must jump, there is no time for reflecting. One must act immediately. Thinking must be reflex and automatic. In other words, the trooper must be free of all inhibitions. Such an attitude demands a certain amount of abandon, almost a disregard for danger, a self-possessing but not necessarily irreverent element of recklessness. As an old trooper would say, "What the hell?" In combat, one man's failure jeopardizes the safety of the entire mission. Among paratroopers, the survival of everyone depends on individualism. Refusals to jump cannot be condoned on any ground.

Among those who jumped at Corregidor, three had parachutes that failed to open. Eleven other men sustained fatal injuries when they crashed into demolished buildings or debris surrounding the drop zones. Fifty troopers were wounded either in descent or after landing. An additional 210 were injured — many receiving severe compound fractures or concussions. The casualties for the 503d RCT troopers on 16 February were 21 killed in action, 267 wounded or injured, and an unknown number unaccounted for.

Combat casualties are never restricted to combat personnel. In armed conflict, there is always the bullet on which is inscribed, "To Whom It May Concern." Old troopers would say *this* bullet was the one that would get you rather than the one with your name on it. Among the noncombatants, Father Powers was wounded during descent and injured upon landing, and Protestant Chaplain Herb received a severe compound leg fracture, resulting in his being placed in a cast from head to foot. The Third Battalion surgeon of the 503d, Capt. Robert McNight,

Men of the 503d Parachute RCT used hand grenades to clean out a Japanese pillbox from a cave position on Corregidor, 17 February 1945.

U.S. Army Photo SC 201373

Two paratroopers of Company C 161st Engineers firing bazooka on enemy pillbox on Geary Point, Corregidor, 19 February 1945. Note the discarded helmet and the folding stock carbine (Model M-1 A3).

151

suffered a severe ankle break that ultimately caused him to be shipped back to the states.

By the time the Second Battalion Combat Team was on the ground, the Japanese on the cliffs around Wheeler Battery and Cheney Battery were inflicting casualties on the troopers, damaging supply planes, and infiltrating the paratroopers' positions. T/5 Lloyd S. Allen, a medic attached to the 462d Parachute Artillery Battalion, treated a seriously wounded trooper who needed more plasma. Leaving his position, Allen ran to an equipment bundle several yards away to obtain the plasma, despite severe enemy fire. He was mortally wounded on his return run. For his bravery, T/5 Allen was awarded the Silver Star posthumously.

Captain Emmet R. Spicer, surgeon for the 462d Parachute Field Artillery Battalion, accomplished an unbelievable feat on 16 February. Captain Spicer set up his aid station, reported to the RCT aid station surgeon, and returned to his station. On his return, he stopped to render aid to a trooper who had lost an eye. He sent this trooper to the Regimental Combat Team aid station and moved on, stopping several times under fire to help the wounded. A single shot from a hidden Japanese rifleman mortally wounded Dr. Spicer. Unbelievably, though dying, he sat down and wrote out his own medical tag. Spicer wrote his name, rank, and serial number, and supplied the diagnosis: GSW (gunshot wound), "perforation left chest. Severe. Corregidor. 16 February, 1945." A patrol later found his body, his open first-aid kit, an empty morphine tube, remains of a cigarette, and his empty canteen. For his gallantry in action, Captain Spicer was awarded the Silver Star posthumously. What a helluva way to die!

Colonel Jones, Rock Force commander, observed that the combined air and naval attacks seemed successful, enemy opposition light, and the defenders surprised and disorganized. Therefore, he requested the Eleventh Corps to cancel the third lift, scheduled for 17 February, for the First Battalion Combat Team of the 503d. Total enemy killed this first day of ground combat was impossible to determine. All combat elements were too occupied with their assigned missions, which were to secure Topside, dig in for the night, and prepare to repel attacks and infiltration by the Japanese. Isolated troopers fought innumerable individual and small group battles with the enemy. Exact body counts had to await a more opportune time. The 503d troopers never gave estimates of casualties inflicted on the enemy by small arms, mortar, or artillery fire. All enemy casualties were body counted by officers. The upper brass apparently regarded the dogfaced troopers as either incompetent or unreliable to count enemy cadavers. It could be difficult to arrive at a correct body count when dozens to hundreds of bodies, many mangled and dismembered, were involved. One could see fingers here, a foot there, another piece of flesh at some other location, and it was difficult to know just how many bodies existed. The Eleventh Corps and Sixth Army Headquarters did make estimates of enemy casualties, usually to account for those who might have disintegrated or been buried in the blasts and tunnel closures.

The third lift of paratroopers, consisting of the First Battalion Combat Team, had been scheduled to be over the objective area at 0830 on 17 February. This lift was to bring the remainder of Regimental Headquarters, the First Battalion of the 503d Parachute Infantry, Battery C of the 462d Parachute Field Artillery Battalion, and a third .50-caliber machine gun platoon of Battery D of the 462d. Following this lift, there were to be daily resupply flights by twelve C-47s until amphibious resupply to San José beach could be provided and a road cleared for use between Bottomside and Topside. Colonel Jones, Rock Force commander, felt secure that enough men already were on the island and wanted to avoid any further drop casualties. He therefore ordered the men scheduled for the third lift to San Marcelino Airfield near Subic Bay and thence to Corregidor by boat. The prepacked supply and equipment bundles were air dropped onto the Corregidor drop zones when the First Battalion Combat Team flew over on the way to San Marcelino. Heavy Japanese antiaircraft fire damaged sixteen of the forty-two troop transport planes and wounded five members of the 317th Troop Carrier Group, thus proving the wisdom of aborting the airlift in favor of a beach assault.

Maj. Robert H. "Pug" Woods's First Battalion Combat Team arrived at San José beach at 1645 hours on 17 February and immediately came under intense enemy fire from the eastern slopes of Middleside. Naval gunfire and support from the Second and Third Battalion troops on Topside soon silenced the Japanese positions. The First Battalion Combat Team then quickly came ashore and hastily moved to Topside to join their fellow paratroopers. Sadly, six of the First Battalion Combat Team's paratroopers were killed coming ashore. The First Battalion, having gained the summit of Topside, became Rock Force Reserve. The First Battalion quickly extended and reinforced the perimeter around the two drop zones, the hospital, and regimental headquarters.

Uncommon valor was an unassumed but accepted behavioral attribute of the troopers on Corregidor. Actions that probably would have been recognized as heroic in regular army divisions were accepted as standard among the troopers of the 503d RCT. The troopers were in the midst of a numerically superior enemy force with no way out. They had to eliminate the foe and establish beachhead points for overwater supplies and evacuation of casualties. A gruesome toll of lives was taken in the course of heated battles, patrolling, closing of caves, caverns, tunnels, and the too frequent detonations of hidden underground caches of explosives by the Japanese. No person had time to stop and record heroic deeds. Leaders of combat teams, who normally would have made nominations of citations for gallantry, were themselves frequent casualties; their observations and notations thereby went unrecorded. But the staunch and determined troopers of the 503d RCT did not mind — their only concern was to get the job done.

To save men when possible, aircraft using napalm or heavily armed naval fire support ships were called upon to strike enemy positions vulnerable to infantry ground attack. The U.S. Navy had assigned the Rock Force two destroyers to support the ground troops. They were on duty around the clock for the following ten days. They maneuvered close to shore, fired directly into caves and menacing gun emplacements, reported Japanese troop movements ashore as they observed them, and fired star shells during the perilous nights to enable troopers to descern enemy movements and help them to repel the numerous nocturnal attacks. The destroyers employed five-inch guns to augment the firepower of the troops on shore.

The 462d Parachute Field Artillery Battalion assembled all its 75mm howitzers on Topside. Its mission was to provide artillery fire to support the operations of the three infantry battalions. Battery D of the 462d, with its .50-caliber machine guns, was assigned one platoon per infantry battalion, serving neck to neck with the attacking infantry. The 462d Parachute Field Artillery batteries did a tremendous job in their close support role of infantry troops on Corregidor. The field artillery batteries not only delivered artillery fire against targets on Corregidor but also placed harassing fire on Japanese forces on Caballo Island to the southeast, at a distance approaching their howitzer's limit of range. The artillerymen also delivered smoke shells to screen the infantry as they positioned themselves for an attack against the enemy.

Company C, 161st Parachute Engineer Battalion, was given the mission of direct support of the RCT. A platoon of engineer troopers was assigned to each battalion combat team on the initial landing but later reverted back to control of its company commander, Capt. James

Pfc. Lyle O. Slaught on rear guard. Note the rifle grenade launcher attachment on the end of his M-1 rifle. This infantryman wears canvas leggings because of the paratrooper jump boot shortage.

155

Closing caves and tunnels required great care, demanded much time, and resulted in dozens of paratrooper casualties.

Byers, of Sarasota, Florida. The heroism of this small engineer company was visibly portrayed throughout the Corregidor operation. The engineers assisted in preparing fortifications, demolishing hazardous structures, and blasting closed the myriads of caves and tunnels on the island, and they also fought as infantry on patrols. In addition to handling explosives, the engineer troopers were in high demand by the infantry for the bazooka and flamethrower services they provided. When conditions permitted, these talented troopers opened, constructed, or improved roads and, with their bulldozers, buried many thousands of decaying enemy cadavers writhing with maggots. Later, the engineers established a water point at the only spring on the island.

With all combat elements of the Rock Force ashore, the plan for the destruction of the enemy on Corregidor was to contain the eastern "tail" end of the island with a bloc by the Third Battalion, Thirty-fourth Infantry, at Malinta Hill. The 503d RCT would then destroy enemy forces on the western end. After this accomplishment, the 503d would move to destroy the Japanese on the eastern sector. Numerous and repeated attempts by the enemy to break through this established blockade were repulsed. On Topside, the 503d had developed a pattern for the destruction of Japanese emplacements. First, aircraft or naval fire would strike accessible enemy positions, using napalm extensively. The troopers would attack as the last shell or bomb exploded. If resistance continued, the 462d Parachute Field Artillery guns would be brought forward to provide direct fire into enemy positions. Behind smoke, phosphorous grenades, flamethrowers, and supporting machine gun fire, the infantry attack would resume. Numerous caves and tunnels were found to be interconnected. To avoid back-flash burns, the flamethrower personnel soon learned to squirt their fuel unignited far into the deep recesses of the caves and caverns and then ignite it with white phosphorous grenades or tracer bullets. Many caves contained baffles that prevented a grenade tossed in from doing any damage. If the Japanese in the caves refused to surrender, which they usually did, demolition experts were summoned to blast the entrances closed.

Topside was divided into two sectors for cleanup by the troopers. The Second Battalion was given the southern half of Topside and the southern approaches of Middleside. The Third Battalion was assigned the northern half of Topside and the northern approaches of Middleside. Even though the First Battalion was a Rock Force reserve force, it was kept busy patrolling bypassed areas of the two assault battalions and mopping up stray enemy troops in the process.

157

The night of 16 February was relatively quiet on Topside, where the Second and Third Battalion combat teams had established a secure perimeter. The men of K Company of the Thirty-fourth Infantry, however, had a rough night sitting atop Malinta Hill. They slew dozens of Japanese attackers trying to "banzai" them from their precocious summit but in turn suffered numerous casualties. On 17 February, enemy positions captured the preceding day had to be recaptured because the Japanese had reoccupied them during the night. This activity persisted throughout most of the campaign and usually resulted in dirty, repetitive combat actions with many casualties. Night infiltration by the Japanese was made easy through the bountiful underground passageways on Topside. The sealing and blocking of these tunnels was a dangerously tedious task for the attacking paratroopers. Nevertheless, steady, relentless, determined, and effective assaults resulted in 300 Japanese killed on the seventeenth and 775 the following day. In the same two days, the Yanks of the 503d Parachute RCT and the Third Battalion, Thirty-fourth Infantry, suffered 30 men killed in action and 110 wounded.

On the 17th, Company G of the 503d and Company I of the Thirty-fourth Infantry attacked from Middleside and Bottomside simultaneously in order to establish an overwater supply and casualty evacuation route for the troopers on Topside. One tank and two M-7 self-propelled guns were used, starting from Bottomside. Japanese rifle and machine gun fire came from caves and defiladed positions, and the vehicles responded by turning and firing point-blank at the enemy. Demolition teams, headed by Lt. William E. Blake of the 503d Regimental Headquarters Company, closed a stretch of roadway covered by six cave openings by late afternoon. Volunteer troops manning the self-propelled howitzers ran the gauntlet from Black Beach to the 503d hospital on Topside to bring in blood plasma, water, and critically needed supplies and to carry out seriously wounded troopers. Sgt. William Hartman and Cpl. Mike Nolan later tried to count the bullet scars on their vehicle but gave up the chore as hopeless. Back on the north side of the island, the action was heating up. Staff Sgt. Walter E. Baker of Company I, 503d covered the strategic withdrawal of his squad while he remained behind with a wounded trooper until help arrived. For this heroic deed, Sergeant Baker was awarded the Silver Star. Neighboring Company H ran into trouble toward nightfall and suffered several casualties who could not be reached safely. Private Herman F. Lackey of Company H volunteered and, under cover of darkness, crawled to within twenty yards of the enemy and made several trips to remove his wounded comrades to safety. For his feats, he was awarded the Silver Star for gallantry in action.

Paratroopers moving into Japanese held territory around Geary Point, Corregidor, 19 February 1945

U.S. Army Photo SC 374603

159

The 18th of February saw the troopers slowly working their way around the rim of Topside, cave by cave, building by building, gun emplacement by gun emplacement. They received active fire support from the 462d pack howitzers, the USAAF planes, and naval gunfire. The task was dirty, nasty, exacting, and demanding of the troopers' energy. Each trooper had jumped or come ashore with two canteens of water, but by the second day, their canteens had been drained; the fierce heat and physically demanding battle actions caused great thirst. Many cans of water dropped from planes were damaged on landing and, as in all previous battle engagements, the "rear area commandos" would take their fill of all water and rations before any trickled out to the combat line companies. Troopers would suck on pebbles, share a tongue-moistening swallow of water with a buddy, and even shake the canteens of the fallen enemy for water. Tongues would swell and parched lips would crack in thirst, but the relentless hunt for the enemy took precedence. On 18 February, Pfc. Fernando B. Valdez of Company I was leading a patrol when he thwarted an enemy ambush. He killed six of the enemy in rapid succession. An exploding land mine killed one trooper and wounded two others. Pfc. Valdez remained in his precarious position, firing at the enemy, until the dead and wounded could be evacuated. For his daring, Valdez was awarded the Silver Star. The Japanese defenders were beginning to realize what their fate would be.

At 0130 hours on 19 February, about forty Japanese committed suicide by blowing themselves up in an ammunition dump — tunnel complex about two hundred yards inland from Breakwater Point. A building directly above the explosion housed the command post of A Company of the 503d. Nearly twenty troopers died or were injured in the blast. This suicidal act presaged greater horrors to come for the attacking paratroopers. The enemy troopers surviving the initial blast came out of the tunnel chanting and soon squatted in circles. They popped pins on grenades, which they then pressed to their stomachs, ceremoniously blowing themselves to the "rising sun." At nearly the same hour, Japanese troops from Wheeler Point and Cheney Ravine began infiltrations and ground attacks against the First and Second Battalion combat teams. The enemy forces were led by a Lieutenant Endo of the *Japanese Imperial Marines*, who had served on Corregidor since October 1944. He commanded a detail of some six hundred troops of six batteries of naval fortress guns. The attacking Japanese propelled their way through the 503d perimeter by sheer weight of numbers. The tough and seasoned paratroopers, staying within their positions, fired only at visible targets.

75mm howitzer shells from the 462d Parachute Artillery Battalion hitting Japanese machine gun positions in support of the attacking parachute infantry. Corregidor, 19 February 1945.

U.S. Army Photo SC 380674

Pvt. Lloyd G. McCarter receives the Congressional Medal of Honor from Pres. Harry S. Truman. The airborne command apparently supplied the uniform and shoulder patch for it is not the 503d emblem. The ovoid infantryman background behind the wings is also missing.

These became numerous — the Japanese ran by their positions faster then the troopers could reload. Primitive hand-to-hand combat was unavoidable. The clank of steel on helmets, the rattle of bayonets on bayonets, the cries of the wounded as trench knives were driven home, and the shrill voices of unit commanders of the opposing forces directing their combatants in this din of hell were terrifying. But the stoic, brave, and steeled troopers held their ground. The enemy broke through the perimeter held by D and F companies of the Second Battalion sector between Wheeler and Cheney batteries. On the First Battalion sector, A Company's positions near Breakwater Point were harassed by feigning enemy attackers.

Company D, stationed around the rim of Wheeler Battery, was hardest hit. The Japanese had made it a fortress within a fortress, and it had changed hands several times since D-Day. This night, Company D found itself enveloped on both sides. Staff Sgt. Nelson Howard managed to work a light machine gune toward the point of attack. Just as dawn was breaking, one of the machine gunners was killed along with twelve other troopers, including their company commander, First Lt. Joseph A. Turinsky, when a grenade was tossed into Battery Wheeler. More than a dozen other troopers were wounded.

Company F, also hard-pressed by the attacking Japanese, was rallied by heroic twenty-year-old Pvt. Lloyd G. McCarter. At about 2200 hours on the 18th, as the Japanese began deploying their forces for the attack, Private McCarter left his secure foxhole for an exposed downhill observation post. Here he remained for the night, pouring relentless fire upon the attackers from his Thompson submachine gun, a rifle, and a BAR. As dawn broke, Lieutenant Endo's main force banzaied. Private McCarter stood up to determine the Japanese machine gun and mortar supporting fire positions. While directing counter mortar fire, he was felled by a Japanese rifle bullet in the chest. Private McCarter refused to be evacuated to safety until he was sure the troopers' mortars had sought out the foe. Sunrise found more than thirty dead SNLF Marines in front of Private McCarter's position. For his action, Private McCarter was awarded the Congressional Medal of Honor, the only one awarded for all forces combined in the recapture of Corregidor (see appendix).

The Japanese attack ultimately infiltrated as far as Topside barracks, where the 503d RCT command post was located. One Nippon marine tossed a grenade into the regimental supply area and wounded four troopers. Private James Edgar of Battery D of the 462d Parachute Field Artillery Battalion, finding himself arguing with a Japanese over

A paratrooper BAR man firing at Japanese on Corregidor, 20 February 1945.

Paratrooper 60mm mortar team fires into a Japanese pillbox position. Note cave in right background. Corregidor, 20 February 1945.

U.S. Army Photo SC 201372

165

a .50-caliber machine gun, pulled the trigger, thus ending a short confrontation. The battle lasted until about 0800 hours. By 1100 hours, the last of the stragglers of the Japanese attack had been killed. Action on 19 February had cost Rock Force thirty-three men killed in action and seventy-five wounded. Japanese dead exceeded five hundred. Three Japanese prisoners were taken in this battle. Mopping up required inspecting every building, recess, and ravine. Many enemy "dead" would rise to throw grenades at patrolling troopers. Enemy cadavers and portions thereof were strewn everywhere about the scene of battle.

The following days saw troopers fighting their way down the ravines to the seashore, sealing caves in the cliffs, and securing artillery and naval batteries that had menaced Allied shipping. Nighttime always brought a sense of loneliness and helplessness in the eerie isolation of the troopers. The human imagination magnifies each sensation received — shadowy outlines, soft but distinct sounds — even Mother Nature appeared hostile to the vigilant paratroopers on watch. Fortunately, the combined operations of the army, navy and army air force established an intercommand communications network on Topside near the RCT command post with a complex network of radio and telephone lines. Each branch of the services was in direct communication with ground forces ashore. Days of attack, continual thirst, unrelenting strain, fatigue, sleeplessness, and the ever-present stench of death began to take a toll on the troopers on Topside.

Suddenly, vast swarms of flies appeared. At first, although flies were present, they disappeared at nightfall. With the presence of thousands of decaying Japanese cadavers (and some Americans in isolated ravines), plus human excrement, the insect pests seemed to multiply in staggering numbers. Additional flies from Caballo Island and Bataan probably also zeroed in on the stench. The large blue flies, corpse-fattened, buzzed, swarmed, and stung at night as well as by day. To meet the imminent danger of diseases being transmitted by these insect vectors, the Sixth Army dispatched C-47s loaded with DDT to spray the entire island.

The succeeding days of combat on Topside Corregidor repeated events of previous days: advance, secure, mop up, close caves, caverns, and tunnels, and count the enemy dead while licking one's own wounds. While the troopers were having their problems, the Third Battalion of the Thirty-fourth Infantry atop Malinta Hill repulsed attacks each night by small but numerous enemy contingents emanating either from within Malinta Hill or from units on the "tail" of the island. The staunch and gallant efforts of these men prevented the thousands of Japanese troops within the Malinta tunnel complex and the eastern end of the island

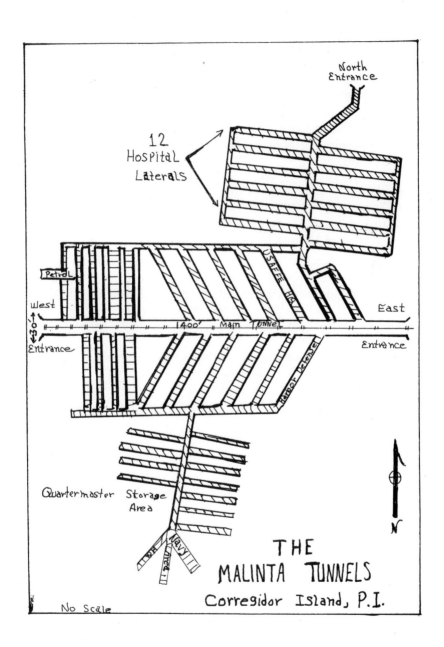

North
Entrance

12
Hospital
Laterals

USAFFE HQ

Petrol

West

East

1400' Main Tunnel

Entrance

Harbor Defense

Entrance

Quartermaster Storage
Area

Navy HQ
Area

N

THE
MALINTA TUNNELS
Corregidor Island, P.I.

No Scale

167

from joining their comrades on Topside, thereby thwarting a potentially dangerous enemy reinforcement and attack effort against the paratroopers. The cavernous openings into Malinta Hill were foreboding to the men of the Third Battalion, Thirty-fourth Infantry. No one knew what lay within the darkened bowels of the hideously unpredictable demon. Intelligence knew that American forces had left great stores of explosives in the tunnels when Wainwright surrendered. The Japanese might have placed additional armaments there. An eerie feeling of suspense engulfed the men atop Malinta Hill. The ominous, "gut felt" sixth sense of impending doom bore down on them during the night of 21-22 February.

At 2130 hours, an earth-shaking explosion rocked the island. Flames erupted from tunnel entrances, rocks and debris flew in all directions, and fissures in the rocky slopes of Malinta Hill opened up. A landslide on the south side of Malinta Hill buried six men of Company K. Realizing they had to break out or die of thirst, the Japanese troops within Malinta's tunnels had become desperate. They decided to detonate some of the huge stores of ammunition to stun the American troops above, blast open the west entrance, which had been closed by earlier landslides, and then rush out, charge Topside, and annihilate the paratroopers. Their plans for a controlled explosion apparently backfired and detonated other stores of the huge cache of explosives within the tunnel complex. The planned banzai fizzled to a stunned fifty-odd Japanese survivors, who marched out the west entrance in a column of twos. All were slain. Nearly a hundred of the enemy ran out the old hospital entrance, heading toward Shore Road. They were either killed or driven back into the tunnel by machine gun, tank, and mortar fire. About six hundred other Japanese escaped from the east entrance and fled toward defenses on the "tail" of the island. Additional explosions deep within the tunnels signified more suicides during the night of 23-24 February.

At day's end, as darkness fell, night perimeters were established. The troopers usually piled rock and debris about themselves for protection because it was difficult, if not impossible, to dig a foxhole in the hard coral prominence they sat atop. During daylight as the troopers advanced, Topside frequently rocked from explosions that signaled the closures of other caves, caverns, and tunnels. After a tunnel entrance collapsed, the trapped Japanese, deep in the cavernous recess, often detonated explosives — grenades, land mines, and so on — in acts of self-destruction. The weary but cautious paratroopers quickly learned to put distance between themselves and the TNT charges used to close a tunnel entrance. On 22 February, a patrol of the Second Battalion Headquarters and Headquarters Company came under fire. One man was killed and one wounded in a withering hail of enemy light machine gun fire. Second Lieutenant Clifford MacKenzie, who was killed plunging through the fire to aid his platoon members, was awarded the Silver Star posthumously. On this same date but on the south side of Topside, Capt. John P. Rucker of Company C risked his life for two hours to direct naval fire on enemy positions while exposing himself to both friendly and enemy fire in order to neutralize harassing enemy fire. For this action, Captain Rucker was awarded the Silver Star.

One evening, a firefight erupted near the mouth of Cheney Ravine. At dusk the troopers of Company E dug in for the night, having failed to retrieve the bodies of two of their fallen comrades because of the intensity of enemy fire. The following morning, patrols into the previous evening's battle area discovered that the bodies of Pvt. Howard J. Jandro and 2d Lt. Emory N. Ball were gone. They could only surmise that the Japanese had carted away the American corpses along with their own dead during the night. Whether the dead troopers were taken to a cave for burial or to the sea for high tide to carry them away remains unknown.

In the meantime, the Third Battalion of the 503d RCT was methodically clearing its assigned sector. An amusing but serious event occurred one morning as Company G advanced down Middleside. A Japanese soldier was flushed from the Lantana bushes. In his haste to escape, he jumped into the mixing bowl of a huge concrete mixer that was nearby. A Yank grenade, placed therein, exploded loudly. Suddenly, out jumped the bleeding and limping Japanese, only to disappear into thick brush downslope. The astonished dogfaces of G Company did not fire a single shot at the fleeing Nippon.

To the north, the Third Battalion combat teams of Companies H and I were busy cleaning out their assigned areas. Company H, led by Capt. Joseph Conway, was confronted by a monstrous and forbidding structure east of Battery Point. It was the old naval storage area for mines, a reinforced concrete emplacement, fronted by an iron fence. Iron doors faced the sea below. The first set of iron doors was blasted open by bazookas. Inside was a small chamber, then another set of steel doors. A check of the inner doors was answered by enemy grenades being chucked through some adjacent openings. Platoon Sgt. Howard Anthony and four other men nearly jammed the door in their rapid exit.

A demolition team, headed by Lieutenant Blake failed to close the openings. Fearing that the oppressing recesses harbored vast stores of explosives, Blake and his demolition section injected napalm and white phosphorous grenades at a vent some two hundred yards south. After galloping to a safe distance, they set off charges. No explosion resulted, but fire and smoke poured from the vents for days.

The metal-hungry Japanese had removed all the railroad tracks and other valuable steel products from the island. Trackways became roadways. Each roadway, track, or trail was traversed and searched out by the hunter-killer paratroopers. As H Company moved east along the shore between Battery Point and North Dock, a trooper stepped on a land mine. With one leg severed and the other shattered, he was evacuated to the regimental collecting station, about a mile away. He died of shock before the carrying party could transport him to the field hospital. Two hours probably passed between the time the wound was inflicted, first aid given, a hasty stretcher constructed, and the wounded man reached the aid station. This primitive care and evacuation process was the best the troopers could provide. The next morning, as H Company pressed east toward the old power plant, the troopers were in a line of squad columns formation, two platoons abreast, one platoon in reserve. A flushed Japanese from the Lantana brush ran into a nearby cave opening. Lieutenant Bonnel Stone, leading the platoon, ran after the Japanese soldier and fired his carbine at the retreating enemy as he fled into the cavern recess. The entire hillside exploded at that instant. I was watching Lieutenant Stone as he fired and observed him vaporizing. A moment later, the hillside rose considerably, felling all to their knees. The hillside then began crumbling and rolling down slope toward the nearby sea. In addition to Lieutenant Stone, four enlisted men were killed by the landslide. Frantic digging by nearby troopers uncovered Staff Sgt. Dominic Dimascio, whose arm was sticking above ground. He had lost an eye, his face resembled raw beefsteak, and he had other injuries. The bodies of two troopers were recovered from the rubble but those of Pfc. James Moore and Pvt. Elbert Lovenguth were never found.

In following days of repetitious, deadly combat between the troopers and the Japanese Imperial Marines on Topside, the paratroopers gained control, ultimately moving down the slopes of Middleside and onto Bottomside to link up with Colonel Postelthwait and his spirited Third Battalion of the Thirty-fourth Infantry. On 23 February, Colonel Postelthwait's men began clearing away debris on the North Shore Road, at the foot of Malinta Hill, in preparation for the final onslaught by the 503d on the Rock's tail. A knoll overlooking the old enlisted men's bathing beach was secured at Engineer Cove. A platoon of men, accompanied by a tank, proceeded to blast the hospital entrance of Malinta Hill, flushing out a group of Japanese, who were promptly mowed down. A few rounds from the tank drove the remaining Japanese back into the recesses of Malinta Tunnel. At long last, after eight days, the men of Company K of the Thirty-fourth Infantry were no longer isolated atop Malinta Hill.

By 24 February 1945, the stage was set for the paratroopers' final assault down the tail or eastern end of the island. Colonel Jones, Rock Force commander, detailed the Second Battalion of the 503d to mop up any bypassed enemy on Topside. He assigned the Third Battalion of the Thirty-fourth Infantry to continue holding Malinta Hill and Bottomside but also to secure any remaining enemy positions on Middleside. A portent of how difficult the assault on the tail of the island would be occurred at 0300 hours on 24 February, the kick-off date for the paratroopers' final drive to rid the island of the enemy. The surviving Japanese in Malinta Tunnel began frantic activities, accompanied by frenzied Oriental chanting and culminating in six deafening blasts that made the subterranean tunnel resemble a volcano.

Preparatory to the early morning paratrooper assault, heavy naval, air, and RCT artillery support began bombarding the tail end of the island in a softening-up exercise. The final attack would be made by the First Battalion of the 503d spearheading the drive, with the Third Battalion of the 503d guarding the flanks of the assault forces and mopping up any bypassed Japanese troops during the advance. The 503d paratroopers began their attack at 0830 hours, moving rapidly past Malinta Tunnel's north entrance, while a rolling barrage from the massed howitzers of the 462d Parachute Field Artillery Battalion whistled overhead. A sudden Japanese banzai out of the hospital tunnel opening caused momentary tension. A supporting tank that had passed the portal wheeled about and, in random machine gun firing, killed four paratroopers. In backing up to pivot to a better firing angle and to cover the tunnel entrance, the tank's treads crushed another trooper, who was prone on the ground, firing at the enemy.

Pfc. Peter C. McCabe, a medic of the 462d Field Artillery Battalion, had volunteered to go on this assault mission with the infantry because medical personnel of the First Battalion had suffered excessive casualties. During the melee, McCabe saw a severely wounded trooper fall into a pile of burning rubble, fully exposed to enemy fire. Although McCabe had already passed the opening of the tunnel, he ran back, moved the wounded trooper to safety while under fire, and stopped a hemorrhage, thus saving the trooper's life. In keeping with the highest traditions of the United States military service, Private McCabe was awarded the Silver Star for his courageous actions.

The Japanese attack was soon quelled, and the remainder of the enemy retreated back into the recesses of the tunnel complex. The tank accompanying the troopers squared itself before the opening tunnel and fired several cannon rounds and machine gun bursts into the abyss. It remained in this position until all friendly troops had passed the danger point. The attack by the first battalion quickly resumed. A short while later, while under intense enemy fire, T/Sgt. Robert Heyer of Company B led an assault that neutralized a machine gun position. For his gallant service, at the cost of his life, Sergeant Heyer was awarded the Silver Star.

On the north side of the island's tail, Company C was mopping up Artillery Point. T/Sgt. John Boyle risked his life to save a platoon from an enemy ambush. For his daring feats, Sergeant Boyle was awarded the Silver Star. The action on Corregidor was so fierce and rapid that heroic feats were often disregarded, to be recalled only later in a lull of the battle. For gallantry in action on 21 and 24 February, Captain William T. Bossert of Company A was awarded the Silver Star.

Meanwhile, back on Topside, the Second Battalion of the 503d had its problems during the day of 24 February. While withdrawing along Cape Corregidor, Company D became pinned down by intense enemy rifle fire from insurmountable cliffs. Pfc. Clifton L. Puckett, although wounded, engaged the enemy in a firefight. He was wounded a second time but continued to engage the enemy. A third, and ultimately fatal, wound caused Puckett to withdraw. For his valor, he was awarded the Silver Star.

Back on the eastern tip of the island, the two attacking paratrooper battalions encountered serious enemy fire at Engineer Point, just off the northeast edge of Malinta Hill. Overcoming this resistance, the troopers advanced some eight hundred yards eastward. An Infantry Point, on the north shore, more than six hundred Japanese massed for a counterattack. Well-placed artillery fire, supplemented by that of the attacking infantry, annihilated more than half of the enemy before their banzai got under way. The surviving Japanese fled eastward. By nightfall of the 24th, the paratroopers had advanced to a line running roughly from Camp Point on the south to just east of Infantry Point on the north. The Third Battalion of the 503d, following, eliminated several nests of bypassed Japanese and sealed numerous tunnels and caves on the flanks along the shoreline and overlooking hillsides adjacent to the main line of offense. The troopers had only three hundred yards to go to end their Armageddon!

As darkness fell on the 24th, Maj. Robert H. "Pug" Woods summoned his unit commanders to his command post in a large bomb crater. About the same time, the unknown Japanese commander of the Imperial Marines on the tail of the island assembled about six hundred troops atop Water Tank Hill. Enemy probing attacks and mortar fire began about 2100 hours. Accurate mortar fire began fallng on the First Battalion's perimeter. One round dropped into the command post, killing Major Woods and two others. Several of his staff were wounded, and Capt. John Rucker, Company C commanding officer, lost an arm. During this long night, while Company A was receiving damaging mortar fire, T/5 Lester R. Pinter, a medic, crawled through the enemy fire and challenging fire from friendly troops to minister to wounded troopers. For his unselfish and heroic actions, he was awarded the Silver Star. The First Battalion executive officer, Maj. John N. Davis, took command. A call to the 462d Parachute Field Artillery Battalion on Topside resulted in a veritable deluge of 75mm artillery shells that began in front of the First Battalion's positions and "walked" to the top of Water Tank Hill. Nearly half of the six hundred Japanese attacking troops were slain in this barrage. During the night, three troopers were killed and another twenty-one were wounded.

To the left rear flank, Company H had sealed several caves and caverns and had gone into perimeter at Infantry Point for the night. While the First Battalion was being harassed, hundred of Japanese assembled from unsealed caves, caverns, and other recesses to converge on the darkened shoreline between Infantry Point and Artillery Point and harass the men of H Company with rifle and mortar fire. Below, on the beach, shouted commands could be heard for an hour or more. The paratroopers braced themselves for an all-out banzai. By midnight, the Japanese were quiet. At dawn, as the troopers scanned the sea in the direction of Bataan, they saw hundreds of bobbing heads — the enemy using various flotation devices in an attempt to swim to Bataan. Aircraft, destroyers, PT boats, barges, and any other Allied sea craft available were hastily summoned to attack the swimmers. The navy had so far in the campaign accounted for 1,014 Japanese trying to escape Corregidor in their several attempts to avoid destruction. The total number of enemy troops killed by strafing aircraft or drowned may only be conjectured, however. At dawn the troopers reconnoitered their perimeters and usually found some enemy infiltrators.

Throughout the island campaign on Corregidor, the enemy employed suicide or hara kiri when unable to escape. Often they pressed grenades to their chests, stomachs, or heads. If hand grenades were not available, they used land mines, dynamite, or other explosives to destroy themselves rather than be captured. One common method of suicide was to place a rifle bore in the mouth and use the large toe to pull the trigger. There were even bizarre self-hangings. The morning of 25 February, H Company flushed a Japanese soldier along the beach on its early morning reconnaissance. He sought refuge under a cliff that projected into the sea. A phosphorous bazooka shell brought him out from cover with hands above head. As the patrol was escorting him back along the shore to company headquarters, a rifle shot rang out from the hillside above. The shot entered the upper right of the soldier's body and exited the lower left abdomen, disemboweling him. An empty fifty-five-gallon petroleum drum lay nearby, having washed ashore. The Japanese Imperial Marine rose onto his knees, removed his stitched tiger marine belt from his waist and laid it across the top of the oil drum. He then removed a pouch of prayer sticks from around his neck and placed it atop his belt on the oil drum. Taking a prayer stick, he muttered some words, bowed to the east, and then pulled several feet of protruding intestine from his abdominal wound. This astounding drama was repeated several times until a large pile of air-inflated intestines was spread out in front of him. A rifle bullet from a trooper ended this grisly melodrama.

Poor communications between commands resulted in a G Company trooper to the east of Infantry Point unintentionally killing an H Company trooper as the latter rounded a projecting precipice of Infantry Point at water's edge. During the course of the battles for Corregidor, there were several isolated and regrettable instances in which comrades inadvertently slew their own comrades.

At dawn of 25 February the First Battalion prepared to advance down the tail from its perimeter. Just before sunrise, a .50-caliber machine gun crew of Battery D ambushed and slew fourteen enemy infiltrators. One of the Japanese marines, a noncommissioned officer or warrant officer, had fallen backwards with his body lying downslope from the trail, his spectacles askew on his face. As the men of Company C began moving out for the assault on Water Tank Hill, a trooper passing by the dead Japanese noted the eyeglasses, stopped short, paused, bent down, and straightened them on the dead man's face. Standing up, the man tilted his head to survey his handiwork, then rapidly hurried forward to join in the attack. First Lt. Jesse Gandee, Battery D

174

executive officer, says that he has always wondered if the paratrooper was an optometrist or, simply a perfectionist.

The attack on Water Tank Hill after the preliminary softening-up by mortars, artillery, and naval fire was accomplished by the troopers of Company C. The uphill charge was a classical military success. By day's end, American lines had advanced nearly one thousand yards, and the perimeter for the night ran from Cavalry Point on the north shore to the southeast, just to the south shore at Monkey Point, a distance of slightly over seven hundred yards across. The First Battalion had met stiff resistance in banzai charges near Monkey Point. In the late afternoon, large numbers of Japanese tried to escape by swimming to Bataan to the north and to Caballo Island to the south. The escapees who failed to surrender to a patrolling naval destroyer were killed by the sailors aboard or by cruising PT boats, LCM's of the 592d Engineer Boat and Shore Regiment, and strafing aircraft.

The valiant Third Battalion of the Thirty-fourth Infantry would not be around to share in the victory, however, because the Twenty-fourth Division was assembling back on Mindoro for operations in the southern Philippines and the battalion had to leave. It was replaced by the Second Battalion of the Thirty-eighth Division's 151st Infantry Regiment, which had come ashore from Mariveles. Major Davis and his First Battalion had gained all the high ground during the day and could view Kindley Field to the east. The Third Battalion troopers were steadily mopping up bypassed Japanese. More than five hundred Imperial Marines had been killed in the past twenty-four hours against the loss of sixteen paratroopers. When darkness fell, the absence of the usual Japanese small arms and mortar fire signified the enemy's heavy losses. As night enveloped the troopers of the First and Third Battalions, they felt a sense of serene confidence that the morrow would end the strenuous conflict for the rock.

Shortly after 0800 hours on 26 February, the First Battalion began to advance to the tail with two Sherman tanks in the vanguard. The previous day, an offshore destroyer had observed well over a hundred of the enemy seek refuge within a large tunnel leading from Monkey Point into the old navy radio intercept complex. With Company C on the north end of the offensive line, Company A was atop the small ridge on Monkey Point, and Company B was downslope toward the south, observing a lower opening. An air attack and artillery preparation were under way to soften up the approach to Kindley Field and the point beyond. While the troopers were squatting, resting, smoking, and exchanging small talk in this preassault pause, one of the Sherman tanks fired into a group of small caves on the ridge. Suddenly, almost as the tank fired its cannon, an explosion of indescribable magnitude lifted the entire ridge above the tunnel. Bodies of paratroopers and Japanese flew everywhere, mostly in pieces. One trooper, cut in half, lived for a minute or two. I observed one man, along with a tree, blown so high into the sky that they nearly disappeared from sight. The blast was even greater than the earlier Malinta Hill blast. Debris of all descriptions rained down for minutes. In addition to bodies and pieces of bodies, there fell pieces of concrete, steel, rocks, trees, and a haze of dust. One chunk of coral landed on a destroyer two thousand yards to the south. Another bit of debris injured a trooper on Topside, a mile or so distant. Untold tons of explosives stored in the arsenal had been detonated by unknown numbers of Japanese in an attempt to kill as many Americans as possible in their ultimate hara-kiri ritual.

One Sherman tank was cartwheeled back some fifty yards. A crew member who survived had to be cut out by acetylene torch hurriedly acquired from the nearby destroyer. Capt. Holger S. Mouritsen, of the Medical Corps of the 462d Parachute Field Artillery Battalion, was wounded in this explosion. Nevertheless, he immediately began to care for the wounded. He saved the surviving tank trooper from death by immediately amputating the soldier's leg. Captain Mouritsen continued his efforts to succor the wounded until he lost consciousness because of his own injuries. For his courageous devotion to duty, Captain Mouritsen was awarded the Silver Star. The scene was one of utter carnage. The little ridge over Monkey Point had vanished. In its stead was a crater some 130 feet long, 70 feet wide, and 30 feet deep.

The Rock Force lost 52 men killed and 144 injured in this action. Surviving troopers called on their skills and past combat experiences to become on-the-scene medics. Several hours were required to clear the site of the 196 casualties. Included among the dead were Silver Star recipients T/5 Pinter and T/Sgt. Boyle, whose heroic deeds were described above. This horrible calamity had halted the First Battalion. But while the enemy was also stunned by the blast, Colonel Jones ordered Colonel Erickson's Third Battalion forward to resume the attack. Company I spearheaded the attack with Company H on the north flank and Company G on the south. These troopers overcame scattered light resistance, overran Kindley field, and had a platoon push all the way to East Point by 1600 hours.

After doubling back on the northern flank to check out possible enemy positions missed in the hurried advance, my men and I traversed the North Shore Road back toward Kindley Field and the night perimeter. The amassed dead from the morning explosion plus those of the assaulting Third Battalion forces were wrapped in ponchos, lying on both sides of the dirt road, perhaps an arm's length apart, their feet pointed toward the tracks of the roadway. The line of bodies probably extended more than a hundred feet. Shadows cast by the setting sun made the gruesome scene even more grim and heartbreaking to the tired paratroopers, heading forward again for the night perimeter.

The First Battalion, licking its wounds, went into the perimeter for the night back on Water Tank Hill. Company A had but two officers and 42 enlisted men left of the 132 men and officers who had come ashore on 17 February. The night of 26 February was relatively quiet. While the First and Third Battalions had been assaulting the tail of the island, the Second Battalion on Topside had been searching out hidden enemy troops and closing endless numbers of caves. A nest of caves near Wheeler Point had cost Company D three troopers killed and five wounded. The navy destroyer would fire above cave entrances, the blasts causing earthslides to close the openings. Near one large cave, a patrol was pinned down so tightly by enemy fire that it had to be evacuated from the beach by one landing craft while another fired into the cavern entrances to keep the enemy in recess. But on 26 February, the two gallant navy destroyers retired from shore support, called for another battle assignment.

The final phase of the campaign — mopping up — began on 27 February. Two battalions on each end of the tadpole-shaped island began the tedious but perilous work. In Company G's mop-up of a ravine northeast of Kindley Field, a trooper fell wounded before one of three supporting enemy caves. Pfc. Arvle C. Maxwell rushed to his fallen comrade, firing his Thompson submachine gun with one hand and carrying his buddy to safety with the other. An enemy bullet cut the sling of his weapon. Pfc. Maxwell was awarded the Silver Star for this action. On the Company I sector, S/Sgt. Ernest J. Debruycker threw a phosphorous grenade into a cave. Out it came, exploding and burning him seriously. Sergeant Debruycher pulled the pin on another and held it for a few seconds before tossing it into the cave, killing four Japanese marines. For his cool actions, Sergeant Debruycker was awarded the Silver Star. In a related clean-up activity, Pfc. Stanley C. Crawford of Company I was mortally wounded as he cleaned out an enemy-infested cave. For this action, Pfc. Crawford was awarded the Silver Star. By 2 March, the 503d Parachute Regimental Combat Team had suffered an additional fourteen men killed in action. But by 1 March, Manila Bay was being used as an anchorage for the Allied naval forces.

Approaching Topside, Corregidor, 2 March 1945. Left to right: Maj. Gen. Marquat, General MacArthur, and Col. Jones. Driver unidentified.

U.S. Army Photo

178

General MacArthur participates in the flag-raising ceremony atop Corregidor as buglers sound "To the Colors" 2 March 1945.

The Eleventh U.S. Army Corps commander, Lieutenant General Hall, decided that Corregidor was sufficiently secure to invite General MacArthur ashore.

At 1000 hours on 2 March 1945, a fleet of PT boats commanded by Lt. Henry Taylor (USN) approached San José beach carrying General Douglas MacArthur and his staff, Lieutenant General Krueger and his staff, Lieutenant General Hall and his staff, and a large number of naval brass and newsmen. MacArthur's party came to the Rock on Pt 373, commanded by Lt. Joseph Roberts (USN). The long line of jeeps carrying the dignitaries finally halted at one end of the old parade ground near where troopers of the 503d RCT had assembled. The surrounding buildings, trees, and shell craters were still dotted with parachutes, the panels of their canopies gently waving in the tropical breeze. The old flagpole, which had once been the mast of a Spanish warship, was still standing, its rigging intact.

Colonel Jones, Rock Force commander, called the troopers to attention. As MacArthur approached, Colonel Jones stepped forward, saluted, and stated to General MacArthur: "Sir, I present you Fortress Corregidor." General MacArthur responded with an acceptance speech, pinned the Distinguished Service Cross on Colonel Jones's chest, and turned to the color guards at the base of the flagpole. Handing them a brand new flag, he remarked, "I see the old flagstaff still stands. Hoist the colors to the peak, and let no enemy ever haul them down." As the buglers sounded the stirring notes of "To the Colors," the Stars and Stripes were raised to the top of the mast. This act officially closed the Corregidor campaign. Sadly, three more troopers died the next day on patrols, and the death of a fourth on 5 March ended the ordeal of the 503d RCT.

The 503d RCT troopers were revisited on 6 March by Lieutenant General Hall, who presented Silver Stars, Bronze Stars, and Purple Hearts to the survivors of the battles who had earned them and still remained on the Rock. On 8 March, the exhausted, grim, but proud troopers boarded LCIs at San Jose for return to their Mindoro Island base of operations. The campaign had been a fierce inferno of Hades for more than two weeks. Total casualties for the Rock Force were 209 killed in action, 725 wounded, and 19 missing. Among these were 164 paratroopers killed in action, 618 wounded or injured, and seven missing in action. A good many of the dead and missing were blown to bits or buried in the numerous explosions.

One bizarre incident of the Corregidor campaign remains as a unique and eerie mystery. Whereas all those missing in action from the

Col. George M. Jones, Commanding Officer of the 503d Parachute Regimental Combat Team, received the Distinguished Service Cross from General MacArthur on 2 March 1945. The colonel, proud and elated, apparently forgot and put his bird on his right jacket lapel backward.

181

503d Infantry are accounted for and their deaths confirmed by witnesses, the single missing in action report of the 462d Parachute Field Artillery Battalion indicates that Cannoneer Harvey R. Huskey of Battery A was never seen again after he parachuted from his plane onto Corregidor. The assaulting paratroopers turned every rock and pebble on the Rock at least twice in their relentless search for the enemy. Yet the remains of this artilleryman were never discovered. He did not drift into the sea; PT boats were watching and would have seen him. Was his body disposed of by the enemy? Did he seek shelter in an enemy-occupied cave and was killed the morning of the jump? Was he captured alive and tortured to death in an enemy abyss? The 462d also failed to locate three .50-caliber machine guns and one entire 75mm pack howitzer that were dropped onto Corregidor on 16 February.

The 503d RCT casualty report is as follows:

	Killed in Action	Wounded in Action	Injured in Action	Missing in Action
503d Infantry	135	229	267	6
462d Parachute Field Artillery	23	31	46	1
Company C 161st Engineers	5	25	18	0

Now the grisly island was eerily quiet. The Angel of Death had departed for other battles. The U.S. Sixth Army had estimated that there were only 850 Japanese troops on Corregidor. But for the first forty-eight hours of the operation, the troopers were outnumbered by more than three to one. The American forces remained outnumbered until Topside was secured and the initial assault on the east end of the island was accomplished. The body count of the Japanese dead was 4,506. The U.S. Navy killed 1,014 Japanese trying to escape. The number of enemy troops killed by the United States Air Force, drowned, eaten by sharks, sealed in the vast numbers of caves, or blown to bits would be impossible to estimate. Total enemy dead, however, would far exceed the six thousand Japanese troops that U.S. Army Intelligence later estimated were on the island.

As the troopships bearing the 503d RCT paratroopers slowly faded from view of Corregidor into the South China Sea, one could almost hear repeated anew General Wainwright's words, this time with pride:

"these troops have accomplished all that is humanly possible and have upheld the best traditions of the United States and its Army."

After the departure of the 503d RCT on 8 March, the Second Battalion, 151st Infantry, departed in mid-April, having been relieved by the First Battalion, 151st Infantry. After May 1945, the island was garrisoned by company-sized elements of the Sixth Infantry Division, which were dispatched there to protect the quartermaster graves registration company from Japanese stragglers. The latter remained on Corregidor for nearly two years searching for American dead of the two campaigns. Curiously, on New Year's Day of 1946, twenty Japanese troops, marching in formation, surrendered to a sergeant of the graves registration unit. Upon departure of American forces from the island, the Philippine government seeded the scorched and empty land of the hellish face of Corregidor. Jungle trees rapidly grew above the gutted buildings. Ipil-Ipil brush and waist-high grass quickly claimed all open spaces. The great rifles and mortars remained as silent reminders of the rain of death that swept the precipices a short while before. The island was formally transferred to the new Philippine government on 12 October 1947.

Thus ended an era of history in which the paratroopers of the 503d Parachute Infantry Regimental Combat Team played a leading and conclusive role. The governments of the United States, the Philippines, and Japan all have monuments or shrines on Corregidor to commemorate the sacrifices made for the conquest of the fortress by their respective armed forces.

Company C 161st troopers T-5 Thompson and Pfc. Adams display their trophy taken on Corregidor following their return to Mindoro.

11
The Negros Island Campaign and War's End

The gaunt and exhausted troopers of the 503d Parachute Regimental Combat Team arrived at their base camp on Mindoro Island and set about reestablishing their tent quarters, licking their wounds, and welcoming several hundred replacements fresh from the states. Unit assignments were made for the replacements, yet they were insufficient to fill all of the vacant positions.

The veterans rested and recuperated from their combat ordeal. Some of the less severely wounded, sick, and injured troopers from Corregidor returned to their respective companies from the various field and general hospitals on Luzon and Leyte.

To herald the return of the 503d troopers to the Mindoro base camp, the island base commander took over the base radio station and sternly announced to all Allied forces that Colonel Jones and his three thousand thieves had returned. This remark was, in trooper parlance, complimentary. Being a bastard regiment, always destitute of normal issue of basic supplies, the troopers staged "midnight requisitions" to obtain the items needed to make their lives more equitable and tolerable, much to the chagrin of their noncombatant neighbors from whom they "borrowed" these items.

Several days were occupied in orienting the new replacements and calming the fears of the Japanese "supermen" their stateside drill instructors had given them. General MacArthur was becoming anxious to reestablish Allied authority within the remaining Philippine Islands. To do so, he wanted to accelerate the destruction of Japanese resistance in the bypassed central and southern islands of the Philippines. The success of such an operation would complete the blockade of the South China Sea, provide air support for an invasion of Borneo, and isolate the East Indies and all of southern Asia. Except for Palawan and the Zamboanga Peninsula of Mindanao, these islands had no strategic importance in the recapture of the Philippines. Political pressure to seize the remaining Philippine Islands still occupied by Japanese forces, liberate Filipinos, destroy the Nipponese, and reestablishing local government dictated the immediate recapture of these islands.

In the center of the Philippines lie a group of islands known as the Southern Visayas; the four larger among them are Panay, Negros, Cebu, and Bohol. The Japanese on these islands were now isolated. To the north, the Allies had secured Luzon, to the east, Leyte, to the south, Zamboanga, and to the west, Palawan. The seizure and liberation of the southern Philippines was given to General Eichelberger and his U.S. Eighth Army. The major units to be involved were Tenth Corps Headquarters, the Americal Division, the Twenty-fourth, Thirty-first, Fortieth, Forty-first Infantry Divisions, and the 503d Parachute Regimental Combat Team. Only under General MacArthur's direct order did General Krueger reluctantly release the 503d to General Eichelberger and his Eighth Army command. The bulk of the Twenty-fourth Division was on Mindoro. The Thirty-first Division had one RCT at Sansapor, Dutch New Guinea, and the remainder on Morotai Island, between New Guinea and Mindanao, Philippine Islands. The Fortieth Division departed Luzon and Sixth Army control in late February. The Forty-first Division, scheduled for Krueger's Sixth Army on Luzon, had been halted at Mindoro after MacArthur had assigned it the mission to reconquer the southern Philippines. The Americal Division was on Leyte involved in mop-up activities in the mountainous interior.

Japanese forces on the southern Visayan Islands were controlled by the Japanese *Thirty-fifth Army*, the defeated defenders of Leyte. In early February 1945, Lt. Gen. Sosaku Suzuki, commander of the *Thirty-fifth Army*, had begun to evacuate his better troops to Negros from Leyte. The *Imperial Fourteenth Area Army* commander, General Tomoyuki Yamashita, had written off the southern Philippines as being strategically unimportant. He had no intention or capability of reinforcing the islands. His final order to Suzuki was to "pin down for as long as possible the Allied Divisions."

The U.S. Eighth Army assault to secure the Central Visayan Islands commenced when the reinforced Fortieth Division (less the 108th RCT, which had been dispatched to Leyte) staged at Lingayen Gulf for the Panay-Guimaras-Northern Negros operation. The attack force for the Visayans departed Lingayen Gulf on 15 March. The convoy stopped over at Mindoro the following day to take in tow a group of the 542d Engineer Boat and Shore Regiment, which had recently arrived from Leyte. The convoy arrived at the landing beaches on the southeast coast of Panay on 18 March. A preassault bombardment was found to be unnecessary because Filipino guerrillas, under command of Col. Marcario L. Peralta of the Philippine Army, met the First and Third Battalions of the 185th Infantry as they landed unopposed about twelve miles west of Iloilo. The enemy had decided to withdraw to the inland mountains. The 185th Infantry had complete control of Iloilo by 1300 hours on 20 March, and patrols that were put ashore on Guimaras Island found no Nippons there. The Eighth Army planned to have the Fortieth Division mount the initial assault of the Japanese home islands from Panay. The Fifth Infantry Division, after redeployment from the European theater of operations, was to gather at Iloilo for reinforcing operations in Japan.

By 24 March, General Eichelberger, commander of the U.S. Eighth Army, concluded that operations on Panay had proceeded satisfactorily enough that the Fortieth Division could launch an attack against the Japanese forces on northern Negros. He set 29 March as the assault date. The 185th Infantry RCT was to make the initial assault, with the 160th Infantry RCT (less its Second Battalion, which would remain on Panay to garrison that island and supervise Colonel Peralta's guerrilla forces) to follow on 30 March. The 503d Parachute Infantry Regimental Combat Team, then staging on Mindoro, would reinforce the Fortieth Division upon orders from the Eighth Army commander. Eighth Army Reserve for the operation was the 164th Infantry RCT of the Americal Division on Leyte. The attack forces for Negros could expect help from the Negros guerrilla forces, commanded by Lt. Col. Salvador Abcede of the Philippine army, which had been inhibited in their activities because of the size and aggressiveness of enemy garrisons.

Japanese forces on northern Negros were under the command of Lt. Gen. Takeshi Kono, commander of the *Seventy-seventh Infantry Brigade, 102d Division.* An additional thirteen hundred Japanese troops of the *174th Independent Infantry Battalion* were concentrated at the southeast corner of the island but were tactically unrelated to General Kono's forces. They reported to Maj. Gen. Takeo Manjome, commander of the *Seventy-eighth Infantry Brigade, 102d Division*, whose headquarters was on Cebu. General Kono commanded about fifty-five hundred troops of the *102d Division*, seventy-five hundred men of the *Fourth Air Army's Second Air Division*, and about five hundred naval personnel. He had about four thousand trained combat effectives, all from the *102d Division*. His major combatants were the *172d Independent Infantry Battalion* (less one company), the *354th Independent Battalion* (less one company), and the *355th Independent Battalion* (less three companies). All battalions and companies were brought up to strength by absorbing men of other attached units by the middle of March 1945.

General Kono, employing the same peculiar defensive tactics used by Japanese commanders on previous Philippine Island invasions, elected

187

not to defend the important airfield areas of the coastal plain of north-west Negros. Instead, he formulated immense plans to withdraw all of his forces into the mountains of north-central Negros for a long siege. He left token forces behind in the coastal plains area to delay the American advance by harassment and to demolish bridges and supplies. Food, ammunition, and other vital supplies were carted into the hinterland for weeks before the American attack and cached in caves, defiles, and other remote hideouts. But General Kono's men were deficient in several crucial areas. Fewer than two-thirds of his men were armed. Small arms ammunition was in short supply; there was food enough for about two months and approximately eight thousand rifles. In other ways the Kono force was well prepared. The *Second Air Division* had the area bristling with antiaircraft weapons, which Kono used for ground defense operations. Many automatic weapons had been removed from planes destroyed on the airfields and remounted for use by the infantry. Fortunately for the American forces, General Kono was unable to transport but a few of the larger antiaircraft guns to the inner highlands and his main line of resistance.

By late March, most of General Kono's forces were either occupying their prepared inland positions or on their way there. When he withdrew from the coast, General Kono took about twenty light machine guns, eight heavy machine guns, thirty dismounted airplane machine guns, seven 75mm antiaircraft guns, twelve antiaircraft machine guns, one 77mm artillery piece, and four 57mm cannons. He established an outpost line of resistance in the foothills, from five to seven miles east of Bacalod, generally running from north to south. His main line of resistance lay another five to six miles deeper into the mountains.

Elements of the American Fortieth Division, commanded by Maj. Gen. Rapp Brush, invaded Negros Island at 0500 hours on 29 March, with a reinforced platoon that went ashore about fifteen miles south of Bacalod, in the vicinity of Pulupandan, and secured a bridge over the Bago River. The remainder of the 185th Infantry RCT began landing at Pulupandan at 0900 hours without any preliminary bombardment. The only enemy resistance was at the Bago River bridge, which had been assaulted at dawn, before the surprised Japanese guards could demolish it. Rapidly fanning out northward and eastward, the 185th Infantry RCT was followed by the 160th Infantry RCT (-) on 30 March. Most of the coastal plain highway of northwestern Negros was secured by midday of 2 April, and Bacalod and Silay airfields had been captured.

The Fortieth Division, reinforced (less the 108th Infantry RCT) included the Fortieth Division Headquarters, the 185th RCT, the 160th

RCT (less its Second Battalion), most of the division artillery, and normal combat and service attachments. Artillery support for the Fortieth Division consisted of two 105mm howitzer battalions, a 155mm howitzer battalion, the 105mm self-propelled mounts, two cannon companies, a 75mm tank company, two batteries of antiaircraft automatic weapons, and two 4.2-inch mortar companies. (On 20 April an additional 90mm antiaircraft artillery gun battalion arrived and was emplaced nearby for use against ground targets). During the first week the 185th Infantry was ashore on Negros and securing the highway north, a United States naval destroyer cruising offshore kept the nights bright with star shells to assist the attacking forces in repelling harassing night probes by the Japanese forces that had been left behind to detain the Allied advance. By sundown of 8 April, the two regiments of the Fortieth Division had made contact with the Japanese outpost line of resistance.

The concrete coastal highway of Negros, which was always visible from the sea, went north from Bacalod and encircled more than half the island. Tanks and self-propelled mounts, led by the Fortieth Reconnaissance Troop, began reconnoitering the length of this highway. As the 185th Infantry RCT on the north and the 160th Infantry RCT (-) on its right flank advanced inland and struck General Kono's line, Maj. Gen. Rapp Brush became unduly concerned and requested immediate reinforcements. Thus began the final saga of the 503d Parachute Infantry Regimental Combat Team as a fighting unit in World War II.

Negros Island, located between the islands of Panay on the northwest and Cebu on the east, is about 135 miles long north to south and 50 miles wide. The central area is extremely mountainous with peaks of eight thousand feet or more in height. There are no large rivers, but innumerable small streams drain the inland. Like most tropical islands, Negros possessed a lush growth of tall kunai-like grass in the coastal plains area, which gave way to progressively heavier jungle growth further inland. Bacalod is the capital city of Occidental Negros; Dumaguette is the capital of the southeast province, or Oriental part. Inasmuch as the enemy airfield sites at Bacalod and Silay had been captured, and there was no need for the paratroopers of the 503d RCT to jump on Negros, General Eichelberger ordered the regiment to be flown to Panay and thence carried to Negros by boat.

The 503d RCT was airlifted from the Mindoro airdromes on 8 and 9 April by the 317th Troop Carrier Group of Col. John Lackey. Flying to Iloilo, Panay, thence to Negros Island by boat, the 503d Parachute RCT (less the First Battalion) assembled ashore north of Bacalod. (The

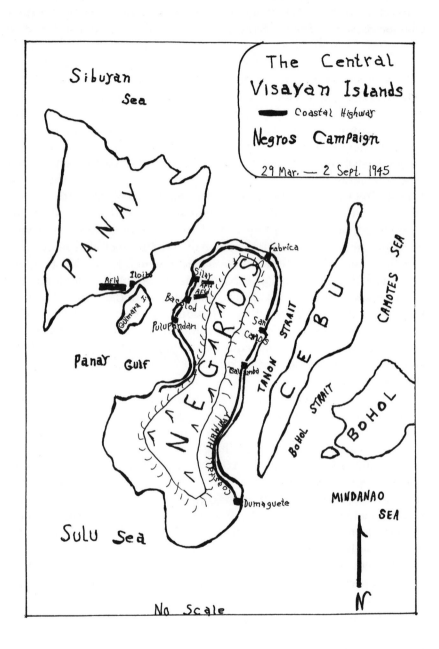

The Central
Visayan Islands
━━━ Coastal Highway
Negros Campaign

29 Mar. — 2 Sept. 1945

Sibuyan
Sea

PANAY

AFld   Iloilo

Guimara I.

Panay Gulf

Silay
AFld
Bacolod
Pulupandan

Fabrica

NEGROS

San
Carlos

Calamba

Coastal Highway

TAÑON STRAIT

CEBU

CAMOTES SEA

BOHOL STRAIT

BOHOL

Dumaguete

Sulu Sea

MINDANAO
SEA

N

No Scale

190

First Battalion, having suffered excessive casualties on Corregidor, remained behind a few days to arm, assign, and orient the many new troopers who had filled its ranks. The First Battalion, as regimental reserve, arrived on Negros on 23 April and rapidly proceeded to the combat area to join the other battalions.)

Beginning on 9 April, the three regiments (less the Second Battalion, 160th Infantry RCT, and the First Battalion, 503d RCT) launched a general offensive aimed at the Japanese-infested mountains lying east of a line running from Silay on the north to near Pulupandan on the south. General Kono's men had prepared caves and concealed artillery positions and countless bunkers or pillboxes, most of the latter being mutually supporting. Many enemy emplacements were connected by tunnels and trenches. The Japanese had dug countless tank traps along the many trailways on the ridgeline escape routes in the mountain foothills. All roads and trails were heavily minded with 250-pound aerial bombs as an antivehicular measure. Antipersonnel mines were planted in grassy areas flanking enemy defense positions. Valleys, draws, creek beds, and other defiladed positions were covered by machine gun fire and mortars. Luckily for the Americans, enemy antipersonnel mine positions were quickly identified. The Japanese removed the grassy turf to implant a mine, then replaced the turf atop the mine. The disturbed grass roots were deprived of moisture, and the grass blades wilted. The troopers would bypass or leap over these grass-wilted sites as they ran forward across the open minefields to attack enemy positions.

The 503d Parachute RCT was assigned the area to the left (north) of the 185th Infantry RCT. Moving rapidly, the troopers of the 503d penetrated perhaps five or six miles inland during their first day ashore. On their first night on Negros Island, they received a portentous preview of the many nights to come. Shortly after dusk, enemy harassment began, ending in primitive hand-to-hand combat, the beginning of a pattern of living hell that was experienced for the remainder of the campaign. The troopers needed a couple of days to become strategically aligned with the already established and holding Fortieth Division in an attack profile. Sadly, the paratroopers were to suffer because of the logistical supply plan of the Eighth Army for the southern Visayan attack.

The fifty-nine-year-old Eichelberger did not follow the standard operating procedures of General Krueger. General Eichelberger had ordered an unprecedentedly meager supply of basic essentials for combat in the Visayan campaign. Instead of a normal sixty-day guaranteed supply of food, munitions, clothing, and other items, General Eichelberger had ordered a mere fifteen-day supply of these essentials

191

to be carried ashore with the assault units. This decision was based on the general's observation of a lone Pacific Island invasion, in the latter part of the war, when insufficient personnel were available to unload a large number of ships that had gone ashore, with the result that the combatants had to be supplied by airdrops. To enhance logistical supply to the invaders of the southern Visayans, General Eichelberger launched what he termed a "floating supply at sea." Theoretically, his supply fleet could have been anyplace between Mindoro and Zamboanga or from Palawan to Cebu. Critical demands for supplies on Negros were met by inexcusable delays in delivery. A fist fight between two troopers epitomized the adverse supply situation. The object of the fight was a new pair of socks.

In the oppressive heat and high humidity of Negros, the three-regiment frontal attack that began on 9 April at the Japanese outpost line of resistance progressed slowly toward the towering, fog-shrouded mountains of the distant interior. General Kono's troops, in possession of the higher terrain, had excellent opportunities to observe the attacking troopers. The rolling hills leading inland to the mountains were open, grass-covered, and steep-sided. During daylight hours, the enemy maintained a static defense. At nightfall, he employed harassing raids, which usually resulted in casualties for the troopers. The troopers of the 503d vigorously attacked and attained their assigned missions by walking, running, fighting, sweating, and cursing each and every uphill yard of terrain gained as their aggressive attack surged forward. The grass-covered plains gave way to grass-covered foothills; tropical palms grew in the valleys. The troopers encountered heavier vegetation as they approached the inland mountains.

On Corregidor, the infantry paratroopers were greatly aided by accurate and abundant fire support from their 462d Parachute Field Artillery brothers. On Negros, for the most of the campaign, the artillery fire supplied to cover the attacking paratrooper infantry was always far short of demand. Lt. Col. Melvin Knudson, commander of the 462d Parachute Field Artillery Battalion on Negros, relates that on arrival on Negros north of Bacalod, the 462d more or less became a part of the Fortieth Division Artillery, which was not a logical deployment for the 75mm pack howitzers. The guns were not suitable for long-range support artillery; they normally operated as short-range, close-in support and sometimes as a direct-fire weapon. Ironically, when assigned to the Fortieth Division Artillery on Negros, the firing batteries of the

462d were directed by the Fortieth Division Standard Operation Procedures and the Fortieth Division Artillery Direction Center. The platoons of .50-caliber machine guns of Battery D of the 462d were assigned to the 503d infantry battalions for front line use.

Near the end of the Negros campaign, when the Fortieth Division was relieved of its positions by the paratroopers of the 503d RCT, the brave and dedicated 462d artillerymen finally were able to operate as a parachute field artillery battalion should. Sadly, in the meantime, too many infantrymen were needlessly slaughtered by the enemy because they received grossly inadequate artillery support from the Fortieth Division Field Artillery Direction Center. This center was not wholly responsible, for it responded to directives from the Fortieth Division commander, Maj. Gen. Rapp Bush. I would still like to know why the 503d paratroopers did not receive their fair share of artillery support. When the artillery support requested by Colonel Jones was inadequate or not forthcoming, why did not the 503d regimental commander protest to the Eighth Army command? Likewise, in planning for this operation, was a demand voiced for equal artillery and aerial support for all assaulting ground troops? Artillery support from the 462d and the attached antiaircraft artillery battalion became overly abundant after the Fortieth Division left Negros; but it was then too late to help the troopers who had been needlessly killed in action because of lack of supporting fire.

The well-fed, aggressive, and numerically superior enemy force fought tenaciously at every encounter. As the campaign progressed, essential artillery and 81mm mortar support became exceedingly scarce, and all support fire diminished as the troopers moved rapidly inland and into the rugged mountains. Regular army units transported up to four hundred artillery rounds per truck, but the two-wheel carts, manhandled by the tough 462d artillerymen when roadways ended, carried but ten rounds. Firepower of the 462d Parachute Field Artillery's 75mm pack howitzers was seldom augmented by the heavy artillery of the Fortieth Division, to which the paratroopers were attached. Several enemy emplacements that the pack howitzers could not breach even by direct fire were encountered. Some assaults were made without preparatory artillery fire. The trooper infantry of the 503d RCT never once experienced the exaltation of a heavy artillery bombardment by the 105mm and 155mm batteries of the Fortieth Division.

The paratroopers frequently made infantry assaults even without preassault mortar and artillery fire. The well-disciplined and aggressive troopers would "go to hell" when given direct orders. Naturally, without prebombardment of the enemy positions, the infantry attacks resulted in unwarranted casualties. From the perspective of history, the point of this campaign may be questioned. The Japanese forces were isolated without hope of reinforcements or evacuation. General Kono's forces were in the mountains, and the Filipino cities had been liberated; why was it deemed necessary to pursue the enemy further? A containment of the Japanese by well dug-in and fortified paratroopers would ultimately have accomplished the same end as constant attack resulting in unnecessary casualties.

As the paratroopers relentlessly pursued the enemy deeper and deeper into his mountainous stronghold, they were fighting uphill all the way. The Japanese, situated on the higher ground and observing the troopers' advance, almost always fired the first shot and inflicted a casualty on the advancing paratroopers. Maj. Logan W. Hovis, Third Battalion surgeon of the 503d, recalled: "We dealt with a lot of casualties, and too many of them were old timers."

While attack efforts were under way on Northwestern Negros, the 164th Infantry RCT, Eighth Army Reserves for the southern Visayan campaign, was released to its mother division on Cebu on 9 April to assist in neutralizing the enemy force on that island. General Eichelberger began pressuring Maj. Gen. William H. Arnold, commander of the Americal Division, to hurry his three-phase campaign commitment to neutralize the enemy on Cebu, Bohol, and southern Negros. On 26 April, the 164th Infantry RCT (less its third Battalion) landed unopposed on the southeastern coast of Negros, near Dumaguette, and very soon thereafter established contact with leading elements of the Fortieth Division's Fortieth Reconnaissance Troop, which had circumnavigated almost the entire island on the coastal highway, since leaving Bacalod on 2 April. The Japanese forces in garrison at this southern end of the island totalled about 1,300, built around the 174th Independent Infantry Battalion, less three rifle companies (plus ground service troops of the Second Air Division) and nearly 150 sailors from sunken naval craft. By 6 May, the 164th Infantry (-) plus a Filipino guerrilla regiment began a concerted attack, which culminated on 28 May, when the last organized enemy stronghold was overcome. By mid-June, no further organized Japanese resistance could be found. Then began the dirty and tedious task of rooting out the hold-out Japanese fanatics. As usual, these mop-up activities saw some of the bloodiest scenes of combat of the war in the Pacific.

Fortunately for the attacking paratroopers on Negros, Japanese army communications systems were primitive, inferior to their American counterparts, and untrustworthy so that enemy commanders rarely possessed an accurate picture or combat profile of opposing forces. The combined Japanese forces on western Negros could have wrecked havoc on the American attackers had they possessed reliable communications systems. Divine Providence had to have been present for the Americans!

Throughout the assault maneuvers of the attacking infantrymen of the 503d RCT, the constant readiness and willing support of the troopers of Company C, 161st Parachute Engineer Battalion were gratefully welcomed. These talented and motivated engineer paratroopers completed countless jobs, many of which were hazardous. They filled in the numerous tank traps that had been dug by the retreating enemy along the many razorback ridges. These tank traps were usually defended by well-concealed automatic weapons systems, supplemented by Japanese sharpshooters equipped with telescopic rifles. Again, as on Mindoro and Corregidor, the troopers would have welcomed the telescopic rifles the 503d brass had caused to be removed from company ranks nearly two years previously. One tank trap on the Third Battalion front resulted in twenty-two paratroopers killed and wounded by a lone Japanese sharpshooter armed with a telescopic rifle. To fill in the tank trap, Company C engineer bulldozer operations sometimes required a guard "riding shotgun" to sit alongside and guard the bulldozer operator. Once I saw both the bulldozer operator and the guard felled by a single enemy shot; one trooper was dead, the other wounded.

Throughout most of the Negros Island campaign, essential food, ammunition, and clothing for the paratroopers were always in short supply. During the first several weeks ashore on Negros the paratroopers were supplied by airdrop onto their forward positions. In this campaign, there were no overcrowded beaches at the beachhead, such as had earlier caused General Eichelberger to formulate his plan of a "floating supply at sea." Rather, the troopers needed supplies that were not soon forthcoming. This situation underscores an apparent lack of foresightedness and planning skill by the Eighth Army and its logistical command.

Upon reaching the base of the Japanese-infested mountains, the Fortieth Infantry Division troops halted their advance, encircled their forward positions with barbed wire, and fired apparently unrestricted numbers of artillery rounds into the dark and ominously jungled mountains. This pattern was repeated day after day and week after week. The Fortieth Division killed the enemy on artillery-derived "paper

Exploding shell in the background marks the end of the roadway constructed along an enemy trail by the troopers of Company C 161st Parachute Engineer Battalion, Negros Island, Philippines, April 1945.

estimates" based upon its unrelenting search and destroy barrages. Yet it saved the dogfaced infantry by its reconnaissance by fire.

Once during the campaign a patrol led by Sgt. Charles H. Wasmund of Farnham, New York, cautiously approached and searched an abandoned native hut. A billy goat was found in one of the rooms. In less than fifteen minutes, the engineer troopers had the goat killed, skinned, and simmering over a hastily built fire. Some swore that they had not feasted so voraciously in recent memory. The hazardous task of defusing the multitudes of antipersonnel mines and bombs planted by the enemy also fell to the brave troopers of Company C, 161st Parachute Engineer Battalion.

Contrary to the Fortieth Division's method of tabulating enemy casualties, the troopers of the 503d always employed the head count method. The paratroopers on Negros ultimately gained the summits of the mountainous heights in their assigned sectors. Sneers of contempt crossed the grimy faces of the paratroopers as they looked down from their hard-won mile high peaks to the men of the Fortieth Division in static defense positions at the mountain base. The Fortieth Division troops at this time obtained and used a new defensive magnesium flare, which could be placed in a shielded parapet forward of friendly positions and ignited by batteries. The troopers, high in the fog-shrouded, dark, cold, and rainy mountaintops, fervently desired these morale-building instruments of war but never received any. Once again the troopers were spurned and denied needed implements of combat by their surrogate mother, the Fortieth Division and its command of logistics and supply.

By mid-May 1945, the combat effectives in the infantry companies of the 503d RCT had been reduced to half strength or less. Men were exhausted, both physically and mentally. The heat, strain, casualties, and physical demands reaped their tolls on the trudging ranks of the plodding troopers. On 21 May, a group of teenaged replacements arrived on Negros. These new troopers were rapidly escorted to their assigned units, although there were too few of them to comfort the old troopers on line. In fact, they were a burden because of the need to alleviate their obvious fears. This was usually attended to by having the new man share his foxhole at night with a seasoned trooper.

The commanding officer of Company H had to write a letter of condolence to the parents of a trooper replacement who was killed before he even reached the company's forward command post. It must have been difficult to write to unfamiliar people news of the death of a man one had never seen. War frequently presented seemingly insurmountable problems. By mid-May, Filipino civilians had been procured to transport forward the daily food and ammunition supplies, which they usually did at the end of the day's advance, and then return with the dead and wounded troopers from the field collecting stations. Before Philippine labor was acquired, parachute drops were made each evening at the forward outposts of the hastily advancing troopers. Bartering between the paratroopers and the native carriers was rapidly established. Parachute silk of various colors would be traded for cooked chickens, eggs, fresh vegetables, or other wares the natives may have possessed that were deemed desirable. The war-ravaged and destitute Filipinos would exchange any reasonable possession for parachute cloth with which to clothe themselves and their families.

Because of the vast distance and terrain covered by the elements of the three battalions of his 503d Parachute Infantry, the support units of the 462d Parachute Field Artillery Battalion, and the troopers of Company C, 161st Parachute Engineer Battalion, Colonel Jones used an artillery spotter plane to survey the advance of the RCT each day and toss grenades at scattered enemy groups. Colonel Jones spent most of the nights in the vicinity of the Bacalod airfield.

By 4 June, General Kono realized that his forces were incapable of stopping the advance of the American forces and directed a withdrawal deep into the mountains. The experiences of the 503d paratroopers for the remainder of the campaign were a repetition of previous combat accounts. The mountain fighting degenerated into deadly, cruel, and demanding warfare of the most primitive description. There were countless series of attacks, delays, regroupings, failures, new problems, casualties, frustrations, and hard-won successes. High in the mountains, the troopers experienced heavy downpours of cold and chilling rain during the late night and early morning hours. These deluges were followed by dense fog that lasted until nearly midday. In early June, Gen. Rapp Brush, commander of the Negros Island Task Force and the Fortieth Infantry Division, reported to General Eichelberger that the last strong enemy outpost line of resistance had been overrun. It is unclear how he justified this statement.

By mid-June, Colonel Abcede's Filipino guerrilla army of nearly fourteen thousand troops had been armed and controlled about two-thirds of Negros Island. Slowly, these guerrillas replaced the paratrooper companies in their mountainous outposts and continued the pursuit of the stubbornly retreating enemy. On 9 June, the 503d RCT troopers relieved all elements of the Fortieth Division in northwestern Negros.

A week later, Colonel Abcede's guerrilla forces began relieving the troopers in their forward positions. The 503d RCT infantry companies were now averaging about a platoon of men in strength. On 10 June, Generals MacArthur and Eichelberger visited Negros Island. During the day, they visited an operations post east of Silay, where as General Eichelberger related, the Americans and Filipinos encircled themselves at night with barbed wire. (How wonderfully serene they must have felt to have been protected from infiltrating Japanese by a gird of barbed wire.) MacArthur praised General Rapp Brush's Fortieth Division troops and decorated three sergeants of the 503d RCT for gallantry during his brief stay on the island.

In war, combat troops display obvious disrespect for rear base noncombatants. To illustrate this point, a tale must be borrowed from Brig. Gen. Robert Shoe, chief of staff in the Eighth Army. In the hottest part of the fighting on Negros, General Shoe made a trip to the front to observe the troopers' progress. Passing a weary group of paratroopers who had been relieved of fighting and were resting alongside a stream, he asked a grimy old trooper of about twenty years of age how things were at the front. The tired trooper "eyeballed" the star on the general's shoulder, clean uniform, and jeep, but said nothing. General Shoe proceeded on to the forward positions and almost immediately received a minor neck wound. As he was being evacuated to the rear by stretcher, he found himself confronting the trooper he had earlier met back at the stream. The dogface was friendly now, and with a broad grin he queried: "General, how are things at the front?"

With the withdrawal of the Fortieth Division from Negros, American troop strength approximated four thousand men, including antiaircraft artillery and service troops personnel. On 20 June, the 164th Infantry RCT departed Dumaguette and a company of paratroopers was dispatched from northwestern Negros to replace the unit and to supervise the guerrillas in their continuing search for remaining enemy troops. The 164th Infantry RCT had lost 35 men killed in action and 180 wounded and had slain 530 of the Japanese defenders. A platoon of Company C, 161st Parachute Engineer Battalion, was sent to Dumaguette a few days later to establish a water purification plant, which was maintained until the war's end.

Troopers who could find an excuse for going to regimental headquarters at Bacalod for food, ammunition, or medical treatment could usually find respite for a few hours before having to go back to the front. While in town, they would amuse themselves at the Philippine national sport of rooster fighting, drinking "Tiger" brand native whiskey, taking in the sights, or participating in other "things that young men like to do." When the various battalions and companies of the 503d were dispatched to different positions recently vacated by the departed Fortieth Division, artillery fire support miraculously became much more abundant. The troopers continued their endless patrolling in conjunction with the Filipino guerrillas' operations.

The battalions and companies of the 503d were hastily shuffled and shuttled from one locale to another about Negros Island, each unit relieving another from time to time to absorb the slack of the Fortieth Division's withdrawal from northwestern Negros and that of the 164th Infantry from Dumaguette, in the extreme southeastern sector. Rotation of "old men" back to the United States began in late June, based on a point system of selection. This system developed by the army allocated a point for each month of military service, an additional point for each month of expeditionary service, points for wounds, and so on. Rotation had been authorized by the War Department for more than two years, but the orders had been kept from the enlisted men by the U.S. Army commanders in the South Pacific and SWPA theaters of war because insufficient replacements were forthcoming from the states. The war in Europe had taken precedence in troop allocations. The First Battalion of the 503d remained in the vicinity of San Carlos after 20 June. The Second Battalion was dispersed to various barrios on the southern reaches of the island. The Third Battalion troopers were dispatched to the northern and western sides of Negros Island. The waning summer days of late June and July slowly passed in the torrid tropical clime as the remaining troopers instituted an attitude of self-preservation. The Filipino guerrilla forces were supervised and supported as they pursured the enemy deep into his formidable strongholds.

On 6 August 1945, the troopers on Negros Island, along with the rest of the world, were stunned by the announcement by Pres. Harry S. Truman that an atomic bomb had been dropped on Hiroshima, Japan, virtually wiping out the city. An ultimatum for the Japanese empire to capitulate unconditionally went unheeded by the enemy. On 9 August, a second atomic bomb was dropped on Nagasaki, Japan. At long last, on 14 August 1945, the Japanese imperial government sued for peace. The power of the atomic bomb was too awesome for the troopers to comprehend. They could hardly envisage an explosion more devastating and earthshaking than those they had witnessed at Malinta Tunnel and Monkey Point less than six months earlier. Hostilities on Negros Island

Lt. Col. Joe S. Lawrie, commander of the 503d RCT on Negros Island, who received General Kono's surrender to the U.S. Army.

were formally ended, but fighting and patrolling continued past the agreed-upon Japanese capitulation date.

Col. George M. Jones, commander of the 503d RCT, rotated back to the United States on 10 August 1945. He was succeeded in command by the regimental executive officer, Lt. Col. Joe S. Lawrie. A 1936 graduate of Lousiana State University, Lawrie was commissioned a second lieutenant by way of the Reserve Officers' Training Program of that university and received his regular army commission on 3 July 1937 at Fort Sam Houston, Texas. He was a charter member of the original 503d Battalion and had served in the battalion and regiment continuously.

The Negros Island campaign had cost more than 370 men killed and 1,025 wounded in action. The 503d had suffered 144 troopers killed in action and 370 wounded during the spring and summer of 1945. Non-battle casualties resulting from heat, exhaustion, and illness totaled 1,028 paratroopers. The last two paratrooper casualties suffered by the 503d RCT during World War II occurred after dark, outside Fabrica, in late October, when two young replacement troopers of Company H, then commanded by Lt. Henry L. Zimon, were returning to their quarters from courting some Filipino maidens. The men were slain from ambush by jealous Filipino suitors. Japanese casualties on Negros by late August had exceeded four thousand killed and nearly thirty-five hundred additional deaths from disease and starvation.

The exultation of the paratroopers at the war's final victory was indescribable. Nevertheless, extreme caution was exercised on unit patrols because the enemy soldiers on Negros were as yet unaware of their empire's capitulation. Various means were employed by the paratroopers to convey the news of the Nippon surrender to the hiding enemy deep in mountain retreats. Jeeps flying white flags patrolled the roadways and trails with loudspeakers blaring the news. Airplanes dispatched from Bacalod and Silay airfields dropped leaflets on suspected enemy positions. Occasionally, in the next few days, an English-speaking Japanese soldier would emerge from a jungle hideout, under security of a white cloth or flag of truce. Radios and instructions for follow-up communications were presented to these soldiers so they would carry the news to their comrades. Numerous additional contacts and affirmations of surrender were soon made in various locales about the island.

Efficient and effective negotiations with the enemy were hindered by a lack of fluent interpreters and mutual distrust between the paratroopers and the Japanese forces. Finally, seemingly endless lines

Unbelievable numbers of healthy Japanese troops filed out of their mountainous retreats.

Japanese officers leading their troops to areas designated for arms disposal and impoundment.

of General Kono's men slowly began winding their way out of the mountains of northwestern Negros Island and surrendering to the paratroopers of the 503d RCT. These Japanese troops had clean uniforms and shaved heads, and their morale was high. Lieutenant General Kono surrendered more than six thousand troops. At Dumaguette, another 880 enemy survivors came out of hiding and surrendered to the paratroopers.

Military victory, in all its glory and manifestations, produced varied but happy reactions among the surviving paratroopers who attended the surrender ceremonies in the various locales about Negros Island. Among the ranks were a few troopers of the original 503d Parachute Infantry Regiment, who had sailed from American shores in the autumn of 1942 with blood in their eyes and revenge in their hearts. Accounts of the surrender activities written by some of those present at the surrender are included here for the benefit of those old troopers who were unable to be at the surrender. These recollections were written in letters to me from former troopers in 1980-82. The surrender time dictated to the Japanese forces on Negros Island was to coincide with the time the representatives of Japan were to sign the surrender documents aboard the USS *Missouri:* 1000 hours, Sunday 2 September 1945.

RECOLLECTIONS:
First Battalion, 503d Parachute Infantry Regiment
The First Battalion covered the San Carlos area until the Japanese surrender. With the news of the Japanese Supreme Command's directive that all enemy forces were to lay down their arms and surrender, the task was to establish communications with the Japs on Negros and substantiate this information for them. After a few attempts with jeeps, white flags, and loudspeakers with interpreters, the enemy received a radio and arranged surrender at various points on Negros. Many of us were outside San Carlos to witness these enemy troops coming in, and when I saw the extremely long column of "two's" moving downhill toward us, I thought this *had* to be all the enemy on Negros. There were some two thousand, plus, and they were very neat and orderly. They stacked their weapons as directed. A colonel led this group and he had an American educated interpreter. He reminded us that under terms of the Treaty, he was a civilian! The Jap colonel refused American rations. A day later, rice and other Jap food arrived. Among the enemy forces were many women . . . some apparently Japanese . . . others, Filipino, but all were neat and clean, and well cared for. I don't recall where they stayed, but a hastily constructed barbed wire fence was erected around the Japanese troops. This was just outside of San Carlos.

This rickety, one strand fence wire, served in essence, as a sort of an imaginary wall. One opening served as a gate, which was used to come and go. We supplied a few guards for outside duty, and I do believe this was to keep the Filipinos from harming the prisoners. The Japs went out on details, to wash their clothing, and to bathe. They pretty well had the run of the place and I witnessed no trouble. This was as I had suspected. We once witnessed a Japanese sergeant reprimanding one of his men. He loudly dressed him down, then called him to "attention" and slammed a right fist into his face. When the victim rolled over, the sergeant again called him to "attention." The Jap private stood rigid. The detail was then sent on its way.

Andrew J. Amaty
Platoon Sergeant
Hq. Co. 1st Bn. 503d
30 November 1981

Second Battalion, 503d Parachute Infantry Regiment

Events of the Japanese surrender are dim in my mind. I do remember the Japanese surrendering at Fabrica and guarding the prisoners in an old lumber compound. There was one huge fire of burning Japanese equipment.

Earl K. Hubbard
Hq. Co. 2nd Bn. 503d
25 November 1981

Company C, 161st Parachute Engineer Battalion, 503d RCT

When the Japs surrendered, we had them breaking rocks along the Bacalod airstrip and placing a new top on the airstrip of this crushed stone. After the airstrip was completed, we were all moved to Dumaguette for a few weeks, and then back to Bacalod. We finally left Negros and landed in San José, California, on Christmas Eve. We stayed aboard ship for three days and were finally taken off and sent to an Air Force Base . . . and from there . . . Home Sweet Home!

Charles H. Wasmund
S/Sgt. Co. C, 161st Para. Eng. Bn.
2 February 1982

Various Japanese unit commanders surrender to the paratroopers of the 503d RCT to end hostilities on Negros Island. The long-sought goal had been achieved.

462d Parachute Field Artillery Battalion, 503d RCT

I did take part in the surrender of Negros and though I did not document the occasion, I have vivid memories of the event; however, I don't remember the exact date. Upon the end of the hostilities and after preliminary arrangements had been finalized with Lt. Gen. Kono, commander of Japanese forces on Negros, a formal surrender of the Japanese occupational forces on Negros commenced. At the time, I was executive officer of D Battery, 462d Parachute Field Artillery Battalion, and was detailed to take all battery transport vehicles, together with one platoon, to act as guards and as security for the prisoners. The entire day before the designated surrender date, was utilized in cleaning and preparation of the vehicles, so as to present the most military appearance possible. The men were briefed in their responsibilities and were instructed to "fall in" the following morning with their equipped arms and in a clean field uniform.

On the morning of the date of the surrender, four men, designated as guards, together with a driver and a non-commissioned officer riding "shotgun," were assigned to each of the eight trucks from Battery D. We formed up, with my Jeep in the lead and fell into the column of vehicles being furnished as transport, by the 462d Parachute Field Artillery Battalion. The column moved out under the command of Lt. Col. Melvin R. Knudson, Battalion Commander. We proceeded to Bacalod city and from there to the appointed place of surrender, about a mile east of Bacalod; arriving about noon. The surrender site selected was a long plateau overlooking a water course and valley. The high mountain range was visible in the distance, where the Japanese had determined to make their last stand. It was not long until I observed in the distance, a white flag, and the advance guard of the surrender detail. An officer of the 503d and a Recon squad was in the forefront of the main force of the Japanese marching to surrender. As they came nearer, their numbers became evident, resembling Army ants as they wove their way to the surrender point.

In the meantime, all of the trucks, including some DUKW's (Ducks), had been placed on line, as if at a parade ground inspection, ready to shuttle the prisoners to the compound established near Bacalod. Upon arrival of the Japanese commander and his staff, the guard detail was formed up, by unit, ahead of the truck fleet. The staff and battalion commanders took their place on center of the 503d formation. Lt. Col. Lawrie took his place at the front of the regiment. The Japanese formed up with their senior officers in two ranks, with Lt. Gen. Kono opposite to Lt. Col. Lawrie. After exchanging salutes of formality, Gen.

Kono presented his Samurai sword to Lt. Col. Lawrie. In like respect, all the Japanese officers presented their sabers to the 503d Regimental Combat Team Staff, Battalion, Company, and Battery Commanders.

Upon conclusion of the formal surrender ceremonies, the Japanese were loaded up, about thirty men to the truck, and the convoy moved out to the compound. Enroute, the Filipinos, at times, became incited to violence at the sight of the Japanese; throwing rocks, and otherwise threatening the safety of the prisoner transport. It became necesary to fire warning shots over the heads of the natives, to restore control. Upon delivering the initial group of prisoners, we returned to the surrender site. Other prisoners were on-loaded and sent on their way. It was becoming apparent that the first arrivals, the hale and hearty, were being followed by the sick and wounded. Some of these unfortunates were at the point of death from their arduous trip from the mountains. Stretcher details were formed, and these infirm individuals, many of whom later died, were delivered to a hacienda near the sugar mill, which had been established as a field hospital for the prisoners.

Jesse B. Gandee
1st. Lt. Btry. D, 462d Para. F.A.
14 November 1981

Third Battalion, 503d Parachute Infantry Regiment

The following is a brief summary of the thoughts that entered my mind while travelling to the Japanese surrender on Negros Island and during the actual ceremony. The date was September 2, 1945. We had been informed that a large group, possibly thousands of the enemy, would come down out of the hills to be interned and face their destiny. Joe Conway and I headed for the designated area in a "borrowed" Jeep. After a short trip from the coastal plains region, we came upon what appeared to be about two companies of Japanese infantry taking a break along both sides of the road. The men practically ignored us, but one or two officers gave a half-hearted salute. Since nearly all of the Japs Joe and I had seen previously were either trying to kill us or we were trying to kill them (with the exception of a very few prisoners), I felt very uneasy, to say the least. After getting by them, we encountered more units on their way to the assembly grounds; but I certainly wasn't getting accustomed to it. After moving about another mile, we saw the main body. There were women and children (some, but babes in arms), and several hundred soldiers. We met a group of men from "H" Company there. They attempted to give the children candy, but the mothers screamed in terror, as only Orientals can. They did their best to hide their young ones. There was just no convincing them of our charitable intentions.

After a few minutes, the paratroopers lined up. Someone, I've forgotten whom, insisted that I get in the front line to possibly receive one of the better swords, as I had made all the missions. A Japanese Major, with a blank expression (but I thought, with a tear in his eye), gave me a beautiful sword which I still have, after all these years. An interpreter later told me it was 130 years old at the time of the surrender. As I looked down at this little man . . . he was completely docile . . . after so many battles; my mind wandered back to Nadzab . . . Hollandia . . . Noemfoor . . . Leyte . . . Mindoro . . . Corregidor . . . here on Negros; and all the fine young Troopers we left along this tortuous route. It now seems impossible, but so many faces flashed in my brain. It appeared to be an entire panorama of the past three years. Perhaps the Major wondered why I, too, had a tear in my eye. The gathering quickly ended and the ex-enemy was marshalled to various internment camps. Company "H" was assigned to guard one of the compounds which was located in a town called San Carlos. The prison had been set up in a large field and was encircled by two rows of barbed wire fencing. Outside the first row, the Japanese furnished a twenty-four hour guard detail; armed with clubs. Outside the second row, Company "H" had a minimal number of armed troopers. Occasionally, one or two prisoners would become delirious from fever and try to wander off. These incidents were the only escape attempts, as the Japs feared being caught by the Filipinos, if they happened to get out.

Letters from home began to arrive fairly often by now, but not necessarily in the order they were written. I had received a letter from my wife, describing a Memorial Mass she had attended; but assuming I had information mailed earlier, didn't mention for *whom* the Mass was for. On the evening of 27 September, another letter arrived. All through the war, I had expected this; but expecting it certainly didn't in any way, prepare me for it. The Memorial Mass had been for my brother, John D. He had died the previous February in a Japanese prison, after surviving the Bataan Death March and two and a half years of suffering. I came very close to making a horrible mistake that night at San Carlos. The thought of revenge hit hard, suddenly. Inside the compound, less than fifty yards from me, were Japanese, who, no doubt, had also mistreated prisoners and caused many of them to die. I told the Troopers around me the sad news. These people, who had faced death so often, seemed to understand more than anyone else. They suspected something. They would not leave my quarters . . . didn't talk

Japanese Lieutenant General Kono with staff studying surrender documents.

Lieutenant General Kono walks that "longest mile" to give his saber to Lt. Col. Joe Lawrie, commander of the 503d RCT on Negros Island, Philippines.

about anything in particular . . . just hung around! After several hours, I realized the futility of such thoughts. Today, I am certainly glad common sense won out and that I was with "H" Company men that night. There never was a time that I couldn't fully depend on each and every one of them. You and I were fortunate to have served in this unit.

James M. Mullaney
1st Lt. Cmndg.
"H" Co. 503d Parachute Infantry
20 February, 1980

The tenseness of combat readiness slowly mellowed to an ecstatic feeling of peace and tranquility. Beyond essential garrison duties, the troopers now became engaged in "town soldiering." Miraculously, prewar American whiskey immediately surfaced in the many villages and barrios. Also, all the barrios provided an ample supply of beautiful, dark-eyed maidens. A bountiful supply of GI food and candy quickly surfaced for bartering with the Filipinos. Native musical festivities erupted spontaneously. Slowly, the "old" troopers of the 503d RCT began transferring to Dumaguette and thence homeward bound! The "low point" troopers were transferred to the Eleventh Airborne Division in Japan.

Lt. Col. Joe Lawrie, commander of the 503d RCT and the last trooper of the 503d to depart Negros Island, was directed to release all 503d records and the hallowed regimental combat team colors to the senior officer of the AAA unit at Dumaguette. Lawrie, a regular army officer, was ordered first to Manila and then dispatched back to Fort Benning, Georgia, and the airborne school. When various units of the Pacific war returned to the United States, parades were held in nearly all the cities of the nation. At one parade in San Francisco, California, the colors fo the 503d were unfurled in the wind but carried by a non-paratrooper, much to the chagrin of the old 503d paratroopers, who were sidelined as bystanders.

The beloved colors of the 503d Parachute Infantry Regimental Combat Team of World War II were encased on 24 December 1945, at Camp Anza (Arlington), California. The original "WILDCAT" emblem of the old 503d Battalion and later the regiment had been replaced by the "ROCK" emblem. The latter was designed by Capt. William Bossert of the First Battalion while recuperating on Mindoro upon his release from the 96th General Hospital at Gua Gua, Bataan, Luzon. The general idea was to depict the heroic contributions of the 462d Parachute Field Artillery Battalion and the troopers of Company C, 161st Parachute

Engineer Battalion. A few minor changes were made by regimental approval before the final product was obtained.

Though the 503d colors had been retired, the camaraderie of the paratroopers they symbolized remained very much alive. Paratroopers, being a unique breed of warriors, are a stolid group, regardless of age, war, or campaign. No other segment of the United States armed forces is as brotherly, faithful, or respectful of each other as the paratroopers. No paratrooper is ever alone and without a buddy. The bonds of trust and friendship are even closer than between blood brothers; for in combat, the trooper knew what his buddy would do; he could not know how his brother might react in a demanding life-or-death situation.

Thus ends the saga of the 503d Parachute Infantry Regimental Combat Team of World War II. The historical feats and accomplishments of this magnificent airborne entity are documented and extends the challenge: "If you cannot follow in our footsteps, don't look at our tracks!"

At this writing, the old troopers of the 503d Parachute Infantry Regimental Combat Team are again preparing for a final patrol. The troopers will once again march down the "Valley of the Shadow." At the terminus of the valley, the trail divides. The troopers will move confidently down the path on this last patrol, but at the point where the trail divides, they will pivot to the one on their right. This path leads into a broad expanse, illuminated by a bright and everlasting light. Here, they will be greeted by former buddies of long ago. The old troopers never once glanced at the trail to their left, leading into a shadowy vale. They had scouted that area before. It led to Hell.

Appendixes

Appendix A
THE 503d SONG

The 503d march or fighting son is traditional. On the forty-two-day voyage to Australia on the old Dutch freighter-turned-troop-transport, the gallant SS *Poelau Laut*, Cpl. Ken Brown wrote the music to this song. Cpl. Brown was a piano player in the Special Services Section of Regimental Headquarters and Headquarters Company. A Sergeant Moore (first name unknown), a guitarist, wrote the words. The 503d band or orchestra was called the Seldom Fed Seven. The group also had a Capt. Charles Rambo on the Hawaiian steel guitar, and troopers Noel and Cates as vocalists. (First names and ranks of the latter are unknown). An unknown trooper with the initials E.S.R. compiled the musical arrangement of the march.

The 503d song has been handed down from songfest to songfest and re-union to reunion with numerous revisions in the lyrics through the decades since its composition. The way the paratroopers sing the song, it does not have much of a march tempo but more closely resembles a college fight song. Nor is the music notated correctly for the rhyme or its rhythm. Nevertheless, the 503d song is reverently and gustily sung by the old troopers of World War II at all their reunions.

Sgt. Larry S. Pierce, Congressional Medal of Honor recipient, First Battalion Recon Platoon, 503d Infantry, in action against the enemy near Ben Cat, Republic of Vietnam, 20 September 1965

Appendix B
LINEAGE AND HONORS

The beloved and revered colors of the 503d Parachute Infantry Regiment of World War II placidly rested encased until 2 March 1951. The involvement of United States armed forces in the Korean conflict caused the 503d Parachute Infantry to be reactivated at Fort Campbell, Kentucky, and assigned to the Eleventh Airborne Division. The 503d did not see combat in Korea, but it did conduct extensive military maneuvers in all of the states of the United States, including Alaska. In 1956, the 503d Parachute Infantry, along with the Eleventh Airborne Division, moved to Germany. On 1 March 1957, the 503d Parachute Infantry was reorganized under the new battle group concept. It was redesignated the First Airborne Battle Group, 503d Infantry. On 1 July 1958, the unit was assigned to its historical former World War II comrades-in-arms of the Twenty-fourth Infantry Division. The First Airborne Battle Group was assigned to the Eighty-second Airborne Division at Fort Bragg, North Carolina, on 7 January 1959. On 25 June 1963, the First Airborne Battle Group was redesignated the 503d Infantry (Airborne) and assigned to the 173d Airborne Brigade on the island of Okinawa.

On 5 May 1965, the troopers of the 173d Airborne Brigade became the first U.S. Army combat unit to be committed to the Vietnam War. One early mission assigned the troopers of the 503d Infantry was to secure the Vung Tau airdrome. The 173d A/B Brigade penetrated the formidable War Zone D in June, a supposedly impregnable fortress of the Viet Cong. In mid-September 1965, the troopers of the 503d again invaded the deadly War Zone D near Ben Cat of the Iron Triangle. The hard-won successes of this second penetration was marred by the death of Sgt. Larry Pierce of the First Battalion recon platoon of the 503d Infantry. While on patrol, his quick actions and shouted warnings saved the lives of three comrades when he threw himself atop an activated Claymore mine. His act of bravery cost him his life. For his valorous feats, Sergeant Pierce was awarded the Congressional Medal of Honor.

On 5 November 1965, the 173d A/B Brigade again invaded the dreaded Zone D in what was termed Operation HUMP. This operation by the troopers of the 503d resulted in numerous close-quarter combat engagements over the next several days. By 9 November, the troopers had decimated a Viet Cong regiment. The undaunted valor of the troopers of the 503d had now earned a second Presidential Unit Citation award for the 503d Parachute Infantry Regiment, this time, the troopers of the First Battalion.

The paratroopers of the 503d later excelled in combat during Operation MARAUDER I and Operation CRIMP. The earlier operation occurred 1-8 January 1966 in the Mekong Delta region. The latter operation destroyed the greater Saigon enemy-controlled area of command. Throughout the year 1966,

Pfc. Carlos J. Lozada, Congressional Medal of Honor recipient for action at Dak To, Republic of Vietnam, 20 November 1967, Company A, Second Battalion, 503d Infantry

the troopers were thwarted by political dampers on their aggressive attack patterns. Hindered by political inconsistency and lack of 100 percent support by the nation's leaders, the gallant troopers held their gains of the previous year. Beginning in February 1967, the 503d paratroopers participated in Operation JUNCTION CITY. For actions during the period of 5 May 1965 to 4 May 1967, the troopers were awarded the Meritorious Unit Citation. By 6 November 1967, the 173d A/B Brigade had been deployed to Dak To. Only the old troopers of World War II and the valiant men of the Vietnam War can fully appreciate or relate to the oppressive heat, the relentless jungle struggles in close combat, the insects, the revolting stench of decaying cadavers, the blood-sucking leeches, and the ominous portent of early morning recon patrols outside the night perimeter suffered in these campaigns.

On 10 November 1967, the troopers of the 503d organized two task forces for search and destroy operations west of Forward Support Base (FSB) 15. Shortly after dawn on 11 November, Company A of the 503d reinforced by one platoon of Company D (First Battalion), engaged a battalion-sized force of the enemy about three kilometers west of FSB 15. Coming under heavy assault, the paratroopers repeatedly repulsed the enemy attacks numerous times at close quarters, in hand-to-hand combat. About 1445 hours, Company C of the reinforced Fourth Battalion of the 503d, arrived and brought in badly needed ammunition. The Fourth Battalion of the 503d Infantry was created by Department of the Army orders. A battalion of the First Brigade of the 101st Airborne Division was used as a cadre nucleus, filled, redesignated the Fourth Battalion of the 503d, and joined the parent regiment, the 503d Infantry. Enemy contact had been broken by 11 November. This battle was the turning point in the battle of Dak To.

On 20 November, while engaging the enemy at Dak To, Republic of Vietnam, Pfc. Carlos James Lozado, a machine gunner of Company A, Second Battalion, 503d Infantry Regiment (Airborne), gave his life at an early warning outpost, slaying the enemy while giving his company time for an orderly withdrawal to a more secure defense position. For his valorous feats, Pfc. Lozado was awarded the Congressional Medal of Honor. For its valorous actions at Dak To, the 173d A/B Brigade, minus the Third Battalion, was awarded the Third Presidential Unit Citation received by the 503d Parachute Regiment.

In March 1968, the 173d A/B Brigade began Operation COCHISE, in which the brigade assumed responsibility for operations in the provinces of Binh, Phu Yen, and Phu Bon. By 1969, the military emphasis had shifted to pacification. The 503d troopers now became engaged in security operations with local forces, built schools, manned the dispensaries, and worked with the villagers and hamlet officials. For its performance of duty during the period 5 May to 27 September 1970, the 503d troopers were awarded the Vietnamese Cross of Gallantry with Palm. Simultaneously, the Vietnamese government awarded the regiment the Vietnamese Civil Action Medal for pacification efforts for the period from 1969 to 1971.

In January 1971, the 503d began Operation GREEN LIGHTNING in the Meiu and Tiger Mountain ranges. At long last, the paratroopers of the 503d began to stand down on 1 April 1971. The stand down was finalized at Landing Zone English in a farewell ceremony on 27 April 1971. On this date, the 503d colors were encased and dispatched to Hawaii.

On 3 September 1971, when the Fourth Battalion was inactivated at Fort Campbell, Kentucky, its assets were used to replenish the remaining 503d Parachute Infantry battalions. The paratroopers of the 503d were released from assignment to the 173d A/B Brigade and reassigned to the Third Brigade (Airborne) of the 101st Airborne Division (Airmobile) on 14 January 1972.

In the six years of green hell in the jungle war of Vietnam, eight Congressional Medals of Honor were awarded to distinguished paratroopers of the 503d Parachute Infantry Regiment. They are as follows:

Name	Unit	Postition	Posthumously
Pfc. Carlos J. Lozado	2/503	Machine Gunner	Yes
SP4 Michael R. Blanchfield	4/503	Rifleman	Yes
SP5 Lawrence Joel	HHC 1/503	Medic	No
SSG Glenn H. English	3/503	Squad Leader	Yes
SP4 Don L. Michael	4/503	Rifleman	Yes
SSG Charles B. Morris	2/503	Squad Leader	No
Pfc. Milton L. Olive	2/503	Rifleman	Yes
SSG Larry S. Pierce	1/503	Squad Leader	Yes

At this writing, the paratroopers of the 503d Infantry are striving to maintain their combat-ready status. The Rock Force stands ready to accomplish any assigned mission with the same esprit de corps displayed by the troopers of the 503d of the past in blood, sweat, and glory.

By the grace of God, may the paratroopers of today and tomorrow experience only the glory of peace among mankind!

503d INFANTRY
(The Rock Regiment)
Heraldic Items

COAT OF ARMS

Shield: Argent, a fort voided azure, pierced to the center by a pile of the second counterchanged with the fort and bearing three parachutes of the first, two and one.

Crest: None.

Motto: The Rock.

Symbolism: The colors, blue and white, are the current and old colors of infantry. The inverted triangle terminating in the broken fort symbolizes the drop on Corregidor during the Luzon campaign, whereas the three parachutes represent the three other campaigns of the organization in World War II.

Distinctive Insignia

The distinctive insignia is the shield and motto of the coat of arms.

LINEAGE

Constituted 24 February 1942 in the army of the United States as the 503d Parachute Infantry (concurrently), First Battalion consolidated with the 503d Parachute Battalion (constituted 14 March 1941 and activated 22 August 1941 at Fort Benning, Georgia) and Second Battalion consolidated with the 504th Parachute Battalion (constituted 14 March 1941 and activated 5 October 1941 at Fort Benning, Georgia) and consolidated units designated as the First and Second Battalions, 503d Parachute Infantry.

Regiment (less First, Second, and Third Battalions) activated 2 March 1942 at Fort Benning, Georgia. Third Battalion activated 8 June 1942 at Fort Bragg, North Carolina. (Second Battalion reorganized and redesignated 2 November 1942 as the Second Battalion, 509th Parachute Infantry, hereafter separate

221

lineage; concurrently, new Second Battalion, 503d Infantry, activated in Australia.) Regiment inactivated 24 December 1945 at Camp Anza, California. Redesignated 1 February 1951 as the 503d Airborne Infantry; concurrently, allotted to the regular army and assigned to the Eleventh Airborne Division. Activated 2 March 1951 at Fort Campbell, Kentucky.

Relieved 1 March 1957 from assignment to the Eleventh Airborne Division; concurrently, reorganized and redesignated as the 503d Infantry, a parent regiment under the Combat Arms Regimental System.

CAMPAIGN PARTICIPATION CREDIT

World War II	Vietnam
New Guinea	Defense
Leyte	Counteroffensive
Luzon (with arrowhead)	Counteroffensive, Phase II
Southern Philippines	(with arrowhead)
	Counteroffensive, Phase III
	Tet Counteroffensive
	Counteroffensive, Phase IV
	Counteroffensive, Phase V
	Counteroffensive, Phase VI
	Tet 69 Counteroffensive
	Summer-Fall 1969
	Winter-Spring 1970
	Sanctuary Counteroffensive
	Counteroffensive, Phase VII
	Consolidation I

DECORATIONS

Presidential Unit Citation (Army), Streamer embroidered *Corregidor* (503d Parachute Infantry cited: WD GO 53, 1945).

Presidential Unit Citation (Army), Streamer embroidered *Bien Hoa* (First Battalion, 503d Infantry cited: DA GO 40, 1966).

Presidential Unit Citation (Army), Streamer embroidered *Phouc Vinh* (Second Battalion, 503d Infantry cited: DA GO 40, 1967).

Presidential Unit Citation (Army), Streamer embroidered *Dak To* (173d Airborne Brigade (less Third Battalion, 503d Infantry) cited: DA GO 42, 1969).

Presidential Unit Citation (Navy), Streamer embroidered *Vietnam 1966* (Fourth Battalion, 503d Infantry cited: DA GO 32, 1973).

Philippine Presidential Unit Citation, Streamer embroidered *17 October 1944 to 4 July 1945* (503d Parachute Infantry cited: DA GO 47, 1950).

Meritorious Unit Commendation. Streamer embroidered *Vietnam 1965-1967* (First, Second, and Fourth Battalions, 503d Infantry cited: DA GO 48, 1968).

Vietnamese Cross of Gallantry with Palm. Streamer embroidered *Vietnam 1965-1970* cited: DA GO 51, 1971 (inclusive dates: 5 May 1965-27 September 1970.)

Vietnamese Civic Actions Medal Unit Citation. Streamer embroidered *Vietnam 1969-1971*, cited: DA GO 5, 1973. Inclusive dates: 15 April 1969-16 March 1971.

First Battalion, 503d Infantry
(The Rock Regiment)

LINEAGE   101st Airborne Division RA

Constituted 14 March 1941 in the army of the United States as Company A, 503d Parachute Battalion. Activated 22 August 1941 at Fort Benning, Georgia. Consolidated 24 February 1942 with Company A, 503d Parachute Infantry (concurrently constituted) and consolidated unit designated as Company A, 503d Parachute Infantry. Inactivated 24 December 1945 at Camp Anza, California. Redesignated 1 February 1951 as Company A, 503d Airborne Infantry, an element of the Eleventh Airborne Division, and allotted to the regular army. Activated 2 March 1951 at Fort Campbell, Kentucky.

Reorganized and redesignated 1 March 1957 as Headquarters and Headquarters Company, First Airborne Battle Group, 503d Infantry, and remained assigned to the Eleventh Airborne Division (organic elements concurrently constituted and activated). Relieved 1 July 1958 from assignment to the Eleventh Airborne Division and assigned to the Twenty-fourth Infantry Division. Relieved 7 January 1959 from assignment to the Twenty-fourth Infantry Division and assigned to the Eighty-second Airborne Division. Relieved 26 March 1963 from assignment to the Eighty-second Airborne Division and assigned to the 173d Airborne Brigade. Reorganized and redesignated 25 June 1963 as the First Battalion, 503d Infantry. Relieved 14 January 1972 from assignment to the 173d Airborne Brigade and assigned to the 101st Airborne Division.

CAMPAIGN PARTICIPATION CREDIT

World War II	Vietnam
New Guinea	Defense
Leyte	Counteroffensive
Luzon (with arrowhead)	Counteroffensive, Phase II
Southern Philippines	Counteroffensive, Phase III
	Tet Counteroffensive
	Counteroffensive, Phase IV
	Counteroffensive, Phase V
	Counteroffensive, Phase VI
	Tet 69 Counteroffensive
	Summer-Fall 1969
	Winter-Spring 1970
	Sanctuary Counteroffensive
	Counteroffensive, Phase VII

DECORATIONS

Presidential Unit Citation (Army), Streamer embroidered *Corregidor* (503d Parachute Infantry cited: WD GO 53, 1945).

Presidential Unit Citation (Army), Streamer embroidered *Bien Hoa* (First Battalion, 503d Infantry cited: DA GO 40, 1966).

Presidential Unit Citation (Army), Streamer embroidered *Dak To* (173d Airborne Brigade, less Third Battalion, 503d Infantry cited: DA GO 42, 1969).

Meritorious Unit Commendation, Streamer embroidered *Vietnam 1965-1967* (First Battalion 503d Infantry cited: DA GO 48, 1968).

Philippine Presidential Unit Citation, Streamer embroidered *17 October 1944 to 4 July 1945* (503d Parachute Infantry cited: DA GO 47, 1950).

Republic of Vietnam Cross of Gallantry with Palm, Streamer embroidered *Vietnam 1965-70* (First Battalion, 503d Infantry cited: DA GO 51, 1971).

Republic of Vietnam Civil Action Honor Medal, First Class, Streamer embroidered *Vietnam 1969-1971* (First Battalion, 503d Infantry cited: DA GO 5, 1973).

Second Battalion, 503d Infantry
(The Rock Regiment)

LINEAGE   101st Airborne Division RA

Constituted 14 March 1941 in the army of the United States as Company B, 503d Parachute Battalion. Activated 22 August 1941 at Fort Benning, Georgia. Consolidated 24 February 1942 with Company B, 503d Parachute Infantry (concurrently constituted) and consolidated unit designated as Company B, 503d Parachute Infantry. Inactivated 24 December 1945 at Camp Anza, California. Redesignated 1 February 1951 as Company B, 503d Airborne Infantry, an element of the Eleventh Airborne Division, and allotted to the regular army. Activated 2 March 1951 at Fort Campbell, Kentucky. Inactivated 1 March 1957 in Germany and relieved from assignment to the Eleventh Airborne Division. Redesignated 1 September 1957 as Headquarters and Headquarters Company, Second Airborne Battle Group, 503d Infantry, assigned to the Eighty-second Airborne Division, and activated at Fort Bragg, North Carolina (organic elements concurrently constituted and activated). Relieved 24 June 1960 from assignment to the Eighty-second Airborne Division and assigned to the Twenty-fifth Infantry Division. Relieved 1 July 1961 from assignment to the Twenty-fifth Infantry Division. Assigned 26 March 1963 to the 173d Airborne Brigade. Reorganized and redesignated 25 June 1963 as the Second Battalion, 503d Infantry. Relieved 3 September 1971 from the 173d Airborne Brigade and assigned to the 101st Airborne Division.

CAMPAIGN PARTICIPATION CREDIT

World War II	Vietnam
New Guinea	Defense
Leyte	Counteroffensive
Luzon (with arrowhead)	Counteroffensive, Phase II
Southern Philippines	(with arrowhead)
	Counteroffensive, Phase III
	Tet Counteroffensive
	Counteroffensive, Phase IV
	Counteroffensive, Phase V
	Tet 69/Counteroffensive
	Summer-Fall 1969
	Winter-Spring, 1970
	Sanctuary Counteroffensive
	Counteroffensive, Phase VII
	Consolidation I

DECORATIONS

Presidential Unit Citation (Army), Streamer embroidered *Corregidor* (503d Parachute Infantry cited: WD DO 53, 1945).

Presidential Unit Citation (Army), Streamer embroidered *Phouc Vinh* (Second Battalion, 503d Infantry cited: DA GO 40, 1967).

Presidential Unit Citation (Army), Streamer embroidered *Dak To* (173d Airborne Brigade, less Third Battalion, 503d Infantry, cited: DA GO 42, 1969).

Meritorious Unit Commendation, Streamer embroidered *Vietnam 1965-1967* (Second Battalion, 503d Infantry cited: DA GO 48, 1968).

Philippine Presidential Unit Citation, Streamer embroidered *17 October 1944 to 4 July 1945* (503d Parachute Infantry cited: DA GO 47, 1950).

Republic of Vietnam Cross of Gallantry with Palm, Streamer embroidered *Vietnam 1965-1970* (Second Battalion, 503d Infantry cited: DA GO 51, 1971).

Republic of Vietnam Civic Action Medal, First Class, Streamer embroidered *Vietnam 1969-1971* (Second Battalion, 503d Infantry cited: DA GO 5, 1973).

Third Battalion, 503d Infantry
(The Rock Regiment)

LINEAGE:

RA
Inactive

Constituted 14 March 1941 in the army of the United States as Company C, 503d Parachute Battalion. Activated 22 August 1941 at Fort Benning, Georgia. Consolidated 24 February 1942 with Company C, 503d Parachute Infantry (concurrently constituted) and consolidated unit designated as Company C, 503d Parachute Infantry. Inactivated 24 December 1945 at Camp Anza, California. Redesignated 1 February 1951 as Company C, 503d Airborne Infantry, an element of the Eleventh Airborne Division, and allotted to the regular army. Activated 2 March 1951 at Fort Campbell, Kentucky.

Inactivated 1 March 1957 in Germany and relieved from assignment to the Eleventh Airborne Division; concurrently, redesignated as Headquarters and Headquarters Company, Third Airborne Battle Group, 503d Infantry. Redesignated 6 February 1967 as Headquarters and Headquarters Company, Third Battalion, 503d Infantry (organic elements concurrently constituted). Battalion activated 1 April 1967 at Fort Bragg, North Carolina, and assigned to the 173d Airborne Brigade. Relieved 14 January 1972 from assignment to the 173d Airborne Brigade and assigned to the 101st Airborne Division. Inactivated 31 July 1972 at Fort Campbell, Kentucky.

CAMPAIGN PARTICIPATION CREDIT

World War II	Vietnam
New Guinea	Counteroffensive, Phase III
Leyte	Tet Counteroffensive
Luzon (with arrowhead)	Counteroffensive, Phase IV
Southern Philippines	Counteroffensive, Phase V
	Counteroffensive, Phase VI
	Tet 69/Counteroffensive
	Summer-Fall 1969
	Winter-Spring 1970
	Sanctuary Counteroffensive
	Counteroffensive, Phase VII
	Consolidation I

DECORATIONS

Presidential Unit Citation (Army) Streamer embroidered *Corregidor* (503d Parachute Infantry cited: WD GO, 53, 1945).

Philippine Presidential Unit Citation, Streamer embroidered *17 October 1944 to 4 July 1945* (503d Parachute Infantry cited: DA GO 47, 1950).

Republic of Vietnam Cross of Gallantry with Palm, Streamer embroidered *Vietnam 1967-70* (Third Battalion, 503d cited: DA GO 51, 1971).

Republic of Vietnam Civil Action Honor Medal, First Class, Streamer embroidered *Vietnam 1969-1971* (Third Battalion, 503d Infantry cited: DA GO 5, 1973).

Fourth Battalion, 503d Infantry
(The Rock Regiment)

RA
Inactive

LINEAGE

Activated 2 November 1942 in the army of the United States in Australia as Company D, 503d Parachute Infantry. Inactivated 24 December 1945 at Camp Anza, California. Redesignated 1 February 1951 as Company D, 503d Airborne Infantry, an element of the Eleventh Airborne Division, and allotted to the regular army. Activated 2 March 1951 at Fort Campbell, Kentucky.

Inactivated 1 March 1957 in Germany and relieved from assignment to the Eleventh Airborne Division: concurrently, redesignated as Headquarters and Headquarters Company, Fourth Airborne Battle Group, 503d Infantry. Redesignated 26 March 1966 as Headquarters and Headquarters Company, Fourth Battalion, 503d Infantry and assigned to the 173d Airborne Brigade (organic elements concurrently constituted). Battalion activated 1 April 1966 at Fort Campbell, Kentucky. Inactivated 3 September 1971 at Fort Campbell, Kentucky.

CAMPAIGN PARTICIPATION CREDIT

World War II	Vietnam
New Guinea	Counteroffensive
Leyte	Counteroffensive, Phase II
Luzon (with arrowhead)	Counteroffensive, Phase III
Southern Philippines	Tet Counteroffensive
	Counteroffensive, Phase IV
	Counteroffensive, Phase V
	Counteroffensive, Phase VI
	Tet 69/Counteroffensive
	Summer-Fall 1969
	Winter-Spring 1970
	Sanctuary Counteroffensive
	Counteroffensive, Phase VII
	Consolidation I

DECORATIONS

Presidential Unit Citation (Army), Streamer embroidered *Corregidor* (503d Parachute Infantry cited: WD GO 53, 1945).

Presidential Unit Citation (Army), Streamer embroidered *Dak To* (173d Airborne Brigade, less Third Battalion, 503d Infantry, cited: DA GO 42, 1969).

Presidential Unit Citation (Navy), Streamer embroidered *Vietnam 1966* (Fourth Battalion, 503d Infantry cited: DA GO 32, 1973).

Philippine Presidential Unit Citation, Streamer embroidered *17 October 1944 to 4 July 1945* (503d Parachute Infantry cited: DA GO 47, 1950).

Meritorious Unit Commendation, Streamer embroidered *Vietnam 1966-1967* (Fourth Battalion, 503d Infantry cited: DA GO 48, 1968).

Republic of Vietnam Cross of Gallantry with Palm, Streamer embroidered *Vietnam 1966-1970* (Fourth Battalion, 503d Infantry cited: DA GO 51 , 1971).

Republic of Vietnam Civil Action Honor Medal, First Class, Streamer embroidered *Vietnam 1969-1971* (Fourth Battalion, 503d Infantry cited: DA GO 5, 1973).

COMPANY C, 161st ENGINEER BATTALION
Lineage and Honors

LINEAGE

Constituted 12 September 1942 in the army of the United States as Company C, 161st Engineer Battalion.

Activated 15 November 1942 at Fort Bliss, Texas, as Company C, 161st Engineer Squadron.

Redesignated 1 May 1943 as the 161st Airborne Engineer Battalion.

Redesignated 2 April 1945 as Company C, 161st Parachute Engineers.

Inactivated 25 October 1945 at Negros Island, Philippine Islands.

Redesignated 24 July 1946 as the 161st Engineer Parachute Company.

Reactivated 1 August 1946 at Fort Benning, Georgia.

Inactivated 14 November 1946 at Fort Benning, Georgia.

Reactivated 15 October 1957 as the 161st Engineer Company.

Inactivated 15 May 1963 in Korea.

CAMPAIGN PARTICIPATION CREDIT
   World War II
      New Guinea
      Leyte
      Luzon (with arrowhead)
      Southern Philippines

DECORATIONS

Presidential Unit Citation (Army), Streamer embroidered *Corregidor* cited: WD GO 53, 1945.

Philippine Presidential Unit Citation, Streamer embroidered *17 October 1944 to 4 July 1945* cited: DA GO 47, 1950.

462d FIELD ARTILLERY BATTALION
Lineage and Honors

LINEAGE
Constituted 25 February 1943 in the army of the United States as the 462d Parachute Field Artillery Battalion.

Activated 15 June 1943 at Camp Mackall, North Carolina.

Inactivated 21 December 1945 at Camp Anza, California.

Redesignated 17 December 1946 as the 462d Field Artillery Battalion, alloted to the Organized Reserves, and assigned to the Second Army.

Activated 23 December 1946 with Headquarters at Toledo, Ohio (Location of headquarters changed 4 June 1947 to Canton, Ohio).

(Organized Reserves redesignated 25 March 1948 as the Organized Reserve Corps; redesignated 9 July 1952 as the Army Reserve).

Inactivated 1 June 1959 at Canton, Ohio.

CAMPAIGN PARTICIPATION CREDIT
World War II
New Guinea
Leyte
Luzon (with arrowhead)
Southern Philippines

DECORATIONS
Presidential Unit Citation (Army), Streamer embroidered *Corregidor* cited: WD GO 53, 1945.

Philippine Presidential Unit Citation, Streamer embroidered *17 October 1944 to 4 July 1945*, cited: DA GO 47, 1950.

APO 321
24 March 1945

SUBJECT: Letters of Commendation

TO: All Officers and Enlisted Men of the 503d Regimental Combat Team, APO
    321.

 1. It is with the greatest pride of my life that I pass on to you the letters reproduced and attached to this letter.

 2. I am fully aware of the many sacrifices and excellent performance of the officers and enlisted men. I believe that the glowing tribute given to the entire Combat Team is well deserved.

 3. May the success we have achieved establish standards from which we will not fail.

GEORGE M. JONES
Colonel, 503d Parachute Infantry
Commanding

Headquarters Sixth Army
Office of the Commanding General

AG 201.22   8 March 1945

SUBJECT: Commendation
TO   : Commanding Officer, 503d Parachute Regiment, APO 73
THRU   : Commanding General, XI Corps, APO 471

     1. Upon the release of the 503d Parachute Regiment from the Sixth Army for another mission, I desire to express to you and to your officers and men my grateful appreciation and official commendation for the magnificent performance of the regiment in the recapture of Corregidor.

     2. The daring aerial assault of the 503d Parachute Regiment into the heart of this historic island fortress on the morning of 16 February 1945, and the subsequent destruction of the strong Japanese forces which defended it with the utmost stubbornness from tunnels and caves, have added a glorious page to the history of the Philippine Campaign. The courage, skill, and gallantry exhibited by all ranks of the regiment is in keeping with the highest traditions of our army and should be a source of great and justifiable pride to each of its members.

     3. The departure of the 503d Parachute Regiment from my command is a source of deep regret to me, and I wish each member of the regiment good luck and God speed.

                                     (Signed) WALTER KRUEGER
                                     Lieutenant General, U.S. Army
                                          Commanding

AG 330.13 A   9 March 1945

Subject: Services of the 503d Parachute Infantry RCT in the landing and reduc-
      tion of Corregidor Island

To   : Commanding General, Eighth Army, APO 343

    1. The performance of the 503d Parachute RCT in the recapture of Cor-
regidor has been recognized by a Presidential Citation which was bestowed
upon all members of the organization by General MacArthur.

    2. This RCT came under my command upon its landing on Corregidor.
I observed it intimately throughout the operation. The job, in my opinion, was
the best handled of any that I have seen during my military career. Both officers
and enlisted men were thoroughly competent, knew what there was to do and
did not hesitate in any instance to close with the enemy and do it. After the
landing, the reduction of Corregidor required carefully planned and methodical
work. The regimental commander, Colonel George M. Jones, knew his job and
the tools with which he had to work. Throughout the operation there was the
most careful planning and fine execution of the methodical attack he made to
clear the island of Nips. The organization clearly showed that it had been well
trained, that its personnel was of a high type and that it was willing and anxious to fight.

    3. I would welcome this organization in any command which I might
hold and for any job, ground or airborne.

(Signed) C.P. HALL
Major General, U.S. Army
Commanding

Headquarters Eighth Army
APO 343

TO   : Commanding Officer, 503d Parachute Infantry Regimental Combat
Team, APO 321

It is a pleasure to add my gratification and appreciation to this recognition of the excellent performance of duty by the personnel of your organization.

(Signed) L. Eichelberger
Lieutenant General, U.S. Army
Commanding

Headquarters
United States Army Forces in the Far East

GENERAL ORDERS)   A.P.O. 501
No .... 112)   8 May 1945

UNIT CITATION

By direction of the President, under the provisions of Executive Order No. 9396 (Sec I, Bulletin 22, WD, 1943) superseding Executive Order No. 9075 (Sec III, Bulletin 2, WD, 1942) and Section IV, Circular No. 333, WD, 1943, the following unit is cited by the Commanding General, United States Army Forces in the Far East:

The 503d Parachute Infantry Regiment with the following attached units:

462d Parachute Field Artillery Battalion
3d Battalion, 34th Infantry Regiment
Company C, 161st Parachute Engineer Battalion
18th Portable Surgical Hospital (Reinforced)
3d Platoon, Antitank Company, 34th Infantry Regiment
3d Platoon, Cannon Company, 34th Infantry Regiment
3d Platoon, Company C 3d Engineer Battalion
Company A 34th Infantry Regiment
3d Platoon, Company C, 24th Medical Battalion
Detachment, Service Company, 34th Infantry Regiment
Battery A, 950th AAA (AW) Battalion
174th Ordnance Service Detachment (Bomb Disposal Squad)
Detachment, 592d Engineer Boat and Shore Regiment
Detachment, 98th Signal Battalion
Detachment, 1st Platoon, 603d Tank Company
Detachment, 592d Joint Assault Signal Company
Detachment, 6th Support Air Party
Combat Photo Unit A, GHQ Signal Section
Combat Photo Unit Q, GHQ Signal Section

These units, organized as a task force, distinguished themselves by extraordinary heroism and outstanding performance of duty in action against the enemy from 16 to 28 February 1945. This force was directed to seize the enemy held island fortress of Corregidor, one of the most difficult missions of the Pacific War. A long prepared and fanatical enemy, strongly entrenched in numerous tunnels, caves, dugouts, and crevices, awaited the assault in commanding and extensively fortified positions. The small dropping area for the parachutists was bordered extensively by sheer cliffs, with resultant variable air currents and eddies; and previous bombings and naval gunfire had cut trees and shrubs close above ground, creating hazardous stakes which threatened to impale descending troops. The approach by sea, through shallow water known to be mined, led to a beach protected by land mines. At 0830 on 16 February, the initial

assault was made by parachute drop on terrain littered with debris and rubble. Heavy casualties were sustained. Two hours later the amphibious elements advanced by sea through the mine field to the beach; and, though many lives were lost and much equipment destroyed by exploding mines, this element moved rapidly inland and under heavy enemy fire seized Malinta Hill. Meanwhile, the Airborne elements, though subjected to intense enemy fire and suffering increasing casualties, were organized into an aggressive fighting force as a result of the initiative of commanders of small units. Advancing doggedly against fanatical resistance, they had by nightfall, secured "The Top of the Rock," their initial objective. On the following morning, the entire task force began a systematic reduction of enemy positions and the annihilation of defending forces. Innumerable enemy tunnels and caves were sealed by demolitions after hand to hand fighting, only to have the enemy emerge elsewhere through an intricate system of inter-connecting passageways. Direct fire of our supporting weapons, employed to seal tunnels, and caves, often resulted in the explosion of enemy emplaced demolitions and ammunition dumps, causing heavy casualties to our troops. Under increasing pressure, the enemy, cut off from reinforcements, exploded demolitions in tunnels, destroying themselves as well as elements of our task force. At the completion of this desperate and violent struggle, 4,509 enemy dead were counted. Prisoners totalled nineteen. Throughout the operation all elements of the task force, combat and service troops alike, displayed heroism of the highest degree. Parachuting to earth or landing on mined beaches, they attacked savagely against a numerically superior enemy, defeated him completely, and seized the fortress. Their magnificent courage, tenacity, and gallantry, avenged the victims of Corregidor of 1942, and achieved a significant victory for the United States Army.
FEXD 200.6
By: COMMAND OF GENERAL MACARTHUR

RICHARD J. MARSHALL
Major General, General Staff Corps
Chief of Staff

OFFICIAL:
    /s/R.E. Fraile
    R.E. Fraile
    Colonel, A.G.D., Adjutant General

PRESIDENTIAL CITATION

X-BATTLE HONORS. As authorized by Executive Order 9396 (Sec. I, WD Bul. 22, 1943), superseding Executive Order 9075 (Sec. III, WD Bul. 11, 1942), the following unit is cited by the War Department under the provisions of Section IV, WD, Circular 333, 1943, in the name of the President of the United States as public evidence of deserved honor and distinction. The citation reads as follows:

The 503d Parachute Infantry Regiment, with the following attached units:
462d Parachute Field Artillery Battalion
3d Battalion, 34th Infantry Regiment
Company "C" 161st Parachute Engineer Battalion
    (Now 161st Airborne Engineer Company)
18th Portable Surgical Hospital (Reinforced)
3d Platoon, Antitank Company, 34th Infantry Regiment
3d Platoon, Cannon Company, 34th Infantry Regiment
3d Platoon, Company "C" 3d Engineer Battalion
Company "A" 34th Infantry Regiment
3d Platoon, Company "C," 24th Medical Battalion
Detachment, Service Company, 34th Infantry Regiment
Battery "A," 950th AAA (AW) Battalion
174th Ordnance Service Detachment (Bomb Disposal Squad)
Detachment, 592d Engineer Boat and Shore Regiment
Detachment, 98th Signal Battalion
Detachment, 1st Platoon, 603d Tank Company
Detachment, 592d Joint Assault Signal Company
Detachment, 6th Support Air Party
Combat Photo Unit "A," GHQ Signal Section
Combat Photo Unit "Q," GHQ Signal Section

These units, organized as a task force, distinguished themselves by extraordinary heroism and outstanding performance of duty in action against the enemy from 16 to 28 February 1945. This force was directed to seize the enemy held island fortress of Corregidor, one of the most difficult missions of the Pacific War. A long prepared and fanatical enemy, strongly entrenched in numerous tunnels, caves, dugouts, and crevices, awaited the assault in commanding and extensively fortified positions. The small dropping area for the parachutists was bordered extensively by sheer cliffs, with resultant variable air currents and eddies; and previous bombings and naval gunfire had cut trees and shrubs close above ground, creating hazardous stakes which threatened to impale descending troops. The approach by sea, through shallow water known to be mined, led to a beach protected by land mines. At 0830 on 16 February, the initial assault was made by parachute drop on terrain littered with debris and rubble. Heavy casualties were sustained. Two hours later the amphibious elements advanced by sea through the mine field to the beach; and, though many lives were lost and much equipment destroyed by exploding mines, this element

239

moved rapidly inland and under heavy enemy fire seized Malinta Hill. Meanwhile, the Airborne element though subjected to intense enemy fire and suffering increasing casualties, were organized into an aggressive fighting force as a result of the initiative of commanders of small units. Advancing doggedly against fanatical resistance, they had by nightfall, secured "The Top of the Rock," their initial objective. On the following morning, the entire task force began a systematic reduction of enemy positions and the annihilation of defending forces. Innumerable enemy tunnels and caves were sealed by demolitions after hand to hand fighting, only to have the enemy emerge elsewhere through an intricate system of inter-connecting passageways. Direct fire of our supporting weapons, employed to seal tunnels and caves, often resulted in the explosion of enemy emplaced demolitions and ammunition dumps, causing heavy casualties to our troops. Under increasing pressure, the enemy, cut off from reinforcements, exploded demolitions in tunnels, destroying themselves as well as elements of our task force. At the completion of this desperate and violent struggle, 4,509 enemy dead were counted. Prisoners totalled nineteen. Throughout the operation all elements of the task force, combat and service troops alike, displayed heroism of the highest degree. Parachuting to earth or landing on mined beaches, they attacked savagely against a numerically superior enemy, defeated him completely, and seized the fortress. Their magnificent courage, tenacity, and gallantry, avenged the victims of Corregidor of 1942, and achieved a significant victory for the United States Army.

OFFICIAL:
    EDWARD F. WITSELL
    Major General
    Acting The Adjutant General

    G.C. Marshall
    Chief of Staff

PRESIDENTIAL UNIT CITATION (ARMY) Award of the Presidential Unit Citation (Army) by the President of the United States of America to the following unit of the Armed Forces of the United States is confirmed in accordance with paragraph 194, AR 672-5-1. The text of the citation, signed by President Lyndon B. Johnson on 4 August 1967, reads as follows:

By virtue of the authority invested in me as President of the United States and as Commander in Chief of the Armed Forces of the United States I have today awarded the Presidential Unit Citation (Army) for extraordinary heroism to:

THE SECOND BATTALION (AIRBORNE), 503D INFANTRY, 173D AIRBORNE BRIGADE (SEPARATE) AND ATTACHED UNITS:

The 2d Battalion (Airborne), 503d Infantry, 173d Airborne Brigade (Separate) with attachments, is cited for extraordinary heroism in connection with military operations against a hostile force near Phouc Vinh, Republic of Vietnam, on 16 March 1966. The Battalion was participating as part of a large force on a search and destroy mission sweeping a portion of War Zone "D" during operation "Silver City," and had been in contact with small groups of Viet Cong during four days of operations in the dense jungle area. On the morning of 16 March the Battalion was deployed in a defensive perimeter in preparation for resuming operations. At approximately 0700 hours a patrol from Company "B" had begun to move from its positions to initiate action against the enemy. At the same time, a resupply helicopter was descending into the landing zone located within the Battalion perimeter. Suddenly the helicopter came under heavy automatic weapon fire from the enemy and was destroyed, and the jungle erupted in gunfire all around the defensive perimeter. The leading elements of the patrol were caught in this initial concentration of murderous fire. The Viet Cong forces, supported by a tremendous volume of automatic weapons, mortar, and artillery fire, attacked all around the perimeter. The enemy exerted considerable force at a point between Company "A" and Company "C" in an effort to effect a breakthrough at this location. Personnel of the two companies, including the wounded, steadfastly remained in their positions, responded at close quarters with fire that was both deadly and accurate, and succeeded in breaking up the determined enemy attack. Maintaining continuous contact around the perimeter, the Viet Cong launched another strong attack to breach the defense. This effort was focused on the center and left flank of Company "B." Time and time again the Viet Cong charged the positions, but the indefatigable and determined Paratroopers of Company "B" exacted heavy casualties and beat back the enemy attackers. Regrouping and concentrating their forces, the Viet Cong made a final assault on the flank of Company "C." This time the desperate Viet Cong ran forward in waves under the protective umbrella of a heavy volume of their supporting fires. Again, however, the gallant and resolute Paratroopers repulsed the enemy, inflicting severe losses, completely disrupting his efforts to destroy the Battalion, and forcing the Viet

Cong to withdraw. Documentary evidence indicates that the attacking force consisted of the entire Viet Cong 271st Main Force Regiment, reinforced by two artillery battalions. A total of 303 Viet Cong dead were confirmed by body count. An estimated additional 150 were killed and numerous Viet Cong were wounded during the battle. The courageous and exemplary actions of the 2d Battalion (Airborne), 503d Infantry, in decisively defeating a determined, numerically superior, and well trained and equipped enemy force reflect great credit on the members of the unit and are in keeping with the finest traditions of the United States Army. By Order of the Secretary of the Army:

CREIGHTON W. ABRAMS
General, United States Army
Chief of Staff

OFFICIAL:
VERNE L. BOWERS
Major General, United States Army
The Adjutant General

General Orders   HEADQUARTERS
No. 42   DEPARTMENT OF THE ARMY

THE PRESIDENTIAL UNIT CITATION. Award of the Presidential Unit
Citation (Army), by the President of the United States of America to the following units of the Armed Forces of the United States is confirmed in accordance
with paragraph 194, AR 672-5-1. The text of the citation, signed by President
Richard Nixon 22 May 1969, reads as follows:

By virtue of the authority invested in me as President of the United States
and as Commander in Chief of the Armed Forces of the United States, I have
today awarded

THE PRESIDENTIAL UNIT CITATION (ARMY)
FOR EXTRAORDINARY HEROISM
TO THE
173d AIRBORNE BRIGADE (SEPARATE)
(LESS THE 3D BATTALION (AIRBORNE), 503D INFANTRY
AND ATTACHED UNITS)

The attached and assigned units of the 173d Airborne Brigade (Separate)
distinguished themselves by extraordinary heroism in connection with military
operations against an armed enemy during Operation MacArthur in Kontum
Province, Republic of Vietnam from 6 November to 23 November 1967. The
173d Airborne Brigade (Separate) and assigned units moved to Dak To in the
central highlands during the period 1 to 6 November 1967 with the mission
of initiating search-and-destroy operations in conjunction with elements of the
United States 4th Infantry Division and allied forces. Opposed by the elite 24th,
32nd, 66th, and 174th North Vietnamese Infantry Regiments supported by the
40th Artillery Regiment of the 1st North Vietnamese Infantry Division, the 173d
Airborne Brigade (Separate) and its assigned and attached units displayed ex-
ceptional gallantry, determination, esprit de corps and professional skill in
defeating a heavily armed, well trained, well disciplined and numerically
superior enemy operating largely from well-prepared and heavily fortified positions. From the combat assault on Hill 823 on 6 November to the final victory
on Hill 875 on Thanksgiving day, the Battle of Dak To was characterized by
countless displays of gallantry, relentless aggressiveness and quick reaction on
the part of all United States Forces involved. During the establishment and
defense of fire support bases and combat assaults into enemy strongholds, individual accounts of unhesitating courage and tenacity to achieve final victory
were made a part of history. For 18 days of continuous combat at point-blank
range, the friendly forces relentlessly pressed the attack against seemingly in-
vulnerable fortified positions until they were reduced and the enemy destroyed.
The separate and combined actions of the Brigade resulted in a hard-fought
and unprecedented victory, rendering the 174th North Vietnamese Infantry
Regiment combat-ineffectives. The Allied defeat of the 1st North Vietnamese
Division frustrated a major enemy attempt to control the Dak To area and the

surrounding highlands. The accomplishment of this mission by the officers and troopers of the 173d Airborne Brigade and assigned and attached units was in keeping with the highest tradition of the military service and reflects great credit upon their units and the United States Army. By Order of the Secretary of the Army:

CREIGHTON W. ABRAMS
General, United States Army
Chief of Staff

OFFICIAL:
VERNE L. BOWERS
Major General, United States Army
The Adjutant General

PRESIDENTIAL UNIT CITATION (NAVY). Award of the Presidential Unit Citation (Navy) to the following United States Army unit for the period indicated is confirmed in accordance with paragraph 194, AR 672-5-1.

4TH BATTALION, 503d INFANTRY (For the period 7 October 1966 to 15 September 1967).

"The President of the United States takes pleasure in presenting the

PRESIDENTIAL UNIT CITATION
TO THE
THIRD MARINE DIVISION (REINFORCED)

for service as set forth in the following:

CITATION:

For extraordinary heroism and outstanding performance of duty in action against the North Vietnamese Army and Viet Cong forces in the Republic of Vietnam from 8 March 1965 to 15 September 1967. Throughout this period, the Third Marine Division (Reinforced), operating in the five northernmost provinces of the Republic of Vietnam, successfully executed its three-fold mission of occupying and defending key terrain, seeking out and destroying the enemy, and conducting an intensive pacification program. Operating in an area bordered by over 200 miles of South China Sea coastline, the mountainous Laotian border and the Demilitarized Zone, the Third Marine Division (Reinforced) successfully executed eighty major combat operations, carrying the battle to the enemy, destroying many of his forces, and capturing thousands of tons of weapons and material. In addition to these major operations, more than 125,000 offensive counterguerrilla actions, ranging from squad patrols and ambushes to company-sized search and destroy operations, were conducted in both the coastal ricelands and the mountainous jungle inland. These bitterly contested actions routed the enemy from his well-entrenched positions, denied him access to his source of food, restricted his freedom of movement, and removed his influence from the heavily populated areas. In numerous operations, the Third Marine Division (Reinforced) demonstrated the great efficacy of combined operations with units of the Army of the Republic of Vietnam. In July 1966, the Third Marine Division (Reinforced) moved to the north to counter major elements of the North Vietnamese Army moving across the Demilitarized Zone into the Province of Quang Tri; its units fought a series of savage battles against the enemy, repeatedly distinguishing themselves, and, time and again, forcing the enemy to retreat across the Demilitarized Zone. Imbued with an unrelenting combat spirit and initiative and undeterred by heavy hostile artillery and mortar fire, extremely difficult terrain, incessant heat and monsoon rains, the Third Marine Division (Reinforced), employing courageous ground, heliborne, and amphibious assaults, complemented by intense and accurate air, artillery, and naval gunfire support, inflicted great losses on the enemy and denied him the political and military victory he sought to achieve at any cost. The outstanding courage, resourcefulness, and aggressive fighting spirit of the officers and men of the Third Marine Division (Reinforced) in battle after battle against a well-equipped and well-trained enemy, often numerically superior in strength, and the great humanitarianism constantly shown to the peoples of the Republic of Vietnam, reflected great credit upon the Marine Corps and were in keeping with the highest traditions of the United States Naval Service."

By Order of the Secretary of the Army:

CREIGHTON W. ABRAMS
General, United States Army
Chief of Staff

OFFICIAL:
VERNE L. BOWERS
Major General, United States Army
The Adjutant General

General Orders
No. 40

HEADQUARTERS
DEPARTMENT OF THE ARMY
Washington, D.C., 31 October 1966

I – DISTINGUISHED UNIT CITATION

Award of the Distinguished Unit Citation by the President of the United States of America to the following units of the Armed Forces of the United States is confirmed in accordance with paragraph 194, AR 672-5-1. The text of the citation as announced by President Lyndon B. Johnson on 20 June 1966 reads as follows:

"By virtue of the authority invested in me as President of the United States and as Commander-in-Chief of the Armed Forces of the United States I have today (20 June 1966) awarded the Distinguished Unit Citation (First Oak Leaf Cluster) for extraordinary heroism to: THE 1ST BATTALION (AIRBORNE), 503D INFANTRY, 173D AIRBORNE BRIGADE (SEPARATE) UNITED STATES ARMY and the Attached Units:

Headquarters and Headquarters Company

Company A, Company B, and Company C of the 1st Battalion (Airborne), 503d Infantry, 173d Airborne Brigade (Separate).

The foregoing companies of the units attached to THE 1ST BATTALION (AIRBORNE), 503D INFANTRY, 173D AIRBORNE BRIGADE (SEPARATE) distinguished themselves by extraordinary heroism in action against hostile forces in the vicinity of Bien Hoa, Republic of Vietnam, on 8 November 1965. The morning after the Battalion had conducted a search operation and learned from patrols that a strong hostile element was in the general area, COMPANY C, the lead Company, encountered a well-entrenched and camouflaged Viet Cong force. When the insurgents opened fire with a volume of automatic weapons fire, the United States forces retaliated. As the battle grew in intensity and it became evident that COMPANY C had engaged a battalion-size Viet Cong element which attempted to surround the flanks of this American unit, COMPANY B was committed to secure the right flank of COMPANY C. Simultaneously, elements of COMPANY A attacked the left flank of the insurgent force. Although COMPANY B met strong resistance and fought at close range in a dense jungle area, it succeeded in penetrating the hostile circle around COMPANY C. Then, as COMPANY B's open flank was being enveloped, the brave men of this Company broke a hostile encirclement for the second time. Despite the constant Viet Cong assaults, their continual attacks in human waves, and the many casualties sustained by the American units, the gallant and determined troops of the 1st BATTALION (AIRBORNE) 503d INFANTRY repulsed the Viet Cong and inflicted severe losses upon them. After a battle which raged throughout the afternoon, elements of the 1ST BATTALION (AIRBORNE), 503D INFANTRY defeated a numerically superior hostile force and on the following morning, counted four hundred and three Viet Cong dead in the immediate area. The devotion to duty, perseverance, and extraordinary heroism displayed by these members of THE 1ST BATTALION (AIRBORNE), 503D INFANTRY and the attached units are in the highest traditions of the United States Army and reflect great credit upon themselves and the armed forces of their country." By Order of the Secretary of the Army:

CREIGHTON W. ABRAMS
General, United States Army
Chief of Staff

OFFICIAL:
VERNE L. BOWERS
Major General, United States Army
The Adjutant General

General Orders
No. 48

HEADQUARTERS
DEPARTMENT OF THE ARMY
Washington, D.C., 13 September 1968

MERITORIOUS UNIT COMMENDATION. By direction of the Secretary of the Army, under the provisions of paragraph 203, AR 672-5-1, the Meritorious Unit Commendation is awarded to the following named units of the United States Army for exceptionally meritorious achievement in the performance of outstanding service during the periods indicated:
The citation reads as follows:

THE 173d AIRBORNE BRIGADE (SEPARATE) and its assigned and attached units:
    1st Battalion, 503d Infantry (Airborne)
    2d Battalion, 503d Infantry (Airborne)
    4th Battalion, 503d Infantry (Airborne)

For exceptionally meritorious achievement in the performance of outstanding service: the 173D AIRBORNE BRIGADE (SEPARATE) and its assigned and attached units distinguished themselves in the conduct of military operations in the Republic of Vietnam during the period 5 May 1965 to 4 May 1967. As the first ground combat unit in-country, the brigade conducted extensive combat maneuvers in the Bien Hoa area and in the Viet Cong strongholds of War Zone D and the Iron Triangle. In every confrontation with the stubborn insurgents, the 173d AIRBORNE BRIGADE (SEPARATE) displayed marked aggressiveness which enabled them to neutralize enemy strongholds and capture thousands of logistical items. In addition to remarkable skill and tenacity in combat, the sky soldiers of the brigade carried on an extensive civic action program characterized by sincere compassion for the suppressed local populace. During each of the brigade's combat operations, the sky soldiers immeasurably aided the allied counterinsurgency effort by winning the hearts and minds of the Vietnamese people. The remarkable proficiency and devotion to duty displayed by members of the 173D AIRBORNE BRIGADE (SEPARATE) are in keeping with the highest traditions of the military service and reflect distinct credit upon themselves and the Armed Forces of the United States.
By Order of the Secretary of the Army:

CREIGHTON W. ABRAMS
General, United States Army
Chief of Staff

OFFICIAL:
    VERNE L. BOWERS
    Major General, United States Army
    The Adjutant General

General Orders   DEPARTMENT OF THE ARMY
No. 47   Washington 25, D.C., 28 December 1950

PHILIPPINE PRESIDENTIAL UNIT CITATION

     I — GENERAL — 1. Under paragraph 2, AR 260-15 the award of the Philippine Presidential Unit Citation to the units of the Armed Forces of the United States listed herein in recognition of the participation in the war against the Japanese Empire during the periods 7 December 1941 to 10 May 1942, inclusive, and 17 October 1944 to 4 July 1945, inclusive, is confirmed.

*   *   *

     II — LIST OF UNITS

*   *   *

     503d Parachute Infantry Regimental Combat Team

*   *   *

     By Order of the Secretary of the Army:

                                   J. LAWTON COLLINS
                                         Chief of Staff
                                   United States Army

OFFICIAL:
     EDWARD F. WITSELL
     Major General, USA
     The Adjutant General

General Orders
No. 51

VIETNAMESE CROSS OF GALLANTRY WITH PALM. The award of the Vietnamese Cross of Gallantry with Palm by the Republic of Vietnam to units listed below is confirmed. (5 May 1965 through 26 September 1970).

173D AIRBORNE BRIGADE and its assigned units:
1st Battalion, 503d Infantry
2d Battalion, 503d Infantry
3d Battalion, 503d Infantry (For the period 22 October 1967 to 26 September 1970)
4th Battalion, 503d Infantry

The citation reads as follows:

The 173d United States Airborne Brigade is a combat-experienced unit, composed of courageous soldiers who always display an enthusiastic anti-Communistic spirit. During its five years of fighting in the Republic of Vietnam, the 173d Airborne Brigade has conducted 15 large-scale operations on battlefields in Military Regions 2 and 3, including Operations IRON TRIANGLE (1965) in the Iron-Triangle area of Binh Duong; HUMP (1965) in War Zone D; NEW LIFE (1965) in Khanh Province; SMASH I (1965) in Phuoc Tuy; MARAUDER (1966) in Han Nghia; CRIMP (1966) in Binh Duong; SILVER CITY (1966) in War Zone D; Bien Hoa, and Long Khanh; NIAGARA/CEDAR FALLS (1967) in the Iron Triangle area; JUNCTION CITY ALTERNATE and JUNCTION II (1967) in War Zone C; GREELEY and MACARTHUR (1967) in Dakato; BOLLING (1969) in Tuy Hoa; WALKER (1969) in An Khe; COCHISE (1969) in Bong Son; and WASHINGTON GREEN (1969) in Binh Dinh, inflicting heavy losses upon the enemy, both in personnel and his war-making material. Furthermore, the 173d United States Airborne Brigade coordinated with and effectively assisted Republic of Vietnam Army Forces units in carrying out civil affairs, pacification and rural development programs in its area of responsibility, such as building military dependent housing areas and hospitals; digging wells; providing desks, chairs, and student materials for schools; and repairing roads, bridges, and culverts, bringing about superior results. The 173d United States Airborne Brigade has made substantial contributions to the struggle against the Communist aggressors in the Republic of Vietnam.

By Order of the Secretary of the Army:

CREIGHTON W. ABRAMS
General, United States Army
Chief of Staff

OFFICAL:
VERNE L. BOWERS
Major General, United States Army
The Adjutant General

General Orders
No. 5

DEPARTMENT OF THE ARMY
Washington, D.C., 5 February 1973

REPUBLIC OF VIETNAM CIVIL ACTIONS MEDAL UNIT CITA-
TION. The award of the Civil Actions Medal Unit Citation by the Republic
of Vietnam to units listed below is confirmed.

For service from 15 April 1969 to 16 March 1971. 173D AIRBORNE
BRIGADE and its assigned and attached units:
    1st Battalion, 503d Infantry
    2d Battalion, 503d Infantry
    3d Battalion, 503d Infantry
    4th Battalion, 503d Infantry
By Order of the Secretary of the Army:

CREIGHTON W. ABRAMS
General, United States Army
Chief of Staff

OFFICIAL:
    VERNE L. BOWERS
    Major General, United States Army
    The Adjutant General

Appendix C
MEMBERS OF THE TEST PLATOON

*An abbreviation of the orders to form the Test Platoon.

HEADQUARTERS TWENTY-NINTH INFANTRY (RIFLE)
OFFICE OF THE REGIMENTAL COMMANDER

Fort Benning, Georgia
1 July, 1940

SPECIAL ORDERS)
No.   127)

5. Pursuant to authority granted by letter Headquarters The Infantry School, file No. 580, subject: "Test Platoon for duty with Infantry Board," dated 1 July 1940, the following named officers and enlisted men of the 29th Infantry are detailed on special duty with the Infantry Board, Fort Benning, Georgia, and will report to the president thereof for duty:

First Lieutenant William T. Ryder, 29th Infantry
Second Lieutenant James Bassett
Sergeant John M. Haley, 6375843, Company A
Sergeant Benedict F. Jacquay, 6657783, Company C
Sergeant Grady A. Roberts, 6382894, Company D
Sergeant B. Wade, 6372146, Company F
Sergeant Norman J. McCullough, 6379058, Company M
Sergeant Lemuel T. Pitts, 6395609, Company B
Private Farrish F. Cornelius, 6399726, Headquarters Co.
Pvt 1cl Specl 6th Cl Obie C. Wilson, 6966177, Headquarters Co.
Pvt 1cl Specl 6th Cl Donald L. Colee, 6393903, Service Company
Private William N. King, 6391164, Hq & Hq Det., 1st Bn.
Pvt 1cl Addison L. Houston, 6384962, Company A
Pvt 1cl Mitchel Guilbeau, 6399296, Company A
Pvt 1cl Joseph L. Peters, 6399384, Company A
Private Thad P. Selman, 6971792, Company B
Private Hugh A. Tracy, 7003695, Company B
Private Jules Corbin, 6386052, Company B
Private Joseph E. Doucet, 6387916, Company C
Pvt 1cl Louie E. Davis, 6966798, Company C
Pvt 1cl Johnnie A. Ellis, 6967763, Company C
Pvt Specl 6th Cl Robert H. Poudert, 6972398, Company D
Private Sydney C. Kerksis, 6388134, Company D
Pvt 1cl Specl 4th Cl Tyerus F. Adams, Company D

Pvt lcl Tullis Nolan, 6927494, Hq & Hq Det., 2d Bn.
Pvt lcl Benjamin C. Reese, 6969901, Company E
Pvt lcl Raymond G. Smith, 6387925, Company E
Pvt lcl Willie F. Brown, 6398865, Company E
Pvt lcl Thurman L. Weaks, 6966916, Company F
Pvt lcl Specl 6th Cl John M. Kitchens, 6394975, Company F
Pvt lcl Louie O. Skipper, 6963804, Company F
Pvt lcl Specl 6th Cl Alsie L. Rutland, 6963778, Company G
Private Frank Kasell, Jr., 6971611, Company G
Private Robert E. Shepherd, 6970095, Company G
Pvt lcl Specl 4th Cl John F. Pursley, Jr., 6396514, Company H
Pvt lcl Lester C. McLaney, 6966537, Company H
Pvt lcl Specl 6th Cl Aubrey Eberhardt, 6920642, Company H
Private Ernest L. Dilburn, 6392470, Hq & Hq Det., 3d Bn.
Private Leo C. Brown, 6384060, Company I
Pvt Specl 6th Cl Albert P. Robinson, 6972295, Company I
Pvt lcl Floy Burkhalter, 6966968, Company I
Pvt 1 Cl Edward Martin, 6963787, Company K
Private John O. Modisett, 6395076, Company K
Private Code E. Barnett, Jr., 6928902, Company K
Private John E. Borom, 6393663, Company L
Pvt 1Cl Specl 6th Cl George W. Ivy, 6399227, Company L
Pvt 1Cl Specl 4th Cl John A. Ward, 6379123, Company L
Pvt 1Cl Specl 6th Cl Steve Voils, Jr., 6967738, Company M
Pvt 1Cl Specl 6th Cl Richard J. Kelly, 6928566, Company M
Private Bura M. Tisdale, 6394981, Company M
By Order of Colonel Griswold:

OFFICIAL:
(Signed)
William H. Craig
1st Lt., 29th Infantry
Acting Adjutant

The below enlisted men were not on S.O.#127 but joined the Test Platoon on separate orders as back-up people in case of drop-outs.
Pvt 1CL Edgar F. Dodd
Private Arthur W. Swilley
Private Charles M. Wilson

Source: Letter from Lem Pitts to author 16 December 1980.

Appendix D
INDIVIDUAL CITATIONS

EUBANKS, RAY E.

Rank and Organization: Sergeant, 503d Parachute Infantry
Place and Date: Noemfoor Island, Dutch New Guinea, 23 July 1944
Entered Service: LaGrange, North Carolina
Birth: Snow Hill, North Carolina

General Order No. 20: 29 March 1945

Citation: For conspicuous gallantry and intrepidity at the risk of his life above and beyond the call of duty at Noemfoor Island, Dutch New Guinea, on 23 July 1944. While moving to the relief of a platoon isolated by the enemy, his company encountered a strong enemy position supported by machine gun, rifle, and mortar fire. Sergeant Eubanks was ordered to make an attack with one squad to neutralize the enemy by fire in order to assist the advance of his company. He maneuvered his squad to within thirty yards of the enemy, where heavy fire checked his advance. Directing his men to maintain their fire, he and two scouts worked their way forward to a shallow depression within twenty-five yards of the enemy. Directing the scouts to remain in place, Sergeant Eubanks armed himself with an automatic rifle and worked himself forward over terrain swept by intense fire to within fifteen yards of the enemy position and opened fire with telling effect. The enemy, having located his position, concentrated their fire with the result that he was wounded and a bullet rendered his rifle useless. In spite of his painful wounds he immediately charged the enemy and using his weapon as a club killed four of the enemy before he was himself hit and killed. Sergeant Eubanks' heroic action, courage, and example in leadership so inspired his men that their advance was successful. They killed forty-five of the enemy and drove the remainder from the position, thus effecting the relief of our beleaguered troops.

McCARTER, LLOYD G.*

Rank and Organization: Private, 503d Parachute Infantry Regiment
Place and Date: Corregidor, Philippine Islands, 16-19 February 1945
Entered Service: Tacoma, Washington
Birth: St. Maries, Idaho

General Order No. 77, 10 September 1945
    Citation: He was a scout with the regiment that seized the fortress of Corregidor, Philippine Islands. Shortly after the initial parachute assault on 16 February 1945, he crossed thirty yards of open ground under intense enemy fire and at point-blank range silenced a machine gun with hand grenades. On the afternoon of 18 February, he killed six snipers. That evening, when a large force attempted to bypass his company, he voluntarily moved to an exposed area and opened fire. The enemy attacked his position repeatedly throughout the night and was repulsed each time. By 0200 hours, all the men about him had been wounded. Shouting encouragement to his comrades and defiance at the enemy, he continued to bear the brunt of the attack, fearlessly exposing himself to locate enemy soldiers and then pouring heavy fire on them. He repeatedly crawled back to the American line to secure more ammunition. When his submachine gun would no longer operate, he seized an automatic rifle and continued to inflict heavy casualties. This weapon, in turn, became too hot to use and, discarding it, he continued with an M-1 rifle. At dawn the enemy attacked with renewed intensity. Exposing himself to hostile fire, he stood erect to locate the most dangerous enemy positions. He was seriously wounded; but although he had killed more than thirty of the enemy, he refused to evacuate until he had pointed out immediate objectives for attack. Through his sustained and outstanding heroism in the face of grave and obvious danger, Private McCarter made outstanding contributions to the success of his company and to the recapture of Corregidor.

---

*Lloyd G. McCarter joined the army in 1940 and later attained the rank of sergeant. He gave up his rank upon transferring to the paratroopers in August 1942. McCarter had been wounded and decorated before Corregidor. While recovering from his wounds in Letterman Army Hospital in San Francisco, California, he received a personal letter from Pres. Harry S. Truman, requesting that he come to the White House in Washington, D.C., to be presented the Congressional Medal of Honor. This he did, and he was soon thereafter discharged because of his wounds. The bullet that entered his chest during the battle on Corredigor lodged too near his heart for surgery. He was in constant pain. In February 1956, greatly depressed by the recent death of his wife and suffering constant pain from his war wounds, Lloyd did what the Japanese could never do: he took his own life. Lloyd G. McCarter was survived by his twin sister, Lillian and brother William.

PIERCE, LARRY S.

Rank and Organization: Sergeant, United States Army. Headquarters and Head-
quarters Company, First Battalion (Airborne), 503d
Infantry, 173d Airborne Brigade (Separate)
Place and Date: Near Ben Cat, Republic of Vietnam, 20 September 1965
Entered Service: Fresno, California
Place of Birth: Wewoka, Oklahoma, July 6, 1941

General Order No.: 7, 24 February 1966
Citation: For conspicuous gallantry and intrepidity at the risk of life above
and beyond the call of duty. Sergeant Pierce was serving as squad leader in
a reconnaissance platoon when his patrol was ambushed by hostile forces.
Through his inspiring leadership and personal courage, the squad succeeded
in eliminating an enemy machine gun and routing the opposing force. While
pursuing the fleeing enemy, the squad came upon a dirt road and, as the main
body of his men entered the road, Sergeant Pierce discovered an antipersonnel
mine emplaced in the road bed. Realizing that the mine could destroy the majority of his squad, Sergeant Pierce saved the lives of his men at the sacrifice
of his own by throwing himself directly onto the mine as it exploded. Through
his indomitable courage, complete disregard for his own safety, and profound
concern for his fellow soldiers, he averted loss of life and injury to the members
of his squad. Sergeant Pierce's conspicuous gallantry, extraordinary heroism,
and intrepidity at the cost of his own life, above and beyond the call of duty,
are the highest traditions of the United States Army and reflect great credit
upon himself and the armed services of his country.

LOZADA, CARLOS JAMES

Rank and Organization: Private First Class, United States Army, Company
                A, Second Battalion, (Airborne), 503d Infantry, 173d
                Airborne Brigade
Place and Date: Dak To, Republic of Vietnam 20 November 1967
Entered Service: New York, New York
Date and Place of Birth: 6 September 1946, Caguas, Puerto Rico

Citation: For conspicuous gallantry and intrepidity at the risk of his life above and beyond the call of duty. Private First Class Carlos J. Lozada, United States Army, distinguished himself by conspicuous gallantry and intrepidity at the risk of his life above and beyond the call of duty on 20 November 1967, in the battle of Dak To, Republic of Vietnam. While serving as a machine gunner with First Platoon, Company A, Second Battalion (Airborne), 503d Infantry, 173d Airborne Brigade (Separate), Private Lozada was part of a four-man early-warning outpost, located thirty-five meters from his company's lines. At 1400 hours, a North Vietnamese army company rapidly approached the outpost along a well-defined trail. Private Lozada alerted his comrades and commenced firing at the enemy, who were within ten meters of the outpost. His heavy and accurate machne gun fire killed at least twenty North Vietnamese soldiers and disrupted their initial attack. Private Lozada remained in an exposed position and continued to pour deadly fire upon the enemy despite the urgent pleas of his comrades to withdraw. The enemy continued to assault, attempting to envelop the outpost. At the same time enemy forces launched a heavy attack on the forward west flank of Company A with the intent to cut the men off from their battalion. Company A was given an order to withdraw. Private Lozada apparently realized that if he abandoned his position there would be nothing to hold back the surging North Vietnamese soldiers and that the entire company's withdrawal would be jeopardized. He called for his comrades to move back and said that he would stay and provide cover for them. He made this decision realizing that the enemy was converging on three sides of his position and was only meters away and that a delay in withdrawal meant almost certain death. Private Lozada continued to deliver a heavy, accurate volume of suppressive fire against the enemy until he was mortally wounded and had to be carried during the withdrawal. His heroic deed served as an example and an inspiration to his comrades throughout the four-day battle. Private Lozada's actions are in the highest traditions of the United States Army and reflect great credit upon himself, his unit, and the United States Army.

MICHAEL, DON LESLIE

Rank and Organization: Specialist 4th Class, United States Army, Company
                        C, Fourth Battalion 503d Infantry, 173d Airborne
                        Brigade
Place and Date: Republic of Vietnam, 8 April 1967
Entered Service: Montgomery, Alabama
Date and Place of Birth: 31 July 1947, Florence, Alabama

    Citation: For conspicuous gallantry and intrepidity at the risk of his life above and beyond the call of duty. Specialist Don Leslie Michael, United States Army, distinguished himself by conspicuous gallantry and intrepidity while serving with Company C, Fourth Battalion, 503d Infantry, 173d Airborne Brigade, in the Republic of Vietnam. On 8 April 1967 Specialist Michael was part of a platoon that was moving through an area of suspected enemy activity. While the rest of the platoon stopped to provide security, the squad to which Specialist Michael was assigned moved forward to investigate signs of recent enemy activity. After moving approximately 125 meters, the squad encountered a single Viet Cong soldier. When he was fired upon by the squad's machine gunner, other Viet Cong opened fire with automatic weapons from a well-concealed bunker to the squad's right front. The volume of fire was so withering as to pin down the entire squad and halt all forward movement. Realizing the gravity of the situation, Specialist Michael exposed himself to throw grenades but failed to eliminate the enemy position. From his position on the left flank, Specialist Michael maneuvered forward with two more grenades until he was within twenty meters of the enemy bunkers, when he again exposed himself to throw two grenades, which failed to detonate. Undaunted, Specialist Michael made his way back to friendly positions to obtain more grenades. With two grenades in hand, he again started his perilous move toward the enemy bunker, which by this time was under intense artillery fire from friendly positions. As he neared the bunker, an enemy soldier attacked him from a concealed position. Specialist Michael killed him with his rifle and, in spite of the enemy fire and the exploding artillery rounds, was successful in destroying the enemy positions. Specialist Michael took up pursuit of the remnants of the retreating enemy. When his comrades reached Specialist Michael, he had been mortally wounded. His inspiring display of determination and courage saved the lives of many of his comrades and eliminated a destructive enemy force. Specialist Michael's actions were in keeping with the highest traditions of the military service and reflect the utmost credit upon himself and the United States Army.

SP4 Don L. Michael, Congressional Medal of Honor recipient (posthumously)

JOEL, LAWRENCE

Rank and Organization: Specialist 5th Class, United States Army, Headquarters
and Headquarters Company, First Battalion, 503d
Infantry, 173d Airborne Brigade
Place and Date: Republic of Vietnam, 8 November 1965
Entered Service: New York, New York
Date and Place of Birth: 22 February 1928, Winston-Salem, North Carolina

G.O. No. 15, 5 April 1967:
Citation: For conspicuous gallantry and intrepidity at the risk of his life
above and beyond the call of duty. Specialist Joel demonstrated indomitable
courage, determination, and profession skill when a numerically superior and
well-concealed Viet Cong element launched a vicious attack that wounded or
killed nearly every man in the lead squad of the company. After treating the
men wounded by the initial burst of fire, he bravely moved forward to assist
others who were wounded while proceeding to their objective. While moving
from man to man, he was struck in the right leg by machine gun fire. Although
he was painfully wounded, his desire to aid his fellow soldiers transcended all
personal feeling. He bandaged his own wound and self-administered morphine
to deaden the pain, enabling him to continue his dangerous undertaking.
Through this period of time, he constantly shouted words of encouragement
to all around him. Then, ignoring the warnings of others and his own pain,
he continued his search for wounded, exposing himself to hostile fire, and as
bullets dug up the dirt around him, he held plasma bottles high while kneel-
ing, completely engrossed in his life-saving mission.
After being struck a second time with a bullet that lodged in his thigh,
he dragged himself over the battlefield and succeeded in treating thirteen more
men before his medical supplies ran out. Displaying resourcefulness, he saved
the life of one man by placing a plastic bag over a severe chest wound to con-
geal the blood. As one of the platoons pursued the Viet Cong, an insurgent force
in a concealed position opened fire on the platoon and wounded many more
soldiers. With a new stock of medical supplies, Specialist Joel again shouted
words of encouragement as he crawled through an intense hail of gunfire to
the wounded men. After the twenty-four-hour battle subsided, the Viet Cong
dead numbered 410. Snipers continued to harass the company. Throughout
the long battle, Specialist Joel never lost sight of his mission as a medical aid-
man and continued to comfort and treat the wounded until his own evacuation was ordered.
His meticulous attention to duty saved a large number of lives and his
unselfish, daring example under the most adverse conditions was an inspiration to all. Specialist Joel's profound courage for his fellow soldiers, his conspicuous gallantry, and his intrepidity at the risk of his life above and beyond
the call of duty are in the highest traditions of the United States Army and reflect
great credit upon himself and the armed forces of his country.

SP5 Lawrence Joel, Congressional Medal of Honor recipient

OLIVE, MILTON LEE III

Rank and Organization: Private First Class, United States Army, Company B, Second Battalion, 503d Infantry, 173d Airborne Brigade
Place and Date: Phu Cuong, Republic of Vietnam, 22 October 1965
Entered Service: Chicago, Illinois
Date and Place of Birth: 7 November 1946, Chicago, Illinois

G.O. No. 18.: 26 April 1966
 Citation: For conspicuous gallantry and intrepidity at the risk of his own life above and beyond the call of duty. Private Olive was a member of the Third Platoon of Company B, Second Battalion (Airborne), 503d Infantry, as it moved through the jungle to find the Viet Cong operating in the area. Although the platoon was subjected to a heavy volume of enemy gunfire and pinned down temporarily, it retaliated by assaulting the Viet Cong positions, causing the enemy to flee. As the platoon pursued the insurgents, Private Olive and four others were moving through the jungle together when a grenade was thrown into their midst. Private Olive saw the grenade and saved the lives of his fellow soldiers at the sacrifice of his own by grabbing the grenade in his hand and falling on it to absorb the blast with his body. Through his bravery, unhesitating actions, and complete disregard for his own safety, he prevented additional loss of life or injury to the members of his platoon. Private Olive's conspicuous gallantry, extraordinary heroism and intrepidity at the risk of his own life above and beyond the call of duty are in the highest traditions of the United States Army and reflect great credit upon himself and the armed forces of his country.

Pfc. Milton Lee Olive III, Congressional Medal of Honor recipient (posthumously)

MORRIS, CHARLES B.

Rank and Organization: Staff Sergeant, United States Army, Company A, Second Battalion (Airborne), 503d Infantry, 173d Airborne Brigade (Separate)

Citation: For conspicuous gallantry and intrepidity at the risk of his life above and beyond the call to duty. Seeing indications of the enemy's presence in the area, Sergeant Morris deployed his squad and went forward alone to make a reconnaissance. He unknowingly crawled within twenty meters of the enemy machine gun, whereupon the gunner fired, wounding him in the chest. Sergeant Morris instantly returned the fire and killed the gunner. Continuing to crawl within a few feet of the gun, he hurled a grenade and killed the remainder of the enemy crew. Although in pain and bleeding profusely, Sergeant Morris continued his reconnaissance. Returning to the platoon area, he reported the results of his findings to the platoon leader. As he spoke, the platoon came under heavy fire. Refusing medical attention for himself, he deployed his men into better firing positions confronting the entrenched enemy to his front. Then, for eight hours, the platoon engaged numerically superior enemy forces. Withdrawal was impossible without abandoning many wounded and dead. Finding the platoon medic dead, Sergeant Morris administered first aid to himself and was returning to treat the wounded members of his squad with the medic's first-aid kit when he was again wounded. Knocked down and stunned, he regained consciousness and continued to treat the wounded, reposition his men, and inspire and encourage their efforts. Wounded again when an enemy grenade shattered his left hand, nonetheless he personally took up the fight and armed and threw several grenades, which killed a number of enemy soldiers. Seeing that an enemy machine gun had maneuvered behind his platoon and was delivering the fire upon his men, Sergeant Morris and another man crawled toward the gun to knock it out. His comrade was killed, and Sergeant Morris sustained another wound, but, firing his rifle with one hand, he silenced the enemy machine gun. Returning to the platoon, he courageously exposed himself to the devastating enemy fire to drag the wounded to a protected area, and, with utter disregard for his personal safety and the pain he suffered, he continued to lead and direct the efforts of his men until relief arrived. Upon termination of the battle, important documents were found among the enemy dead, revealing a planned ambush of a Republic of Vietnam battalion. Use of this information prevented the ambush and saved many lives. Sergeant Morris's conspicuous gallantry and intrepidity at the risk of his life above and beyond the call of duty were instrumental in the defeat of the enemy, saved many lives, and were in the highest traditions of the United States Army.

Sgt. Charles B. Morris, Congressional Medal of Honor recipient

ENGLISH, GLENN H., JR.

Rank and Organization: Staff Sergeant, Company B, Third Battalion, 503d Infantry, 173d Airborne Brigade (Separate), United States Army

Place and Date: Phu My District, Republic of Vietnam, 7 September 1970

Citation: For conspicuous gallantry and intrepidity in action at the risk of his life above and beyond the call of duty. Sergeant English distinguished himself on 7 September 1970, while serving as a squad leader in Phu My District, Republic of Vietnam. Sergeant English was riding in the lead armored personnel carrier in a four-vehicle column when an enemy mine exploded in front of his vehicle. As the vehicle swerved from the road, a concealed enemy force waiting in ambush opened fire with automatic weapons and antitank grenades, striking the vehicle several times and setting it on fire. Sergeant English escaped from the disabled vehicle and, without pausing to extinguish the flames on his clothing, rallied his stunned unit. He then led it in a vigorous assault, in the face of heavy enemy automatic weapons fire, on the entrenched enemy position. This prompt and courageous action routed the enemy and saved his unit from destruction. Following the assault, Sergeant English heard the cries of three men still trapped inside the vehicle. Paying no heed to warnings that the ammunition and fuel in the burning personnel carrier might explode at any moment, Sergeant English raced to the vehicle and climbed inside to rescue his wounded comrades. As he was lifting one of the men to safety, the vehicle exploded, mortally wounding him and the men he was attempting to save. By his extraordinary devotion to duty, indomitable courage, and utter disregard for his own safety, Sergeant English saved his unit from destruction and selflessly sacrificed his life in a brave attempt to save three comrades. Sergeant English's conspicuous gallantry and intrepidity in action at the cost of his life were an inspiration to his comrades and are in the highest tradition of the United States Army.

Sgt. Glenn H. English, Jr., Congressional Medal of Honor recipient (posthumously)

BLANCHFIELD, MICHAEL R.

Rank and Organization: Specialist 4th Class, United States Army, Company
A, Fourth Battalion, 503d Infantry (Airborne), 173d
Airborne Brigade (Separate)
Place and Date: Binh Dinh Province, Republic of Vietnam, 3 July 1969

Citation: For conspicuous gallantry and intrepidity in action at the risk
of his life above and beyond the call of duty. Specialist Michael R. Blanchfield
distinguished himself on 3 July 1969, while serving as a rifleman in Company
A, Fourth Battalion, 503d Infantry, 173d Airborne Brigade, on a combat patrol
in the Binh Dinh Province, Republic of Vietnam. The patrol surrounded a group
of houses to search for suspects. During the search of one of the huts, a man
suddenly ran out toward a nearby tree line. Specialist Blanchfield, who was
on guard outside the hut, saw the man, shouted for him to halt, and began
firing at him as the man ignored the warning and continued to run. The suspect
suddenly threw a grenade toward the hut and its occupants. Although the exploding grenade severely wounded Specialist Blanchfield and several others,
he regained his feet to continue the pursuit of the enemy. The fleeing enemy
threw a second grenade, which landed near Specialist Blanchfield and several
members of his patrol. Instantly realizing the danger, he shouted a warning
to his comrades. Specialist Blanchfield, unhesitatingly and with complete
disregard for his own safety, threw himself on the grenade, absorbing the full
and fatal impact of the explosion. By his gallant action and self-sacrifice, he
was able to save the lives and prevent injury to four members of the patrol and
several Vietnamese civilians in the immediate area. Specialist Blanchfield's extraordinary courage and gallantry at the cost of his life above and beyond the
call of duty are in keeping with the highest traditions of the military service
and reflect great credit upon himself, his unit, and the United States Army.

SP4 Michael R. Blanchfield, Congressional Medal of Honor recipient (posthumously)

GLOSSARY

AA	Antiaircraft
AAA	Antiaircraft Artillery
A/B	Airborne
AAF	Army Air Force
AIF	Australian Imperial Force
AKA	Cargo ship, attack
AKE	Transport, ammunition
Alamo Force	The code name for the U.S. Sixth Army while working under GHQ SWPA
AP	Transport ship
APA	Transport, attack
APC	Transport, coastal
APD	Transport, destroyer, high speed
Aussie	An Australian
BAR	Browning automatic rifle
Bazooka	Portable rocket launcher used as a shoulder weapon
Blitzkrieg	Lightning war (German). A closely coordinated surprise offensive by air and ground forces
Bn	Battalion
BCT	Battalion Combat Team
Brig.	Brigadier
CA	Heavy cruiser
Canteen	Recreation facility for servicemen
Chute	Short for parachute
CL	Light cruiser
CM	Mine layer
Col.	Colonel
Corps	A tactical military unit consisting of two or more divisions plus auxiliary forces
CV	Aircraft carrier
CVE	Aircraft carrier escort
DD	Destroyer
DE	Destroyer escort
DMS	Destroyer, mine sweeper
DSC	Distinguished Service Cross
DUKW	2½ ton, 6 x 6 truck, amphibious
FA	Field artillery
Fly Boys	Combat airmen

271

FO	Forward observer
G-1	Personnel officer of division or higher staff
G-2	Intelligence officer
G-3	Operations officer
G-4	Supply officer
Gen.	General
GHQ	General Headquarters
GI	Army vernacular denoting an elisted man from the term Government Issue
GO	General order
Goldbrick	Soldier who shirks assigned duties
Grog	An alcoholic beverage, any of which would make one "groggy"
Hara-Kiri	Japanese for suicide
Honey Bucket	Galvanized containers used in the tent cities during World War II for urinating or vomiting into; the odoriferous contents were sarcastically referred to by the GI's as "honey" smelling
Hootch	Paratrooper colloquialism for any alcoholic beverage
IJN	Imperial Japanese Navy
IMB	Independent Mixed Brigade (Japanese)
Inf.	Infantry
KIA	Killed in action
Kilroy	A GI graffito of World War II
LCI	Landing craft, infantry
LCI(G)	Landing craft, infantry, gunboat
LCI(L)	Landing craft, infantry, large
LCM	Landing craft, mechanized
LCP(R)	Landing craft, personnel (Ramp)
LCS	Landing craft, support
LCT	Landing craft, tank
LCV	Landing craft, vehicle
LCVP	Landing craft, vehicle and personnel
LMG	Light machine gun
Love III	Codeword for the Mindoro invasion plan
MC	Medical Corps
MG	Machine gun
MIA	Missing in action
MLR	Main line of resistance
Napalm	Flammable naphthalene mixture, used as a bomb, to burn away jungle foliage or incinerate entrenched Japanese enemy forces
NEI	Netherland East Indies
Noncom	A noncommissioned officer
OCMH	Office of the Chief of Military History
PBY	A twin-engine U.S. Navy patrol bomber (Black Cat)
PB4Y4	U.S. Navy designation of the U.S. Army B-24 bomber
PF	Patrol vessel, frigate
PIR	Parachute infantry regiment

POW	Prisoner of war
PT	Motor torpedo boat
QM	Quartermaster
RAAF	Royal Australian Air Force
RAN	Royal Australian Navy
RCT	Regimental Combat Team
S-1	Personnel officer of regimental or battalion staff
S-2	Intelligence officer
S-3	Operations officer
S-4	Supply officer
SC	Submarine chaser
Sly grog	Alcoholic beverages sold after closing hours or in violation of rationing regulations
Snafu	In GI vernacular, the term roughly meant "situation normal — all fouled up"
SNLF	Special Naval Landing Force (Japanese). Also referred to as Imperial Marines and Tiger Marines
SWPA	Southwest Pacific Area
Tiger Marine	Japanese SNLF or Imperial Marine. So called because each marine had an embroidered cloth waistband outlining a tiger: the outline supposedly contained one thousand stitches, a prayer for each stitch
Trooper	Paratrooper
US	United States
USA	United States Army
USAAF	United States Army Air Force
USAFFE	United States Armed Forces in the Far East
USN	United States Navy
USNR	United States Naval Reserve
WD	War Department
WIA	Wounded in action
Yard bird	A GI colloquialism. As fowl of the air meander across open lots picking up items, so did the soldier, the items usually being discarded cigarette butts, paper, and so on, with heads down and rear ends up, like chickens, or "yard birds."
YMS	Minesweeper

BIBLIOGRAPHY

Books

Anonymous. "Combat over Corregidor, 16 February 1945, Carried out by the 503d Parachute Combat Team." Office of the Chief of Military History Files.

Baker, A. J. *Yamashita*. New York: Ballatine Books, 1973.

Belote, James H., and Belote, William M. *Corregidor: The Saga of a Fortress*. New York: Harper & Row, 1967.

Bulkley, Capt. Robert J., Jr., USNR. *At Close Quarters: PT Boats in the United States Navy*. Washington, D.C.: Naval History Division, 1962.

Cannon, M. Hamlin. *Leyte: The Return to the Philippines*. United States Army in World War II. Washington, D.C.: U.S. Government Printing Press, 1954.

Craven, Wesley Frank, and Cate, James Lea, eds. *The Army Air Forces in World War II*. Vol. 4, *The Pacific: Guadalcanal to Saipan*. Chicago: University of Chicago Press, 1950.

_____. Vol. 5, *The Pacific: Matterhorn to Nagasaki*. Chicago: University of Chicago Press, 1953.

Devlin, Gerard M. *Paratrooper*. New York: St. Martins Press, 1979.

Eichelberger, Lt. Gen. Robert L., and Mackaye, Milton. *Our Jungle Road to Tokyo*. New York: Viking Press, 1950.

Gavin, Maj. Gen. James M. *Airborne Warfare*. Washington, D.C.: Infantry Journal Press, 1947.

Heavy, Brig. Gen. William F. *Down Ramp: The Story of the Army Amphibian Engineers*. Washington, D.C.: Infantry Journal Press, 1947.

Huston, James A. *Out of the Blue: U.S. Army Airborne Operations in World War II*. West Lafayette, Ind.: Purdue University Press, 1972.

Karig, Capt. Walter, USNR; Harris, Lt. Cmdr. Russel L., USNR; and Manson, Lt. Cmdr. Frank A., USN. *Battle Report: Victory in the Pacific.* New York: Rinehart and Company, 1949.

Krueger, Gen. Walter. *From Down Under to Nippon: The Story of Sixth Army in World War II.* Washington, D.C.: Combat Forces Press, 1953.

Miller, John, Jr. *Cartwheel: The Reduction of Rabaul.* United States Army in World War II. Washington, D.C.: U.S. Government Printing Press, 1959.

Milner, Samuel. *Victory in Papua.* United States Army in World War II. Washington, D.C.: U.S. Government Printing Press, 1957.

Morison, Samuel Eliot. *History of United States Naval Operations in World War II.* Vol. 8, *New Guinea and the Marianas.* Boston: Little, Brown, and Company, 1953.

_____. Vol. 12, *Leyte.* Boston: Little, Brown, and Company, 1958.

_____. Vol. 13, *The Liberation of the Philippines.* Boston: Little, Brown, and Company, 1959.

Morton, Louis. *The Fall of the Philippines.* United States Army in World War II. Washington, D.C.: U.S. Government Printing Press, 1953.

Public Information Division, Department of the Army. *The Medal of Honor of the United States Army.* Washington, D.C.: U.S. Government Printing Press, 1948.

Raff, Edson D. *We Jumped to Fight.* New York: Eagle, 1944.

Smith, Robert Ross. *The Approach to the Philippines.* United States Army in World War II. Washington, D.C.: U.S. Government Printing Press, 1953.

Templeman, Harold *The Return to Corregidor.* New York: Strand Press, 1945.

Wainwright, Gen. Jonathan Mayhew, and Considine, Robert. *General Wainwright's Story.* Garden City, N.Y.: Doubleday and Company, 1946.

OTHER SOURCES

After Action Reports: These reports submitted to the adjutant general of the U.S. Army in Washington, D.C., were filed through the army commander assigned, after each major battle engagement, per paragraph 10, AR 345-105, dated 18 November 1929. They graphically summarized the operations of the 503d PIR and later those of the 503d RCT in all actions against the enemy.

Articles: The Static Line, edited by Don Lassen and published monthly at Box 87518, College Park, Georgia 30337, an airborne newspaper, included several articles pertinent to early airborne history and names of paratroopers who were knowledgeable of unit histories.

Interviews: The interviews conducted with members of the 503d PIR and later of the 503d RCT are too numerous to mention. They included persons in all command positions from privates to generals. Both personal and telephone interviews were held. Representatives of all line companies, batteries, and the engineers of Company C, 161st Parachute Engineer Battalion, were interviewed — anyone having pertinent data in reference to the 503d operations, who was willing to share that information for the sake of history.

Letters: Letters replying to inquiries or evaluating the manuscript in rough draft were received from the following officers: Lt. Gen. John J. Tolson III; Lt. Gen. Matthew B. Ridgway; Maj. Gen. William M. Blake; Maj. Gen. Joe S. Lawrie; Brig. Gen. George M. Jones; Col. John B. Pratt; Col. Joe Conway; Col. John N. Davis; Col. Robert M. Atkins; Col. Harris T. Mitchell; Col. William D. Ziler; Col. Lester H. Levine; Lt. Col. Henry T. Capiz; Col. Melvin R. Knudson; Col. Ernest C. Clark; Maj. William P. Brazil; Maj. C. W. Plemmons; Maj. Logan W. Hovis, M.D.; Capt. Lemuel T. Pitts; Capt. James M. Mullaney; Capt. Jesse B. Gandee; Capt. William Bossert; Department of the Navy, Naval Historical Center; Congressman from Oklahoma, The Honorable Mike Synar; Registrar, University of Nebraska; Registrar of Archives, West Point Military Academy; Royal Netherlands Embassy, Historical Naval Staff, the Netherlands; U.S. Department of Commerce, Maritime Administration; Harold M. Templeman; Lou Varrone, and most important of the correspondents, the dogfaced enlisted men who fought and won the battles: George F. Brown, Mike A. Hostinsky, Mike Matievich, Andrew J. Amaty, Carl G. Ballard, Richard F. O'Brien, and Charles H. Doyle of the 509th Battalion (original Second Battalion of the 503d); Joseph R. Heidt, Jerry B. Risely, and Phil Hand (original

Company C of the 501st Battalion but helped organize the 551st Parachute Battalion); Norman F. Petzelt, Max E. Spangle, Gene B. Stautberg, David D. Whiting, Bernard M. O'Boyle, Richard E. Broadwell, Charles H. Wasmund, John S. Hall, Ted L. Alex, Earl K. Hubbard, Guadalupe Escobedo, Herbert Abernathy, Cameron L. Thompson, and Frank D. Hanks, Jr.

Pamphlets: The 503d — Gordonvale Area. Mulgrave Shire Historical Society, Norman Street, Gordonvale, North Queensland, Australia.

First Battalion (Airborne) 503d Infantry THE ROCK 3d Brigade (Airborne) 101st Airborne Division Ft. Campbell, Kentucky. This pamphlet obtained by the courtesy of Col. Hudson C. Hill through Public Relations Department, 101st Airborne Division (Airmobile).

Lineage and Honors: Office of the Chief of Military History, United States Army, Washington, D.C., 1972, Army Lineage Series, *Infantry, Part I: Regular Army,* by John K. Mahon and Romana Danysh.